Defending Traditional Islam in Indonesia

Defending Traditional Islam in Indonesia examines the rise of young preachers of Arab descent (*habaib*) and their sermon groups in the region and shows how Islam and politics coexist, flourish, interlace, and strive in Indonesia in complex, pragmatic, and mutually beneficial relationships.

The book argues that the emergence of Arab preachers in the late 1990s, when traditional forms of Islamic authority came under growing challenge from a diverse array of Muslim groups and ideologies, is closely tied to contestation between traditionalists and their puritanical rivals, the Salafi-Wahhabi. Not only have the *habaib* featured prominently in defending traditionalism, they have also used this contestation as an opportunity to build their authority and religious capital through marketisation and their ties to the Middle East. The author explores the ways in which *habaib* promote themselves to the mostly young urban, Muslim community, and also analyses the use of new media and marketing strategies by *habaib* to attract young followers. The use of merchandise utilising popular culture and group identity markers is especially salient in the preachers' outreach to urban audiences. In addition, public staging and entertainment during preaching activities are means by which the *habaib* cast their Islamic preaching (*dakwah*) as the Prophet's mission and encourage their followers' participation.

A novel sociocultural and religious study and a contribution to the growing discussion on new media, market, and religion, this book will be of interest to anthropologists, social scientists, and area studies scholars interested in Indonesia, Southeast Asia, and Islamic studies.

Syamsul Rijal is a Professor of Sociology of Islam at both Syarif Hidayatullah State Islamic University and the Indonesian International Islamic University.

Routledge Series on Islam and Muslim Societies in Indonesia

Published in cooperation with the Ministry of Religious Affairs of the Republic of Indonesia

Series editors: Noorhaidi Hasan, *UIN Sunan Kalijaga Yogyakarta, Indonesia and Indonesian International Islamic University (UIII)*, **Yanwar Pribadi**, *UIN Sultan Maulana Hasanuddin Banten, Indonesia and Indonesian International Islamic University (UIII)*, **Akh. Muzakki**, *UIN Sunan Ampel Surabaya, Indonesia*

International editorial advisory board: Etin Anwar, Hobart and William Smith Colleges, USA; Ismatu Ropi, UIN Syarif Hidayatullah Jakarta, Indonesia; Arif Zamhari, UIN Syarif Hidayatullah Jakarta, Indonesia; Moch. Nur Ichwan, UIN Sunan Kalijaga Yogyakarta, Indonesia; Martin Slama, Austrian Academy of Sciences; Kostas Retsikas, SOAS, University of London, UK; Eva Fahrun Nisa, Australian National University; James B. Hoesterey, Emory University, USA.

This series publishes empirical and critical studies on Islam and Muslim societies in Indonesia. Home to the largest Muslim population and the third largest democracy in the world, the interaction between Islam and politics is defined by increasing globalisation and a growing public visibility of Islam. This series thus explores the complex status and socio-politics of Indonesian Muslims in the local, global, and neoliberal contexts. Employing comparative and interdisciplinary perspectives, the books in the series analyse the impacts of historical and political legacies as well as socio-economic change on Muslims' activism, culture, and politics in Indonesia. These original contributions offer a broad analysis of how Islam and politics coexist, flourish, interlace, and strive in complex, pragmatic, and mutually beneficial relationships.

For more information about the series, please see our website: https://www.routledge.com/Routledge-Series-on-Islam-and-Muslim-Societies-in-Indonesia/book-series/RSIMSI

1 **Islamic Law and Society in Indonesia**
  Corporate Zakat Norms and Practices in Islamic Banks
  Alfitri

2 **Defending Traditional Islam in Indonesia**
  The Resurgence of Hadhrami Preachers
  Syamsul Rijal

Defending Traditional Islam in Indonesia
The Resurgence of Hadhrami Preachers

Syamsul Rijal

LONDON AND NEW YORK

First published 2024
by Routledge
4 Park Square, Milton Park, Abingdon, Oxon OX14 4RN

and by Routledge
605 Third Avenue, New York, NY 10158

Routledge is an imprint of the Taylor & Francis Group, an informa business

© 2024 Syamsul Rijal

The right of Syamsul Rijal to be identified as author of this work has been asserted in accordance with sections 77 and 78 of the Copyright, Designs and Patents Act 1988.

All rights reserved. No part of this book may be reprinted or reproduced or utilised in any form or by any electronic, mechanical, or other means, now known or hereafter invented, including photocopying and recording, or in any information storage or retrieval system, without permission in writing from the publishers.

Trademark notice: Product or corporate names may be trademarks or registered trademarks, and are used only for identification and explanation without intent to infringe.

British Library Cataloguing-in-Publication Data
A catalogue record for this book is available from the British Library

Library of Congress Cataloging-in-Publication Data
Names: Rijal, Syamsul, 1978– author.
Title: Defending traditional Islam in Indonesia : the resurgence of Hadhrami preachers / Syamsul Rijal.
Description: New York : Routledge, 2023. | Includes bibliographical references and index.
Identifiers: LCCN 2023033787 (print) | LCCN 2023033788 (ebook) | ISBN 9781032415352 (hardback) | ISBN 9781032415345 (paperback) | ISBN 9781003358558 (ebook)
Subjects: LCSH: Islamic preaching—Indonesia. | Daʻwah (Islam) | Muslims—Indonesia. | Islam—Social aspects—Indonesia.
Classification: LCC BP63.I5 R56 2023 (print) | LCC BP63.I5 (ebook) | DDC 306.6/9709598—dc23/eng/20230823
LC record available at https://lccn.loc.gov/2023033787
LC ebook record available at https://lccn.loc.gov/2023033788

ISBN: 978-1-032-41535-2 (hbk)
ISBN: 978-1-032-41534-5 (pbk)
ISBN: 978-1-003-35855-8 (ebk)

DOI: 10.4324/9781003358558

Typeset in Times New Roman
by codeMantra

For Nisa, Salwa, and Milan
My late parents,
Abdul Rauf Sulaiman and Sitti Aisyah

Contents

List of illustrations		*ix*
Acknowledgements		*xi*
A Note on Spelling and Transliteration		*xiii*
Glossary and Abbreviations		*xv*

1 Introduction   1

2 Internal Dynamics within Hadhrami Arabs in Indonesia:
From Social Hierarchy to Doctrine   18

3 Defending Traditional Islam: *Habaib* and Anti-Salafism   41

4 Performing Arab Saints and Marketing the Prophet   61

5 Reviving Yemeni Traditionalist Networks: The Assertion
of Authenticity and Authority   82

6 Following Arab Saints: *Muhibbin*, Popular Piety, and Youth
Expression   105

7 Conclusion   123

Appendix   *129*
Bibliography   *131*
Index   *145*

Illustrations

Figures

3.1	Front Covers of Habib Noval's books	49
4.1	Logo of the MR and the Nurul Musthofa	77
5.1	A special public sermon for welcoming Habib 'Umar at Monas, Jakarta, 25 November 2013	93

Map

5.1	Paths of Hadhrami diaspora routes. Source: CartoGIS CAP-ANU	83

Acknowledgements

The completion of this book could not have been accomplished without the support of and contributions from several individuals and institutions. First and foremost, I would like to express my sincere gratitude to my PhD supervisor, Emeritus Professor Greg Fealy of the Department of Political and Social Change (PSC), Australian National University (ANU), for his exceptional guidance and continuous support throughout the writing process. His invaluable advice and constructive criticism have played a pivotal role in shaping my argument and refining the analysis presented in this book. Furthermore, beyond the academic realm, Pak Greg, as he is fondly referred to by Indonesian students, has also been a trusted confidant, offering a sympathetic ear for personal concerns and sharing invaluable insights and rumours concerning religious and political matters in Indonesia. Additionally, I extend my thanks to my advisors, Associate Professor Marcus Mietzner and Associate Professor Ronit Ricci, for their critical views and invaluable suggestions that helped me develop my argument, structure, and chapter drafts.

This book is a contribution to the Routledge series on Islam and Muslim societies in Indonesia, with the support of the Directorate of Islamic Higher Education, the Ministry of Religious Affairs (MORA) of Indonesia. In the light of this, I would like to express my sincere gratitude to the dedicated editors from MORA, Professor Noorhaidi Hasan and Dr Yanwar Pribadi who nominated this work for publication by Routledge. I would also like to extend my appreciation to Routledge team and xii *Acknowledgements*

their reviewers, whose invaluable feedbacks and meticulous editing have significantly elevated the overall quality of this book.

I embarked upon my academic journey at State Islamic Institute of Antasari, Banjarmasin, and later transitioned to the State Islamic University of Syarif Hidayatullah Jakarta. For the past two years, I have had the privilege of serving as a lecturer and heading the PhD Programme of Islamic Studies at the Faculty of Islamic Studies, Indonesian International Islamic University (IIIU). Consequently, I am immensely grateful to these three esteemed institutions, as they have played a crucial role in shaping my academic career and fostering my intellectual growth. The universities have consistently offered me supportive environments for both teaching and scholarly endeavours.

It would not have been possible to complete this book without the cooperation and participation of the Hadhrami community, especially the *habaib* and their followers in Jakarta and several cities in Indonesia when I did my fieldwork. I would like to thank the executive boards of Hadhrami-related institutions such as Rabitah Alawiyah, Jamiat Khair, Darul Aitam, Al-Irsyad, alKisah, and several sermon groups (*majelis taklim*) for allowing me to interview staff and followers and also for sharing their documents and publications. I would also like to thank several *habaib* who generously gave their time for interviews amidst their busy schedules. Among them are Habib Muhsin b. Idrus Al-Hamid, Habib Nabiel b. Fuad Al-Musawa, Habib Ahmad Zein Al-Kaff, Habib Mahdi Alatas, Habib Jindan b. Novel, Habib Ahmad b. Novel, Habib Bagir b. Yahya, Habib Muhammad Rizieq Syihab, Habib Jamal b. Ba'agil, Habib Novel b. Muhammad Alaydarus, Habib Syech b. Abdul Qadir Assegaf, Habib Mahmud b. Umar Al-Hamid, Habib Abdullah b. Ja'far Assegaf, and Habib Muhammad b. Alwi Al-Kaff. I also thank *majelis'* staff and young participants (*muhibbin*) for their willingness to be interviewed and to share their experiences. Their kindness in adding me in their virtual groups, such as mailing list and WhatsApp group, enabled me to better understand their personal views, discourses, and debates within their community. Several staff, young followers, and students in Hadhramaut have been kindly answering my many questions through WhatsApp after my fieldwork.

I would like to extend my heartfelt grateful to my late parents, Siti Aisyah and Abdul Rauf Sulaiman, whose unwavering support enabled me to pursue my dreams. They consistently encouraged me to advance my studies and fervently prayed for my success in both my academic pursuits and family life. Finally, I am profoundly indebted to my beloved wife, Khoirunnisa, my daughter Salwa Zhafira Syamani, and my son Aydin Milan Kamali who have been with me every step of the way and have provided unwavering encouragement throughout the completion of this book. It is to them that I would like to dedicate this work.

Acknowledging the contributions of numerous individuals and institutions, I take sole responsibility for any flaws present in this book.

A Note on Spelling and Transliteration

This book utilises many texts that are written in Indonesian language and Arabic. The spelling of Indonesian terms follows that of the *Ejaan Baru Bahasa Indonesia* (1972), except for personal names and titles of books or articles, which are rendered according to the original spellings. Likewise, all Arabic words that are in common Indonesian usage will be given in standard Indonesian spelling, without their Arabic diacritical signs, such as *dakwah*, instead of *da'wa*; *majelis taklim*, instead of *majlis al-ta'līm*; *habaib*, instead of *habāib*; and al-Irsyad, instead of al-Irshād. However, for un-Indonesianised Arabic terms, I have used the transliteration system of the *International Journal of Middle East Studies*, but diacritics have been kept to a minimum.

Where Indonesian words have the same single and plural form, such as ulama and *pesantren*, I retain that practice in this text. The plural of Arabic words is formed simply by adding 's' to their more familiar singular forms: *sayyids*, instead of *sāda*; irsyadis, instead of *irshadiyyūn*; and salafis, instead of *salafiyyūn*. However, I keep using *habaib* as a plural form of *habib* as it is popular in Indonesian use.

For my informant's names, especially those with Arabic names, I follow the customary Indonesian practice of referring to them by their first name rather than their last name. The main reason is to differentiate between individuals, many of whom have similar family or clan names such as Assegaf, Shihab, Alaydarus, and Al-Musawa. However, for the names of authors, I use their last name to be consistent with those in the ordering of the bibliography.

Glossary and Abbreviations

ahl bayt	literally, 'people of the house'; family of the Prophet Muhammad
akidah (Ar. *aqida*)	creed
'alawi (pl. *alawiyyin*)	a collective family name of the descendants of the Prophet Muhammad living in Hadhramaut
aswaja	*ahl al-Sunna wa al-Jama'a*, followers of the example of the Prophet and the [majority] community: Sunnis. In Indonesia, *aswaja* particularly refers to traditionalist Sunnism linked to Nahdlatul Ulama
Ba'alawi	literally 'Children' of 'Alawi'; a collective term used to describe the Hadhrami *sayyids* who traced their descent to 'Alawi b. 'Ubaydillah
berkah (Ar. *baraka*)	blessing or grace; a quality possessed by holy men such as *habib* or *kiai*
Betawi	local ethnic group of Jakarta
bid'ah (Ar. *bid'a*)	literally 'innovation'; a practice or belief not sanctioned by the Qur'an or Sunna
bid'ah hasanah	lawful innovation
bid'ah mazmumah	unlawful innovation
dakwah (Ar. *da'wa*)	Islamic propagation
dakwah nabawi	the Prophet's dakwah
Dalwa	Dar al-Lugah wa al-Da'wah (Educational Institution for Language and Proselytisation). A *pesantren* in Pasuruan, East Java
daurah (Ar. *dawra*)	training in Islamic studies for several days
dzikir (Ar. *dhikr*)	remembrance of God through repetition of formulas
fikih (Ar. *fiqh*)	Islamic jurisprudence
FPI	Front Pembela Islam (Islamic Defenders' Front); a conservative and militant organisation founded in 1998
habib (pl. *habaib*)	beloved; a noble tittle of the *sayyids*
hadhrah	Hadhrami traditional music that includes tambourines and drums

xvi   *Glossary and Abbreviations*

Hadhrami	people from Hadhramaut, Yemen
Hadith	tradition related by the Prophet and relayed to the Muslim community; the second most authoritative source of Islamic law
haul (Ar. *hawl*)	Annual commemoration of a religious scholar/leader's death
ijazah	a certificate given by a scholar to his student granting authority to teach a particular text or give instruction in a particular ritual
ijtihad (Ar. *ijtihad*)	literally 'effort'; individual analysis of interpretation of Islamic law
imamah	turban
Irsyadi (Ar. *Irshadi*)	a member or follower of Al-Irsyad, the Arab Association for Reform and Guidance
isbal	wearing trousers that reach below the ankle
jalsatul itsnain	Monday meeting
jubah	a long robe with wide sleeves worn in Arab society
karamah (Ar. *karama*)	literally 'dignity'; a sign of miracles performed by a *wali*
kitab kuning	literally 'yellow books' (a reference to the colour of the pages); commentaries on the Qur'an and Islamic law
kopi darat	to meet and talk with friends from internet
kiai	religious leader and scholar
LBM	Lembaga Bahtsul Masail, a body within Nahdlatul Ulama that deals with religious matters, particularly Islamic law and *fatwa*
Mabadi' (sing. *mabda'*)	principles
madzhab (pl. *madzahib*)	school of Islamic law
majelis taklim	literally 'council of learning'; religious educational gatherings
maulid (Ar. *mawlid*)	the celebration of the Prophet Muhammad's birthday
muwallad	a person of mixed ancestry
MR	Majelis Rasulullah (the Assembly of the Prophet)
Muhammadiyah	a modernist Islamic organisation founded in 1912
muhibbin	the devotees of the Prophet and His descendants
musyrik (Ar. *mushrik*)	polytheists, idolatrous
NM	Nurul Musthofa (the Light of the Chosen); name of one of the largest *majlis taklim* in Jakartae
NU	Nahdlatul Ulama (Revival of the Religious Scholars); Indonesia's largest Islamic organisation founded in 1926

Glossary and Abbreviations xvii

PAI	Persatuan Arab Indonesia (Indonesian Arab Union); later changed into Partai Arab Indonesia (Indonesian Arab Party)
PBNU	Pengurus Besar Nahdlatul Ulama, the central board of NU, comprising the Syuriah and Tanfidziyah
pengajian	an informal religious learning in a group of people
peranakan	half-blood; born in the Indies
pesantren	traditional Islamic schools under the leadership of *kiai*
PKS	Partai Keadilan Sejahtera (Prosperous and Justice Party)
ratib	formulae of *zikir* and prayers formulated by a Sufi teacher
ribat/rubat (pl. *arbita*)	a learning centre for traditional Islamic studies in Yemen
salaf (pl. *aslaf*)	literally 'predecessors'; usually referring to the companions of the Prophet and the following two generations of Muslims. Within the *sayyid* community, the term is also used to describe the *sayyid* ancestors
Salafi	a person who follows the path of the Salaf or pious ancestors
salawat	religious formulas in praise of the Prophet
salawatan	chanting salawat
sanad	chain of narrators or scholars connected to the Prophet
Sarkub	Sarjana Kuburan (scholars of the grave). It refers to a group of traditionalist activists who defend *aswaja* teachings against Salafi attacks
sarung	a garment consisting of a length of cloth that is wrapped around the body and tied at the waist. Popularly worn by men and women in Indonesia and Malaysia, especially among traditionalist Muslims
sayyid (pl. *sada*)	a male descendant of the Prophet
sayyida or *sharifa*	a female descendant of the Prophet
Shi'a	literally 'party' or 'faction'; the second largest branch of Islam after Sunni
Shi'i	a follower of Shi'a
syirik (Ar. *shirk*)	idolatry
siwak	a natural toothpick made from a twig of a tree
Syafi'i (Ar. *shafi'i*)	one of the four *mazhab* of Sunni Islam, and the dominant school of Indonesia's traditionalist Muslims
Sufi (Ar. *sufi*)	Muslim mystic
Sunni	A person who adheres to the Sunni theology or *ahl sunna wa al-jama'ah*

xviii   *Glossary and Abbreviations*

syafa'at	advantages granted by Allah to the Prophet Muhammad to help mankind on the Day of Judgment
tabarruk	to seek blessings (*baraka*) from the Prophet Muhammad and other pious persons through touching any object related to them
tahlilan	recitation of the creed, *la ilaha illa 'llah* (There is no god but God), at ceremonies to commemorate the dead
takfiri	declaring Muslims to be apostate
talkin (Ar. *talqin*)	whispering instructions in the ear of the dead at the close of a funeral with the objective of providing answers to the questions asked by the angels of death. Practiced only by traditionalists but rejected by modernists
tariqa	a mystical order
Tariqa 'Alawiya	the Sufi path of *sayyids* or the Ba'alawi
tawassul	supplication requesting intercession
totok	full-blooded
ulama	Muslim scholars
usalli	pronouncing intention before performing prayers (*salah*); a practice rejected by modernists
ustadz	Islamic teacher of preacher
Wahhabi	a person who adheres to Wahhabism
Wahhabism	Saudi-based religious purification and social reform movement founded in the late 18th century by the scholar Muhammad ibn 'Abd al-Wahhab (1703–1987)
wali	protégé of God, saint, holy man
wulaiti	full-blood; born in Hadhramaut
Wali Songo	literally 'nine saints'; the semi-mythical figures who are credited with Islamising Java
yasinan	recitation of *sura yasin* from the Qur'an; usually after a Muslim's death
ziarah (Ar. *ziyara*)	literally 'visit'; devotional visit to a holy place, usually the tomb of a saint, seeking spiritual intercession with God

1 Introduction

Background

On New Year's Eve, 2013, thousands of young Muslim men and women flocked to the National Monument (Monas, *Monumen Nasional*) in Jakarta, many of them in convoys of motorcycles. They had come to attend a mass religious gathering organised by the prominent sermon group, the Assembly of the Prophet (Majelis Rasulullah [MR]). Most of the audience wore sarongs and the distinctive black jackets of MR with the image of the Prophet Muhammad's Mosque in Medina emblazoned on the back. The atmosphere was like a night festival, a bustling, cheerful meeting of bazaar, entertainment, and religion. A large stage with green bunting dominated the open field. MR flags, huge loudspeakers, banks of lights, and an array of cameras surrounded the stage, with the cameras feeding live images to several large screens at either side. Traditional Arab songs of praise to the Prophet were broadcast to the milling audience. Around the outside of the field were a myriad of vendors selling religious products, snacks, and drinks. Some stalls sold MR merchandise such as jackets, DVDs of MR sermons, books, helmets, and stickers and posters of MR preachers. While waiting for the programme to begin, many attendees spent their time shopping, eating food, and catching up with friends. High-spirited conversations, often interspersed with laughter, could be heard all around.

Around 8 pm, some in the crowd began excitedly saying that Habib Munzir b. Fuad Al-Musawa, the founder and main preacher of MR, had arrived, signalling that the programme would soon commence. *Habib* (sing.) or *habaib* (pl.) is an honorific title given to religiously learned men of Arab descent who claim a genealogical link to the Prophet Muhammad. Like most Indonesian *habaib*, Habib Munzir's family originated from Yemen, and he had been educated in one of Yemen's most famous traditional Islamic schools. As Habib Munzir emerged from his car, dozens of nearby admirers rushed to shake or kiss his hand to receive his blessings. MR staff were forced to hold back the crowd so the *habib* and his entourage could make their way to the stage.

As Habib Munzir with his fellow guests came up on stage, many in the audience sang a *salawat* (a hymn of praise to the Prophet) to welcome the preachers. Following some welcoming words, Habib Munzir invited his special guest, Jakarta Governor Joko Widodo (now president), to give a short speech. The preaching

DOI: 10.4324/9781003358558-1

2 Introduction

programme then began with the recital of texts praising the Prophet (*buku maulid*) composed by the pre-eminent contemporary Yemeni preacher, Habib Umar b. Hafiz. Traditional Arab music was performed by MR's own professional percussion ensemble (*tim hadrah*). After some 30 minutes of text recitation, Habib Munzir asked different preachers to give short sermons before he delivered the final oration. The *salawat* was repeated each time a new preacher took to the podium to give their sermon. Habib Munzir and his fellow preachers called on the audience to spread and uphold the teachings of traditional Sunni Islam or *ahl sunna wa al-jama'a*. He enjoined the audience to always remember God and His Prophet, rather than celebrating the New Year in a secular way with trumpets and fireworks. He also urged the audience to attend important rituals, especially the celebration of the Prophet's birth (*maulid*) conducted by MR, and expressed the hope that MR's next *maulid* event would be the world's biggest. After almost two hours, the programme closed with prayers and the audience soon dispersed.

* * *

Events such as this are held with growing frequency in Indonesia's large cities and represent a new form of Islamic expression and outreach. The events have at their centre a celebrated Islamic scholar or preacher of Yemeni descent and also feature extensive use of social media and bespoke merchandising. The religious message extols the virtues of traditional Islam and, though socially conservative, criticises puritanical 'Salafi' Islam.

Habaib have long held a special position among traditionalist Muslims. Their adherence to traditionalist Islam aligns them with the non-Arab traditionalist mainstream in various regions across Indonesia. *Habaib* have enjoyed particular reverence due to their high status. Firstly, they have Arab blood that connects them to Islam's birthplace; hence, their understanding and practice of Islam are perceived as more authentic than those of non-Arabs. Secondly, they can trace their lineage back to the Prophet. For traditionalist Muslims, *habaib* have inherited the Prophet's blessings through their descent. Therefore, most lay traditionalists view *habaib* not only as *ulama* (experts in Islamic knowledge) but also as *wali* (friends of God or Muslim saints). Their prayers are believed to expedite God's approval; kissing their hands and their robes could bring blessings and luck to the supplicant.

Weber argued that traditional religious practices will decline as modernisation and rationalisation increase (Weber, 1978). This approach was taken up by numerous scholars of Muslim communities. Ernest Gellner's study on Moroccan society, for instance, argued that traditional Islam, which he called 'the tribal style of religion', was no longer relevant in the face of increasing urbanisation and modernisation. He claimed that modernist Islam would replace the authority of Saints because "the scripturalist style of faith is modernisable; the tribal and saintly one is not" (Gellner, 1981, p. 58). Likewise, Clifford Geertz was pessimistic about the role of the Javanese *kiai*. He pointed out that these religious leaders would be incapable of guiding the new and modern Indonesia unless they 'renovated' their traditional role. One suggestion he offered to the *kiai* was to

Introduction 3

carry out "a reformation of Java's oldest scholarly tradition even more profound that it experienced in changing from a Hindu-Buddhist monastery to a Moslem *pesantren*, i.e. the creation of truly modern rural religious school" (Geertz, 1960, pp. 248–249). Clearly, Geertz was looking at traditional Muslim societies and their leaders through the Western modernisation lens. The aforementioned approach has been criticised by several scholars (Soares, 2004, 2005; Bruinessen & Howell, 2007) due to the fact that traditional practices of Islam such as Sufism and saint veneration are widespread in urban areas across the Muslim world. Howell (2001, 2008, 2014, 2015a, 2015b) has shown in her works that various forms of Sufism, ranging from the formal Sufi path (*tarekat*) to Sufi-inspired study clubs, have existed and survived in Indonesia since the 1990s not only in rural areas but also in urban ones.

The increasing popularity of *habaib* in the major cities, especially Jakarta, also points to the prevalence and influence of traditional Islam. However, unlike Sufi groups, preaching by *habaib* only gained popularity after the fall of Soeharto's regime in 1998. The followers of *habaib* are young urban Muslims, most of whom are from traditionalist backgrounds and lower income families. Stressing the necessity of following traditional Islam, they eagerly participate in the *habaib*'s public preaching and perform traditionalist rituals such as visiting saints' graves and celebrating the Prophet's birthday (*maulid*), which are seen as problematic by modernist Muslims who want to purify Islam of local practices and beliefs. Such traditionalist piety is in contrast to previous studies which found that Indonesian urban Muslims are prone to consume forms of preaching which allow them to be pious and modern at the same time (Hariyadi, 2013; Parker & Nilan, 2013). Moreover, the general trend of urban preaching tends to minimise traditionalist rituals and prefers to regard Islam as a moral manual on modern lifestyle.

The popularity of *habaib* preachers and their sermon groups has attracted the attention of sociologists and anthropologists of religion and the Hadhrami diaspora. There are two streams of analysis. The first group sees the popularity of *habaib* as connected to the revival of Sufism in urban areas (urban Sufism). Studying two of the largest sermon groups in Jakarta, MR and Majelis Nurul Musthofa, researchers Arif Zamhari and Julia Howell contend that these movements are new forms of Sufi piety that use popular mediums and culture to spread their message (Zamhari & Howell, 2012; See also Howell, 2014, 2015). Another scholar, Alatas, specifically regarded the two *habaib* sermon groups as the continuation of the older Sufi path of Majelis Habib Ali Kwitang in Jakarta, which have adapted their ways to suit a changing Indonesia (Alatas, 2009). Like Howell, Alatas also sees the rise of *habaib* preaching activities in the context of the Indonesian Sufi revival.

The second group analyses the *habaib* revival in Indonesia through the lens of the Hadhrami diaspora. Martin Slama, for instance, argues that the growing connection to Hadhramaut is due to structural factors, i.e. the restoration of Indonesian-Yemen relations since 1990. He points out that such reconnection has led Indonesian Hadhrami to revive their cultural heritage by visiting their families, sending their children to study in Hadhramaut, or going on pilgrimages to sacred

4   *Introduction*

graves of saints in Tarim (Slama, 2005). Therefore, his analysis suggests that the *habaib* resurgence in Indonesia is largely driven by Hadhrami Arab cultural revival.

This book seeks to explain the emergence of *habaib* in contemporary preaching (*dakwah*) and their growing popularity among young urban Muslims. I agree with the preceding scholars that *habaib dakwah* is closely connected to Sufism, but that is not the main concern of this study. In this study, I view *habaib* in the broader context of Islamic traditionalism in Indonesia and locate them as traditionalist leaders competing with other Muslim groups for religious authority. I will argue that the rise of *habaib* is a reaction to puritanical reformist Muslim groups that challenge the authority and practices of traditionalists. The growing concern among traditionalist communities has pushed *habaib* to defend traditional Islam through various forms of *dakwah*. By defending traditional Islam, *habaib* preachers also gained opportunities to build their religious capital and prestige emerge, through both marketisation and their use of Yemeni legitimacy.

Who Are the Hadhrami, *Sayyid*, and *Habib*?

Hadhrami means 'people from Hadhramaut'. In this study, it refers to Arab immigrants from Hadhramaut, a region in Yemen, who formed a large diaspora especially from the late 18th century in countries around the rim of the Indian Ocean including Southeast Asia (mainly in Indonesia, Malaysia, and Singapore), India, and East Africa. The *sayyids* are the top stratum in the traditional hierarchy in Hadhramaut comprising people who claim a direct bloodline to the Prophet Muhammad via his grandson Husayn (Bujra, 1971, p. 13). They are also called *ba'alawi* or children of 'Alawi, a grandson of their clan ancestor Ahmad b. 'Isa known as al-Muhajir ('The Emigrant'), who moved from Basra in Iraq to Hadhramaut in the 10th century (Jonge, 1993, p. 76). Due to their high social status, which can easily be recognised through customs such as hand-kissing, they are addressed by the honorifics *sayyid* (literally, 'master' or 'lord') and *habib* (literally, 'beloved', signifying 'beloved of God') for men, and *sharifa, habiba, and sayyida* for women (Boxberger, 2002, p. 20). Furthermore, marriage between the daughter of a *sayyid* and a member of a lower stratum is absolutely forbidden (Mobini-Kesheh, 1999, p. 25). In Hadhramaut, this group enjoys a privileged religious and social position, "supervising the observance of religious duties, leading religious activities and ceremonies, and caring for Islamic education" (Jonge, 1993, p. 76). Many *habaib* were seen as saints (*wali*) who possess mystical powers, and, after their death, their tombs become popular sites for pilgrimage and religious rituals (Mobini-Kesheh, 1999, p. 25).

Hadhrami Arabs have settled for several centuries in Indonesia. The difficult conditions in Hadhramaut, such as poverty, drought, and political and tribal conflicts, were major push factors for Hadhrami emigration, while the trading opportunities and missionary work in the Indian Ocean region were pull factors (Jacobsen, 2009, p. 2; Manger, 2010, p. 1). Furthermore, the technological advances in transportation and communication in the 19th century also accelerated the movement and contact of Hadhrami between their diasporic locations and homeland. While many

Introduction 5

Hadhrami acted as religious teachers and prayer leaders in the host societies, the chief goal of their emigration at the outset was to earn money for supporting their relatives at home (Boxberger, 2002, p. 40).

With their claim of genealogical descent from the Prophet, the *sayyids* had many religious roles and political opportunities in their diasporas. Many historians argued they played an important role in the spread and development of Islam in Southeast Asia through migration and international trade networks (Alatas, 1997, pp. 19–34). In this respect, besides working as traders, many Hadhrami acted as preachers and wandering scholars in host societies (Riddel, 2010, p. 122). Their special genealogy not only granted them religious authority but also gave them access to the nobility through marriage with royal families; a few among the *sayyids* evenly successfully established their own dynasties and kingdoms in Southeast Asia (Bajunid, 1996, p. 22). In Indonesia, for instance, the *sayyids* played leading roles in the ruling elites, such as the sultanate of Aceh, Perlis, Siak, and Jambi, while a member of the Al-Qadri family established the sultanate of Pontianak in West Kalimantan (Mandal, 1994, p. 2).[1]

This study looks at *habaib* in contemporary Indonesia. Many scholars consider *habaib* and *sayyid* to be a similar entity denoting the descendants of the Prophet through the line of Husayn. Berg (1889), for instance, considered *sayyid* to be a social status for descendants of the Prophet, while *habib* is a title preceding a *sayyid*'s name. However, his definition is at odds with the fact that many ulama in colonial times used *sayyid* before their names instead of *habib*. This indicates that the usage of *habib* and *sayyid* in the past was interchangeable. In contemporary times, the usage of these terms has changed. In general, Indonesian Muslims tend to associate *habib* with Islamically learned scholars, while this is not the case for *sayyid*. Therefore, in this study, I will use *habaib* in the same way that Indonesian Muslims use the term. It is worth considering the view of the former chairman of Rabithah Alawiyah, Sayyid Zein Umar b. Smith, who distinguishes between *sayyid* and *habib* in the following way. For him, *sayyid* refers to social status or group identity, while *habib* refers to a *sayyid* who is erudite in Islamic sciences, and whose piety and good personality (*akhlak*) are recognised by Muslim society. In his view, "all *habaib* are *sayyid*, but not all *sayyid* are *habaib*" (Republika, October 11, 2014). However, this ideal definition is not widely held. For Indonesian Muslims, *habaib* is simply identified as learned Muslims regardless of whether or not their piety and behaviour are recognised. Like *kiai* (a title for a Javanese traditional leader), the term *habib* has been commodified; many new *sayyid* preachers now claim to be *habib*. Therefore, in this study, I simply use *habib* or *habaib* to refer to *sayyid* religious scholars and preachers through either self-attribution or recognition from the community.

Book's Aims and Contribution

This book aims to analyse the rise and the sociocultural significance of Hadhrami Arabs by making a particular reference to the *habaib* preachers and religious entrepreneurs in several cities in Indonesia. The reason for selecting *habaib* instead

6 Introduction

of other preachers is that they are the elite religious group that has continued to maintain their Arab identity and traditions inherited from Hadhramaut; a number of these leaders and preachers have even asserted their '*habib*-ness' to the Indonesian public. Researching this group leads me to examine the internal development and dynamic of the Hadhrami in post-colonial Indonesia. This book particularly looks at the popular *habaib* preachers who have become religious elites, especially those who publicise their *habib* identity through the media, *dakwah*, and religious teachings. It examines why there has been a resurgence of *habaib dakwah* and how these preachers market themselves to the Muslim public. In addressing this question, the book looks into the dynamic of their interaction with fellow *habaib*, their connection to Hadhramaut, and their interaction with the local Muslim population. Firstly, this book will assess the internal dynamics within the Hadhrami community. Secondly, it will investigate the influence of Hadhramaut on Indonesian *habaib* by looking at the forms of their connection as well as its meaning and importance to them. Thirdly, it will examine how the *habaib* promote themselves and wield their religious authority in Indonesia. In this regard, this book will attempt to establish whether they deliberately emphasise their difference or 'specialness' to garner more followers. It will also examine how young followers view the *habaib* and why they participate in *habaib* movements and religious gatherings.

This book is a sociocultural and religious study of *habaib* in contemporary Indonesia. It contributes to the growing scholarship on reconfiguration of religious authority in Indonesia. This reconfiguration happened as the result of the social, political, and economic changes in Muslim countries, including Indonesia (Feener, 2014, p. 501). Several scholars argue that the spread of mass education and new media technologies has contributed to the diversification of religious authority (Robinson, 1993; Eickelman & Anderson, 2003; Kramer & Schmidtke, 2006; Mandaville, 2007). This diversification makes religious authority a matter of competition between an increasing number of groups and individual actors (Azra & Kaptein, 2010, p. xiv; Meuleman, 2011; Feener, 2014). The emergence of new Islamic movements and individual celebrity preachers in Indonesia, especially in the post-New Order era, has challenged the more established Muslim organisations such as Nahdlatul Ulama (NU) and Muhammadiyah (Feillard, 2010, pp. 167–169). Several works have been written to analyse a single case of new authority. Unlike some scholars who emphasise the importance of new preachers from secular educational background, this study focuses on traditionalist preachers, namely *habaib*, who have been long recognised and revered by traditionalist Muslims in Indonesia. It will analyse how they succeeded in elevating their authority in contemporary Indonesia in the face of challenges from the Salafis.

This study also contributes to the growing discussion on new media, market, and religion. There has been a general tendency among many preachers and religious entrepreneurs in Indonesia to avoid explicit traditionalism and adopt modern styles and more pluralistic religious orientation to gain a wider audience. My study shows that traditionalist Islam has also become a significant market in urban areas, even though it is segmented. By using self-promotion in the form of media and popular culture, *habaib* could attract large numbers of young urban followers.

Introduction 7

The Map of Hadhrami Studies in Indonesia

The Hadhrami Arabs in Indonesia have attracted scholars from various disciplines such as history, anthropology, sociology, and Islamic studies. Their focus ranges from Hadhrami in their hometown, Hadhramaut, to countries where the Hadhrami immigrants reside. Based on my reading of various works on Indonesian Hadhrami, I have identified two categories of analysis: firstly, Hadhrami as immigrants and a distinctive social group, and, secondly, Hadhrami individuals as religious authorities such as religious leaders, scholars, saints, and preachers. I will review each category of these works and then locate my research in the body of Hadhrami scholarship.

Hadhrami as Immigrants and a Distinctive Social Group

Most studies have used immigration or diaspora as the framework of their analysis. According to Sheffer, diaspora refers to "ethnic minority groups of migrant origin residing and acting in host countries, but maintaining strong sentimental and material links with their countries of origin" (Sheffer, 1986, p. 3). These studies look at Hadhrami communities around the Indian Ocean and the interaction or interplay between the host society and their homeland. In this respect, the issue of identity maintenance or integration with local societies has received major attention; this framework has dominated the analysis of scholars from colonial to contemporary times.

The first detailed work on the Hadhrami community was by the scholar of Islam in the Dutch government service, L.W.C. van den Berg (1886), entitled *Le Hadhramout Et Les Colonies Arabes Dans L'archipel Indien*. Published in French in 1886, it provides a detailed account of the conditions and lives of the Hadhrami in the Netherlands East Indies. The book begins by analysing the difference between the Arabs in the Netherlands East Indies and those in Hadramaut, then explores the economic, social, and religious impact on the indigenous people as a result of the arrival of the Arabs. It also describes the conditions of the *muwallad* (Indonesian Arabs) and the ways the original Arabs (*wulaiti*) assimilated with the local people in the host country. Through this work, Berg tried to correct the widespread perception in the Dutch government that Arab Muslim migrants were a threat to their authority. He argued that, far from opposing the Dutch, these Arab migrants were quite cooperative and even became the mediator between the colonial authority and the native society. Berg also maintained that Arab migration to the region was primarily about trade and the accumulation of wealth, and had little to do with religious proselytisation (Berg, 1989, pp. 79, 103).

The Hadhrami community and their identity in the Netherlands East Indies have also been studied by several historians such as Huub de Jonge (1993), Husain Haikal (1986), Sumit Kumar Mandal (1994), and Natalie Mobini-Kesheh (1999). Although each scholar has a different focus, they share the argument that the Hadhrami experienced shifting social identities in the Netherlands East Indies from maintaining Arab identity (Hadhramaut as their motherland) to integration with

8   Introduction

Indonesian nationality during the period from 1900 to 1942. Viewing the Hadhrami as an immigrant group with a distinctive national and ethnicity is relevant to my historical study as in the past the community strongly identified with Hadhramaut and its rigid cultural hierarchy. However, this kind of analysis is not relevant for the post-independence period, as most of the Hadhrami have become fully integrated into the new Indonesian society.

Several studies of the Hadhrami community in post-colonial Indonesia also use diaspora analysis by emphasising assimilation and adaptation. This trend of study views the Hadhrami as a separate and distinct community. The works of Adlin Sila (1998, 2001, 2015), for instance, deal with *sayyid* and local Muslims in a stratified community in Cikoang, South Sulawesi. Exploring the distinctive characteristics of Hadhrami adaptation within a Makassarese cultural context, he argues that the *sayyid* utilised Makassarese material culture in a modified form as a medium for adaptation in the dissemination of Islamic teaching. Examples given in Sila's works include the use of *perahu* (boat) in the festivity of the Prophet's birth (*maulid*) in Cikoang as a symbol of both salvation and livelihood for the local population. In spite of this local accommodation, he found that the *sayyid* still maintain their exclusive tradition in *kafa'ah* (equality of marriage partner). Sila's account of the Hadhrami's success in adapting to local cultural and religious traditions has been confirmed by Frode F. Jacobsen (2009) who deals with social-cultural trends in contemporary Hadhrami societies in Eastern and Central Indonesia, focusing on Bali, Lombok, and Sumbawa. Borrowing a phrase from Huub de Jonge, he describes the Hadhrami identity as 'an Indonesia-oriented group with an Arab signature'. In this account, he provides details on aspects of local adaptations and local forms of cultural creativity undertaken by Hadhrami healers who combine Sufi and Hindu elements in their practice.

Martin Slama researched the dynamics of Hadhrami Islamic organisation 'Al-Khairaat' in Palu, Eastern Indonesia. In one of his articles, Slama explores the institutionalisation of Hadhrami diaspora and illuminates how the translocal networks of Hadhrami members of al-Khairaat in North-Eastern Indonesia have developed differently from those in Java, especially Jakarta, producing many national elites in the post-Soeharto era. He describes this kind of translocal connection as 'globalisation' within Indonesia (Slama, 2011, p. 255). In another work, Slama (2011) also compares Hadhrami communities in Java and Sulawesi. He shows that the Hadhrami community in Sulawesi is distinctive and did not experience division, unlike the community in Java where conflict between *sayyid* and non-*sayyid* led to severe tensions. Al-Khaeraat has become an Islamic organisation for all local Muslims, rather than exclusively for Arabs.

The Hadhrami diaspora analysis in independent Indonesia has a different focus from the preceding studies. If historical studies analysed their group identity and their orientation to Yemen, contemporary studies treat the community as a distinctive social group that has successfully retained its cultural and religious traditions. In this regard, identity maintenance or assimilation is central in their analysis. However, diaspora analysis can no longer be applied to all groups within the community. Like other Indonesians, they have experienced social and religious

Introduction 9

transformations that alter their views and behaviour. I agree with previous scholars that *sayyid* groups still maintain their group identity, especially in terms of marriage and genealogy. However, the non-*sayyid*, especially those who affiliate to Al-Irsyad, no longer regard Hadhramaut as a source of identity. The weakness of diaspora study lies in its treatment of Hadhrami as a minority group which is isolated from local communities. My study will show that to understand this community, we must see not only their culture but also their religious aspirations.

Habaib *as Individual Religious Authorities*

Habaib *in Colonial Period*

The second trend regards *habaib* as religious leaders, scholars, and preachers. It locates individual *habaib* in the context of Indonesian Islam. Some scholars have studied individual *habaib* in the colonial period, including Reid (1972), Azra (2002), and Kaptein (2014). They focused on a religious leader and explore his role in religion and politics in the Netherland East Indies. Their works are somewhat similar to the present study since they regard individual *habaib* as simply religious leaders rather than the representation of an Arab group. These scholars, however, paid little attention to the issue of Islamic preaching (*dakwah*) and traditional Islam, nor were they concerned with how the *habaib* maintain their religious authority.

On the whole, these studies share a view that the *habaib* leaders and scholars in colonial times played significant roles in Islamisation and politics. Reid's biographical account of Habib Abdurrahman Az-Zahir is an excellent example. Due to his profound Islamic knowledge and diplomatic skills, Habib Abdurrahman Az-Zahir was appointed as head of religion and Imam of the Great Mosque, the Sultanate envoy, *wazir* (minister), and finally war commander of the Acehnese army against the Dutch. In spite of his great contribution to Aceh, Reid (1972, p. 37) argues that the whole life of Habib Az-Zahir was a testimony to Islamic internationalism rather than to any particular country or people. Azra (2002), by focusing on Sayyid 'Uthman's biography and religious teaching, suggests that the Hadhrami *ulama* played a prominent role in the course of Islam in the Malay-Indonesian archipelago. A more comprehensive study of Sayyid 'Uthman was written by Kaptein (2014). The author examined how Sayyid 'Uthman viewed the position of Islam during his service as an advisor for Muslim affairs for the colonial government. Unlike some scholars who see Sayyid 'Uthman as merely a henchman of the colonial government, Kaptein portrayed him in a more positive light as a religious scholar who used his position to interpret Islam and publish his works with the financial assistance of the colonial government.

Habaib in Post-Independent Indonesia

Some research has also been carried out on *habaib* preachers and scholars in contemporary Indonesia. A few of these studies are concerned with *dakwah* issue, while others with Sufism. Mona Abaza's article (2004), for instance, looks at the

10 *Introduction*

dakwah of Hadhrami preachers based in the Islamic center in Kwitang, Jakarta. It examines the importance of these Arab preachers in Islam and politics and the new *dakwah* styles among what she calls the "newly gentrified Jakartans" (Abaza, 2004, p. 173). Borrowing the term "Islamic chic" from Jenny White's study of preachers in Turkey, Abaza explores the success of this kind of *dakwah* among the middle class in Jakarta. She traces the continuation of *majlis taklim* in Kwitang from its founder, al-Habib Ali al-Habsyi to his grandson, Habib Abdul Rahman, including their close links with Soeharto's family. Abaza argues that when the *majelis taklim* was handed to Habib Muhammad b. Ali al-Habsyi (i.e. the second generation), the *majelis* played an important role in elections and campaigning for Soeharto. She sees the importance of *majelis* as a meeting site for politicians, businessmen, and military leaders who identify themselves as strongly Islamic. It is also a place for networking among Jakartan preachers. She argues that "Jakartan *dakwah* has become a lucrative business with its own star system. Charisma and popularity among the followers are essential in the marketing of *ustadz*" (Abaza, 2004, p. 183). She gives some examples of popular preachers who rose to popularity and made *dakwah* a lucrative business. For Abaza, what is new with this *dakwah* phenomenon is "the upgrading and gentrification of preaching which touches new audiences of the emerging middle class" (Abaza, 2004, p. 201). Abaza's research is similar to the present study in dealing with *dakwah* and religious markets of *habaib*. Although I agree with her findings about the importance of charisma and popularity in the marketing of preachers, Abaza's analysis is too market oriented. She overlooked the religious and cultural dimensions within the Hadhrami and Muslim society in explaining the *habaib*'s popularity. It is also worth noting that Abaza focused only on the older generation of *habib* preachers, while the current study examines the younger generation. Her findings, therefore, have limited applicability to contemporary young *habaib*.

Woodward and his colleagues (2012) have considered the two faces of Hadhrami *dakwah* in contemporary Indonesia. They compare Habib Syech b. Abdul Qadir Assegaf (Habib Syech) and Habib Muhammad Rizieq b. Syihab (Habib Rizieq) as the representation of peaceful preacher and violent preacher, respectively. The former is portrayed as spreading Sufi piety and rejecting religious and political violence, while the later stresses fear and hatred in upholding shari'a and morality. While Woodward and his colleagues succeeded in analysing the contrasting approaches of the two preachers, their research failed to capture the commonality between them. It is apparent that these scholars distinguish both preachers in binary position. During my research, I found that there has been a commonality between the two: they are both greatly motivated to defend and promote traditional Islam (*aswaja*). Despite their different approaches, the two preachers continue to endorse and praise each other. On several occasions, they preached and performed together on stage. Habib Syech even sang the Islamic songs composed by Habib Rizieq at several *dakwah* events. Although Habib Syech has so far remained silent on controversial issues such as Islamic liberalism and Ahmadiyah, there is a tendency in his *dakwah* to support the social conservatism that Habib Rizieq preaches.

Introduction 11

The second group of researchers is concerned with studying the connections between *habaib* and urban Sufism in Indonesia. Alatas's MA thesis (2009), for instance, examines the historical development of *habaib* in post-colonial Indonesia by observing their Sufi path, *tariqah Alawiyyah*, and their adaptation to changing contexts. By looking at the Hadhrami community in modern Indonesia, Alatas has shifted the focus from the dominant diaspora studies paradigm to the context of Indonesian Islam. Using many case studies from Majelis Ali Kwitang in the colonial era to MR and Nurul Musthofa in contemporary Indonesia, he argues that Indonesian *sayyid* succeeded in adapting their Sufi tradition by articulating it in the idiom of Prophetic piety, i.e the definition of Islam as imitation of the Prophet, exemplified by modern reformist concern with Hadith and the institution of expanded *sayyid* textual community to include local scholars. Alatas (2009) asserts that this creative adaptation and manipulation was needed to secure the place of the *sayyid* community in the wider perception of Indonesian nationhood while protecting their genealogical eminence. Alatas, however, largely relied on the MR to generalise the recent trend of sermon groups. In fact, sermon groups have a commonality in terms of religious mission and diversity in terms of approach. As the findings of this book show, the allegiance to traditional Sunnism has become the general platform of *habaib* sermon groups. While it may be true that contemporary *habaib* have adapted to the growing Muslim consumption, Alatas has overlooked the deeper phenomenon behind this trend, namely the doctrinal contestation within *sayyid* and Muslim society.

Like Alatas, Zamhari and Howell (2012) have also analysed two current *majelis* in Jakarta, MR and Nurul Musthofa, as the distinctive case of urban Sufi groups in Indonesia. Further, they compared the characteristic of rural *majelis*, as represented by Wahidiyyah in Kediri, East Java, and urban ones, as represented by the two *majelis* already mentioned above. Unlike the Wahidiyyah, they found that MR and Nurul Musthofa are less tightly organised and more showy by staging their religious gathering as festivals with impressive staging and "emotive speaker voice modulation" (Zamhari & Howell, 2012, p. 68). In another article, Howell (2014) analyses *habaib dakwah* as a new phenomenon of religious mobilisation through 'televangelism and mass prayer rallies'. Using comparative analysis between religiosity in North America and Indonesia, she found similarities of 'late modernity' theory in terms of "seeker spirituality, fluidity of participation, the importance of religious experience, the prominence of lay leaders and preference for an immanent God" (Howell, 2014, p. 234). While these works are important and useful for studying the sociology of religion, they bear little relevance to the broader issue of traditional Islam and its contestation with other Muslim groups.

The latest work on contemporary *habaib* in Indonesia is written by Ismail Fajrie Alatas. His book deals with broader issues on Islamic religious authorities and their roles in cultivating Muslim communities by looking at various Hadhrami and non-Hadhrami actors, from either the premodern or contemporary era, yet concentrating more on Habib Muhammad b. Luthfi b. Yahya from Central Java as the prominent case of his study. Questioning the Weberian notion of religious

12 *Introduction*

authority, Alatas borrows the concept of 'articulatory labors' from the political philosopher, Hannah Arendt, in understanding the formation and maintenance of religious authority and community. Drawing on historical and anthropological approaches, Alatas analyses how Habib Luthfi and his counterparts "have been able to become religious authorities, as living connectors to the Prophetic past" (Alatas, 2021, p. 6). In his analyses, he shows the importance of infrastructure, genealogy, and mobility for Muslim saints in creating and maintaining their religious authority.

The scholars above have researched a specific case of *habaib* scholars and preachers in contemporary Indonesia, yet none of them explores the relationship between Sunni doctrines, traditional Islam, and religious authority, which is central to the present study. My research is concerned with the factors that triggered the emergence of *habaib*. Alatas's work is closer to my book as it discusses several recent *habaib* preachers in Jakarta; however, his focus is more specifically on the continuation and adaptation of the Hadhrami Sufi path. Although Alatas has provided short profiles of two influential young *sayyid* preachers, namely Habib Munzir Al-Musawa and Habib Hasan b. Ja'far Assegaf, he did not connect their resurgence to the internal dynamics within the *sayyid* community, their ideological division, and their contestation with other Muslim groups.

My study locates *habaib* as individual religious authorities within contemporary Indonesian Muslim society. It considers *habaib* as traditionalist leaders like *kiai* in Java, *tuan guru* in Nusa Tenggara Barat and South Kalimantan, and *gurutta* in South Sulawesi. Since many young *habaib* preachers have emerged at a similar time, this book views their resurgence as a new collective phenomenon although each has their own sermon group and media. The main plank in their religious platform is defending traditional Islam (*aswaja*) and its propagation to Muslims. This book suggests that diaspora theory cannot fully explain the rising popularity of *habaib* in Indonesia due to its limited analysis of ethnicity and group identity. The coming chapters in this book will show that the Hadhrami have faced external challenges from Salafi and other Muslim groups that later led them to reassert traditionalist Sunni Islam within their community. This is concomitant with similar trends within traditionalist Muslim society. In this context, *habaib* express themselves as traditionalist leaders who aspire to defending and popularising traditional Islam in Indonesia.

Book's Argument

This study argues that the resurgence of *habaib* in contemporary Indonesia is a reaction to external 'threats' which challenge their tradition and religious authority. These threats primarily come from puritanical Salafi. *Habaib* defend their tradition and turn the threats into opportunities to buttress their own authority among the Muslim population. In so doing, they promote traditional Islam that meets accords with the beliefs of traditionalist Muslims in Indonesia. In reasserting traditional Islam, *habaib* have undertaken two approaches. Firstly, they validate traditional Islam through doctrines and Arabness, and, secondly, they promote and popularize tradition in creative ways which meet the aspirations of Muslim youths

Introduction 13

in urban areas. Their outreach works to not only strengthen traditional Islam but also enhance their religious standing. Therefore, my study suggests that the more *habaib* promote traditional Islam to Indonesian Muslims, the more they enhance their social status and authority.

In analysing the resurgence of *habaib* in contemporary Indonesia, my study draws on Pierre Bourdieu's theory on 'religious field'. He defined religious field as an arena where "various religious claimants, individual or institutional, can mobilize religious capital in the competition for the monopoly over the administration of the goods of salvation and over the legitimate exercise of religious power..." (Bourdieu, 1991, p. 22). In other words, it is an arena of competition for power among religious leaders and institutions. Bourdieu exemplified the opposition between "the Church (Eglise) and its priests versus the prophet (or 'heresiarch') and his believers, or orthodoxy versus heterodoxy, over the production, administration, and consumption of religious capital and the adherence of the laity to whom it is marketed" (Rey, 2007, p. 82). The church and its priests use a bureaucratic spiritual hierarchy to monopolize the goods of salvation, whereas the Prophet arises as a "petty independent entrepreneur of salvation" who claims to produce and distribute new and better spiritual products that devalue the church's old ones (Bourdieu, 1991, pp. 22–24; Urban, 2003, p. 362).

The idea of field cannot be separated from Bourdieu's broader idea of understanding the nature of human practice. This is related to what people think, how they perceive, and what they do (Wacquant, 1987, p. 50; Rey, 2004, p. 331). In his view on practice, Bourdieu confronted dualism between the individual and society that was debated by previous Western scholars. For him, individual and society are integrated and relational as if "they are two dimensions of the same social reality" (Swartz, 1997, p. 96). From this, he created the concept of *habitus* which he saw as a system of structure that shapes the dispositions of human practice.[2] For Bourdieu, practice is the result of interrelation between three aspects, namely field, *habitus*, and capital. In other words, practice is "the sum product of a person's engagement of capital in any given field" (Rey, 2007, p. 50). It is worth noting that for Bourdieu capital or interest is not only material but also non-material (symbolic). Therefore, he crafted various forms of capital, including economic capital, cultural capital, social capital, and symbolic capital.[3] In his view, as interpreted by Swartz, "all cultural symbols and practices, ranging from artistic tastes, styles in dress, and eating habits to religion, science and philosophy...embody interests and function to enhance social distinction" (Swartz, 1996, p. 72).

This book locates the resurgence of *habaib* preachers in the religious field. In post-New Order Indonesia, the competition between preachers and *dakwah* groups has intensified (Meuleman, 2011). In my study, the rivalry has occurred between traditionalists and Salafis who compete for being 'authentic' Sunni authority among the population. Traditionalist Islam has long existed in Indonesia, while Salafi Islam came later in the 19th century. Due to the size and influence of both institutions, we could equate the former as the 'church' and the later as the 'Prophet' in Bourdieu's theory. As the new comer, the Prophet or new preachers challenged the legitimacy of the church. The Salafi expansion and their attacks on

14 *Introduction*

tradition has become a concern among traditionalists, especially the traditionalist leaders such as *kiai* and *habaib*. The challenges to Islamic tradition threatened their established authority and their special social status. Therefore, the *habaib*'s resurgence through various *dakwah* activities could be analysed as attempts to defend their authority and status through reassertion of traditional Islam in Indonesia. Like Mark Woodward (2012), I regard *habaib* as symbols of religious qualification or religious capital which is ascribed through lineage. This special lineage, however, is not sufficient to drive a person to be a popular preacher. It needs to be enhanced by social capital, such as connection with state officials and Yemeni ulama, and cultural capital, such as being a graduate of traditionalist education in Hadhramaut or performing as traditionalist ulama and Arab saints. Accumulating and expending such capitals can allow *habaib* to maintain and enhance their religious legitimacy, and later inculcate *habitus* among his lay followers (*muhibbin*).

Methodological Notes

This study uses eclectic approaches to analyse the emergence of *habaib* in contemporary Indonesia. It combines historical, sociocultural, and religious study in analysing the motivation and experience of *habaib* and their followers. The data collection was primarily derived from literature research and ethnography. The literature research was undertaken for analysing the history and development of the Hadhrami, especially the *sayyid*, in Indonesia which is documented in books, thesis, and scholarly articles. I also accessed internal collections of various Hadhrami organisations that represent their insider views such as documents and publications of Rabithah Alawiyah, those of the *sayyid* school (Jamiat Khair), and those of the modernist Hadhrami organisation, Al-Irsyad. Moreover, I collected *habaib* books, magazines, and DVDs which are hard to find in bookstores. They are usually sold by vendors or official outlet of a sermon group during a public preaching. Basma Press and *alKisah* magazine are among two important publishers from which I could collect publications by and on *habaib*. By following their publications, I could familiarise myself with the discourse of traditional Islam which are voiced by *habaib* and their sympathisers. In addition to this, I also collected publications from Salafi media and other groups in order to see opposing perceptions of *habaib*.

Most of the data for this study is ethnographic. My fieldwork was conducted from December 2012 to November 2013 in several cities in Indonesia with some data updates in 2023. The selection of cities was based on the presence of *habaib* popular preachers and *sayyid* community in the area. They include Jakarta, Malang, Solo, Surabaya, Bangil, and Makassar. In these cities, *habaib* are considered to play an ongoing role in social, political, and religious spheres. I spent more time in Jakarta (nine months) than other cities for two reasons. Firstly, the central organisations of Hadhrami and their schools are located in Jakarta. These include Rabithah Alawiyah, Jamiatul Khair, Darul Aitam (Orphanage), Al-Irsyad Al-Islamiyyah, and Perhimpunan Al-Irsyad. Besides, several Islamic groups and Islamic media led by *habaib* could also be found in the city. They include the Islamic Defender Fronts, Ahlul Bait Indonesia (a Shia organisation led by a *habib*), and *habaib* media office (*alKisah*). Secondly, Jakarta is the home of numerous *habaib* sermon groups (*majelis taklim*), both old and new. In fact, the two largest sermon groups, MR and Nurul Musthofa, are located in the capital city. To capture the general trend of *habaib* sermon groups in Indonesia, I also made a short visit (three months) to Makassar and several cities in Java where I could interview the sermon group leaders and participate in their religious activity programmes.

My ethnographic research consisted of in-depth interviews, informal conversations, and participatory observation. I employed an in-depth interview when meeting with *habaib* leaders, preachers, and their staff in order to reveal their motivation, their cultural and religious connection, and their experience in establishing their *dakwah* institutions. To build an initial contact with my key informants, especially *habaib* preachers, I went to their offices and sermon group headquarters. Gaining direct access to popular *habaib* in Jakarta was difficult. This was due to various reasons including high schedule, health problem, and suspicion. To solve this problem, I regularly participated in public sermons at their headquarters, and, at the end of the sermons, I would directly come to *habib* or their staff and introduce myself. This method often helped to build trust and to gain an appointment for an interview. Interestingly, making an appointment for interview in other cities in Java was relatively easier than in Jakarta. This can be explained by the fact that *habaib* in other cities have a less busy schedule and not much mobility for *dakwah* compared to those in Jakarta.

To gather data from *habaib*'s followers (*muhibbin*), I attended a number of sermon group's programmes such as public preaching, the annual commemoration of a saint's death (*haul*), the celebration of the Prophet's birthday (*maulid*), and visiting the saints' graves (*ziarah*). While participating in these events and activities, I took notes and photos, and recorded various public sermons. These events allowed me to observe, feel, and experience their rituals as well as building a good rapport with the followers. Before, during, and after the events, I made an informal conversation with them. This initial contact also led me to have an in-depth interview with them. In the interview, I used the life-history technique to comprehend their backgrounds of education, family, economic class and cultural-religious orientation as well as exploring their motivation and experiences in their sermon group. To update or follow up communication with them, I usually asked for their phone number and social media account. Some of them kindly invited me to join their mailing list group, mobile messaging group such as WhatsApp, and community page group in Facebook. Through real and online engagement, I could observe their aspiration, their interaction, and their internal discussion to support *habaib dakwah*.

The selection of *habaib* figures was based on their popularity as religious leaders and preachers in their own community. I mostly focused on young *habaib* who emerged after 1998. During my research, I interviewed 12 popular preachers, 40 leaders from various Hadhrami organisations and their staff, 20 followers of sermon groups, and 2 Indonesian students studying in Tarim, Hadhramaut. With regard to the followers, I focused on those from the MR and the Majelis Nurul Musthofa in Jakarta due to their popularity.

16   *Introduction*

Structure of Book

This book comprises seven chapters. Chapter 1 is an introduction which includes background, key terms, objective and contribution, map of Hadhrami studies, methodological note, and book structure.

Chapter 2 explores the current landscape of the Hadhrami community by comparing their solidarity and divisions between colonial and post-colonial Indonesia. It particularly examines factors that have unified and divided the community in contemporary Indonesia. It begins by giving an overview of the Hadhrami community and their traditional stratification in Hadhramaut. It then moves on to discuss the shift of identity of Indonesian Hadhrami immigrants in changing social political contexts: from the colonial era to post-independence. Finally, the chapter discusses and analyses the current relationship within sub-Hadhrami group by examining two major social groups, namely *sayyid* and Al-Irsyad. It argues that while the old division was driven by disputes between *sayyid* and non-*sayyid*/Irsyadis due to the question on the traditional social hierarchy in the diaspora, the current division that has occurred within Hadhrami subgroups is largely due to doctrinal issues.

Chapter 3 seeks to analyse how *habaib* and traditionalist preachers have defended their traditions by calling for the strengthening of traditionalist Sunni faith (*aswaja*). It starts by providing a short description of traditional Islam and the social-political context of the rising anti-Wahhabism in Indonesia. The chapter then examines three cases of traditionalist groups: popular preachers, NU scholars, and *aswaja* online media activists. It discusses their profiles, their organisation, and the various types of communication medium they use to propagate their religious ideas. Lastly, it analyses the way they define, construct, and brand traditionalist Sunni (*aswaja*) and the way they see their main rival group, namely the Salafi.

Chapter 4 examines the rising popularity of *habaib* preachers by taking the case of the two largest sermon groups in Jakarta: MR and Nurul Musthofa. It discusses the profiles of two popular *habaib* preachers, the late Habib Munzir b. Fuad Al-Musawa and Habib Hasan b. Ja'far Assegaf. It analyses their family and educational background, their *dakwah* method, and how they became popular preachers in their sermon groups. The chapter ends with an analysis of the approaches they use in bolstering their authority and popularity and in attracting audience from traditionalist Muslims.

Chapter 5 discusses transnational factors that contribute to the growing influence of *habaib* in contemporary Indonesia. It firstly analyses the political development in Yemen and its impact on religious freedom and Hadhrami mobility from the socialist regime to the Yemeni unification in 1990. The chapter then looks at the forms of reconnection between Hadhramaut and Indonesia, especially in the sphere of education and preaching network. It particularly raises the case of the rising star ulama, Habib 'Umar b. Hafiz, and his influence in Hadhramaut and in Indonesia. It also analyses the roles of his students in promoting Yemeni scholars and Hadhramaut in Indonesia.

Chapter 6 analyses the experience and engagement of young followers (*muhibbin*) in two *habaib*'s sermon groups in Jakarta. It firstly discusses the social composition of the followers including their economic class, age, and religious orientation. Next, the chapter discusses the problem of poverty in Jakarta and how it relates to the condition and aspiration of young followers of *habaib*. It then moves to explore the followers' views on *habaib* who are seen as charismatic saints and moral exemplars. It also analyses how the followers view the sermon group with regard to youth issues. It finally analyses the narratives of their motivation and experience in supporting the *habaib*'s *dakwah*.

Chapter 7 provides the conclusion of the study.

Notes

1 For further discussion on *sayyids*' influence in the 18th century, see Jeyamalar Kathiri Hamby-Wells (2009), 'Strangers' and 'Stranger-kings': The *Sayyid* in Eighteenth-Century Maritime Southeast Asia, *Journal of Southeast Asian Studies, 40* (3), 567–591.
2 In one of his books, Pierre Bourdieu defined *habitus* as

> systems of durable, transposable dispositions, structured structures predisposed to function as structuring structures, that is, as principles which generate and organize practices and representations that can be objectively adapted to their outcomes without presupposing a conscious aiming at ends or an express mastery of the operations necessary in order to attain them.
>
> (Bourdieu, 1990, p. 53)

3 For further discussion on forms of capital, see Bourdieu in Richardson (1986, pp. 46–56).

2 Internal Dynamics within Hadhrami Arabs in Indonesia

From Social Hierarchy to Doctrine

Introduction

Since the early 20th century, Hadhrami communities in the Netherlands East Indies have experienced a changing relationship within their own communities. The traditional social strata, which had been transplanted to the Indies from Yemen, came under growing attack. The dispute over the *sayyids'* privileged status divided the Hadhrami into conservative and reformist groups. Jamiat Khair and Rabithah Alawiyah represented the conservative Hadhrami, while Al-Irsyad represented the reformists. These groups continue to exist today. Several scholars have analysed the changing identities of Hadhrami community during the colonial era (Haikal, 1986; Jonge 1993; Mobini-Kesheh, 1999). However, the contemporary relationships within the community have attracted the attention of few scholars (e.g. Bamualim, 2011; Slama, 2014). In the contemporary era, when the Hadhrami have become more integrated into Indonesian society, there have been fewer conflicts within the community compared to the past. The community is currently experiencing internal division over doctrinal issues caused by the expansion of Shi'ism and Salafism. The conversion of Hadhrami individuals to Shi'ism has also divided the *sayyid* community, which strongly identifies itself as traditional Sunni or *aswaja*. In the meantime, non-*sayyids* who are affiliated with Al-Irsyad have also been divided in response to growing Salafi influence within the organisation.

This chapter explores the current landscape of the Hadhrami community in Indonesia by examining the contestation from colonial to post-colonial times. It aims to show the internal fissures that affect the resurgence of *habaib* and to analyse factors that have united or divided the community in contemporary Indonesia. It argues that while the conflict in the colonial era was centred on the issue of Hadhrami traditional hierarchy and nationalist orientation, the current conflict has been largely driven by the competition for religious authority. It includes the conflict between Sunni and Shi'i *sayyids* as well as between two competing groups of Al-Irsyad: Al-Irsyad Al-Islamiyah and Perhimpunan Al-Irsyad. In this regard, both *sayyids* and Irsyadis feel that their religious and cultural identity has been challenged by Shi'ism and Salafism. This situation has led Hadhramis to assert their religious and communal identity.

DOI: 10.4324/9781003358558-2

Internal Dynamics within Hadhrami Arabs 19

The first part of this chapter provides a short background of Hadhrami and their stratification system in Hadhramaut. The second part gives an account of the internal conflict between *sayyid* and Irsyadi communities in the Netherlands East Indies. The third part discusses the division between the old generation (*wulaiti*) and the young generation (*muwallad*) of Hadhrami with regard to Indonesian nationalism. The last part examines the current discord within Hadhrami communities by comparing the internal conflict in both *sayyid* and Irsyadi communities. It also analyses factors that caused friction and tension within each Hadhrami group.

Hadhrami and Social Groups in Hadhramaut

The majority of Arab communities in Indonesia originally came from Hadhramaut. Hadhrami society comprises several groups who "largely married among themselves, shared a common array of occupational statuses, and bore tangible and intangible markers of group identification" (Boxberger, 2002, p. 17). According to Bujra, stratification is an important aspect of the society (Bujra, 1971, p. xiv). The stratification system divides the population into three general strata based on their descent: the *sayyids* (*sada, syeds, alawiyyin,* or *ba'alawi*), *mashaikh* (scholars) and *qabail* (tribesmen), and the *masakin* (poor) and *du'afa'* (weak) (Bujra, 1971, p. 13; Mobini-Kesheh, 1999, p. 25). The top class among the social groups are the *sayyids*. This group consists of people who claim to be descendants of the Prophet Muhammad through the line of his grandson Husayn and is therefore considered to have the strongest lineage and highest religious status in society (Bujra, 1971, p. 13). In tracing their genealogy to the Prophet, all Hadhrami *sayyids* refer to their common ancestor Ahmad b. Isa al-Muhajir, who is the eighth generation of the Prophet's descendant through his daughter Fatimah (Mobini-Kesheh, 1999, p. 25). Originally from Basra, Iraq, he migrated to the Hadhramaut around AD 950 (Bang, 2003, p. 12). The Hadhrami *sayyids* identify themselves as Ba'alawi, 'Alawi *sada,* or the 'Alawiyyin (plural of 'Alawi) in reference to their ancestor Sayyid 'Alawi b. 'Ubaydillah b. Ahmad b. Isa, the grandson of al-Muhajir (Boxberger, 2002, p. 19; Bang, 2003, p. 12).

Due to their noble lineage, the *sayyids* came to be revered in Hadhramaut as teachers of Islam, imams (prayer leaders), and mediators in tribal conflicts (Mobini-Kesheh, 1999, p. 25; Boxberger, 2002, p. 20). According to Boxberger, "they prided themselves on piety and the acquisition of religious education, even though many did not live up to the devout and scholarly image that was idealized among their group" (Boxberger, 2002, p. 20). The *sayyids* were distinguished symbolically from other groups by the honorifics *sayyid* (literally 'master') and *habib* (beloved) for men and *sharifa, habiba,* and *sayyida* for women (Mobini-Kesheh, 1999, p. 25; Boxberger, 2002, p. 20). Members of the community also showed their respect by kissing the *sayyid*'s hands (*taqbil*) and greeting them before others in social and religious settings (Boxberger, 2002, p. 21). Bujra reported that when he visited Hureida in 1963, he found that a family group of *sayyids*, al-Attas, wore a special dress of a long white robe with a white hat as an identity marker. The religious

20   *Internal Dynamics within Hadhrami Arabs*

elites wore a green turban over the white hat or draped a green cloth over their shoulders (Bujra, 1971, p. 15).

The second stratum in Hadhrami society included the *mashaikh* (scholars) and *qabail* (tribesmen). Both groups traced their descent from a distant ancestor known as Qahtan, the eponymous ancestor of the Southern Arab (Bang, 2003, p. 13). The *mashaikh* refers to "groups of people who claim descent from well-known and reputed Hadhrami scholars and holy men in the past" (Bujra, 1971, p. 13). They enjoyed their status as religious elites and leaders in Hadhramaut before the coming of *sayyids*, who displaced them as the pre-eminent religious leaders. Nevertheless, they continued to maintain their status as religious specialists in either religious education or ceremonies (Mobini-Kesheh, 1999, p. 25; Boxberger, 2002, p. 25). *Qabail* (sing. *qabila*) are tribesmen who "occupied and controlled most of the countryside, carried arms, and were considered less devout" (Mobini-Kesheh, 1999, p. 25). Lineage has defined the identity and affiliation of tribal members, and with blood connection they are expected to receive mutual support and protection (Boxberger, 2002, p. 25). This group is also known for the high importance they placed on *sharaf* (honor), which was associated with the ability to bear arms and defend one self and one's family. The best example of *qabail* is the Kathiri and Qu'ayti, two ruling tribes which competed for power in historical Yemen (Mobini-Kesheh, 1999, pp. 25–26; Boxberger, 2002, p. 26).

The third level of stratification was occupied by the *masakin* (poor) and *du'afa'* (weak). They have no descent connection either to the Prophet nor to al-Qahtan. Besides, they also had no ancestors who served as religious leaders (Bujra, 1971, p. 14). According to Boxberger, *masakin* did not mean 'poor' but 'inhabitants' since most of the Hadhrami inhabitants of towns and villages were merchants and craftsmen (Boxberger, 2002, p. 31). In the category of *du'afa'* lie workers in earth or clay such as farmers, builders, potters, and field labourers (Mobini-Kesheh, 1999, p. 26). The lowest stratum among all was occupied by *'abid* (slaves) who were of African origin and had been brought to Yemen in the 1860s. Some of them served as soldiers under the Qu'ayti and Kathiri sultanate, while others served as household servants under private families (Boxberger, 2002, pp. 34–35).

Hadhrami and Internal Conflict in Colonial Indonesia

Equality and Revival

The identity of the Hadhrami in the Netherland East Indies was shaped by social-political factors related to both domestic and global developments. The colonial system in Indonesia as well as the spread of Islamic reformism in the 20th century influenced the undermining of the stratification system of Hadhrami. The *sayyid* group, who enjoyed elevated religious and social statuses from their fellow Hadhrami and local Muslim societies, were caught up in such developments. This happened against the backdrop of the Hadhrami awakening (*nahda hadhramiyya*) at the dawn of the 20th century (Mobini-Kesheh, 1999, p. 34). In colonial times, the Hadhrami community was categorised as Foreign Orientals and placed under the

Internal Dynamics within Hadhrami Arabs   21

European class but above the 'natives'. They were also subject to Dutch policies that limited their mobility (Jonge, 1993, p. 79). The Hadhrami awakening aimed to bring awareness to Arabs regarding social equality and progress by adopting modern ideas and institutions. In the early 20th century, the Hadhrami came to assert their belonging and allegiance to their homeland, Hadhramaut (Mobini-Kesheh, 1999, p. 34).

There were three modern social institutions that characterised the Hahrami awakening: voluntary organisations, modern schools, and newspapers (Mobini-Kesheh, 1997, p. 233). The earliest enactment of Hadhrami awakening was the establishment of the first modern organisation for their community, Jamiat Khair (the Association for the Good) in Batavia in 1901. The founders of the organisation were *sayyid*, but in the leadership structure there were a few non-*sayyids*. Since the core programme of the organisation lay in the field of education, they established Islamic schools in Batavia and Bogor that adopted a modern approach with textbooks and Western sciences, as well as maintaining the teaching of traditional religious subjects (Mobini-Kesheh, 1997, p. 233). To ensure the quality of religious studies and Arabic, they recruited a number of teachers from the Middle East (Noer, 1980, p. 69).

Discord among Hadhrami started when teachers recruited from the Middle East came to teach in the Jamiat Khair School. The most influential figure was the Sudanese Ahmad Surkati who had studied and taught in Mecca. During his long stay in Mecca, Surkati adopted the Egyptian ideas of Islamic reformism and became active in the modernist movement (Jonge, 1993, p. 81; Mobini-Kesheh, 1999, p. 54). The idea of Islamic reformism was propagated by Egyptian reformers such as Jamal al-Din al-Afghani (1838–1897), Muhammad 'Abduh (1849–1905), and Rashid Rida (1865–1935) at a time when the Muslim world was largely under European colonialism. The main aspiration of this movement was to reform Islam from within, arguing that the decline of Islamic civilisation was due to the degeneration and corruption of Islam. It therefore promoted a return to the pure sources of Islam, the Qur'an and Hadith, while adopting the modern development (Leaman, 2015, p. 3–4). Surkati came to take up a position as inspector of Jamiat Khair schools, thereby contributing to the growth of the schools. He and other intellectuals infused the spirit of Islamic reformism in the schools. His reformist view became the immediate cause of conflict within the Hadhrami society. In 1912, he went to Solo to visit his friend, Awad Sungkar Al-Urmei. In a meeting with his friend, he was told about a female *sayyid* (*sharifa*) in Solo who lived with a Chinese man outside marriage due to economic reasons. Surkati suggested helping the *sharifa* by separating her from her partner and seeking a Muslim man to marry her. Asked about the marriage status between a *sharifa* and a non-*sayyid*, he pronounced that such marriage is allowed according to Islamic law (Badjerei, 1996, pp. 28–29). On another occasion, he criticised the practice of hand-kissing for *sayyids* and attacked what he saw as the self-exaltation and delusion of their holiness (Jonge, 1993, p. 81). His views aroused indignation among conservative *sayyid* leaders of Jamiat Khair in Batavia eventually forcing Surkati to resign from his position in Jamiat Khair (Mobini-Kesheh, 1999, p. 55).

22　*Internal Dynamics within Hadhrami Arabs*

The resignation of Surkati triggered a deeper division within the Hadhrami community and led to the creation of new Hadhrami organisation with a reformist outlook. He gained support mostly from non-*sayyids*. Persuaded by reform-minded Hadhrami, most notably the Arab *kapitein* (a community leader appointed by the Dutch) Shaikh Umar Yusuf Umar Manggus, Surkati cancelled his intention to return to Mecca and later founded his own school, Madrasah al-Irsyad al-Islamiyyah (Islamic School for Guidance) (Badjerei, 1996, p. 32; Affandi, 1999, p. 13). Following this, in 1914 Surkati and his friends established an organisation for supporting the operation of the schools under the name Jamiyat al-Islah wal-Irsyad al-Arabiyyah (Arab Association for Reform and Guidance) (Mobini-Kesheh, 1999, p. 56). Although there were a few *sayyids* among its members, this organisation became "the bastion of anti-*sayyid*" (Jonge, 1993, p. 81). Echoing the reformist movement in Egypt, Al-Irsyad sought to purify Islam of superstition and innovations as a result of its interaction with localities and return to the religious foundation, i.e. the Qur'an and the Hadith. At the Arab community level, the organisation strove to abolish the traditional Hadhrami stratification system that was inherited from Hadhramaut. In so doing, Al-Irsyad emphasised education by establishing modern schools with subjects that maintained Arab language and culture as well as disseminating the Irsyadi reformist principles (Noer, 1987, p. 12; Jonge, 2004, p. 378).

The rapid development of Al-Irsyad and its continuing challenge to *sayyids* created a long period of hostility between them. Established in Batavia, Al-Irsyad spread rapidly to other cities in Java and other islands of the Indies. Given the success of Al-Irsyad in Batavia, several requests to establish branches were made by a number of groups of Hadhrami from Tegal (1917), Pekalongan (1917), Bumiayu (1918), Cirebon (1918), and Surabaya (1919) (Mobini-Kesheh, 1999, p. 60). As a response to the success of Al-Irsyad, in 1927 several *sayyids* established an organisation for their community called Rabithah Alawiyah, the Union of the Descendants of the Prophet. This organisation opposed attempts by the Irsyadis (followers of Al-Irsyad) to remove privilege position of the *sayyid* (Jonge, 2004, p. 378). Rabithah has an institution called al-Maktab al-Daimi (Daily Office) which serves to preserve *sayyid* history and record their genealogy. In 1940, the institution recorded 17,764 *sayyids* with their genealogies from various parts of Indonesia (AD-ART Rabithah Alawiyah).

The different stance between Al-Irsyad and Rabithah Alawiyah led them to oppose each other through either words or actions. Their debates were published in Arabic papers, pamphlets, and brochures where each group defended their position and attacked their rival (Jonge, 1993, p. 82). The debate revolved around three main areas of Hadhrami custom: "the kissing of *sayyid*'s hands, the ban on marriage between a *sayyid*'s daughter and a non-*sayyid*, and the use of the title '*sayyid*'" (Mobini-Kesheh, 1999, p. 92). Mobini-Kesheh (1999) observed that the debate over *sayyid* status was expressed in terms of Hadhrami-ness. In this sense, each group claimed that they were more Hadhrami than others. For *sayyids*, obedience to the traditional stratification system was the essence of Hadhrami identity, while, for non-*sayyids*, the tradition was imposed by *sayyids* whom they regard as 'intruders' to Hadhrami society. In this regard, Irsyadis sought to be 'modern' while maintaining their Hadhrami identity (Mobini-Kesheh, 1999, p. 92). A culminating point of the debate was the decision of Al-Irsyad to desacralise the title '*sayyid*'. Al-Irsyad's congress in 1931 in Batavia decided that the title *sayyid* was not exclusive to a particular group (*sayyids*) but could be addressed to anyone who deserves respect, regardless of their lineage. For them, the title '*sayyid*' should be equated to 'mister' or 'sir' in general use. By this, Al-Irsyad suggested that any person has the right to use such a tittle. This decision appalled the *sayyids* who feared the loss of their aristocratic privileges (Jonge, 1993, p. 82). The *sayyids* fiercely rejected the idea and argued that "the title *sayyid* was long established by custom in Hadhramaut, in the Indies, and other parts of the Islamic world" (Mobini-Kesheh, 1999, p. 105). Moreover, they contended that the title had to be preserved in order to follow Islamic law that especially applies to descendants of the Prophet, such as the law of *kafa'ah* (equivalence) in marriage. The title was important for *sayyids* because it could remind their offspring to undertake their religious responsibility in societies (Mobini-Kesheh, 1999, p. 106). The polemic between the two groups resulted in serious riots and violence. In Bondowoso, for instance, several Irsyadis who pushed forward during prayer in a mosque were killed by *sayyids* (Jonge, 1993, p. 84).

Both *sayyids* and Irsyadis petitioned the Dutch government on the issue of *sayyid* status. The *sayyids*, under the Rabithah organisation, sought legal recognition of their title, but the Irsyadis asked the government to be neutral in the conflict by rejecting the *sayyids'* demands. The government finally decided that it would not fulfil the *sayyids'* wishes. According to Mobini-Kesheh, with this failed *sayyids'* petition, it could be said that the Irsyadis had won the title fight. The conflict was finally over due to the role of new generation of *sayyids* who preferred to focus on the issue of education rather than extending their battle with Irsyadis (Mobini-Kesheh, 1999, p. 107). In the meantime, younger generation Irsyadis, along with some progressive *sayyids* who were born in Indonesia (*muwallad*), opposed the division within the Hadhrami community and sought to integrate them into Indonesian society by establishing the Persatoean Arab Indonesia (PAI), the Union of Indonesian Arabs (Jonge, 1993, p. 86).

Orientation to Hadhramaut or Indonesia?

Attitudes towards Indonesian nationalism and independence was another issue that divided the Hadhrami community in colonial times. This idea was proposed by Indonesian-born Hadhrami (*muwallad*) who were caught between Alawi-Irsyadi disputes. The *muwallad* saw themselves as a different group from their parents who were born in Hadhramaut. *Wulaiti* were 'pure-blood' Hadhrami migrants from Hadhramaut, while *muwallad* were born in the diaspora with mixed descent (Mobini-Kesheh, 1999, p. 128). *Muwallad* mothers were local women, as Hadhrami women could not migrate, indicating that they were mixed descent. *Muwallad* regarded the conflict among Hadhrami as actually continuing the conflict in Hadhramaut (Haikal, 1986, p. 327). They advocated unity among *muwallad*, both

24   *Internal Dynamics within Hadhrami Arabs*

sayyids or Irsyadis, and called them to orient their nationalism to Indonesia. However, this movement was opposed by the Hadhrami. This led to a new division between the two generations: *wulaiti* versus *muwallad*.

A young *muwallad* who played a central role in this movement was the former Irsyadi member, Abdurrahman Baswedan (1908–1986). He was born into non-*sayyid* family in 1908 in Sunan Ampel Surabaya. After spending a few years studying with Sayyid teachers in a Hadhrami school in Surabaya, he was sent to study at the al-Irsyad school in Batavia under Shaikh Ahmad Surkati. Being educated in a reformist school, he was familiar with the idea of equal rights. Since a young age, he showed his passion in writing. When he was 18 years, he began writing a series of articles for Hadhrami periodicals in Surabaya (Jonge, 2004, p. 381). Since 1931, Baswedan worked as an editor in periodicals led by Hadhrami who sought to unite opposing groups of Hadhrami. He later became an editor-in-chief of the Chinese newspaper *Sin Tit Po*. This newspaper belonged to a progressive Chinese, Liem Koen Hiam, who supported Indonesian nationalism. According to Mobini-Kesheh (1999, pp. 134–135), his engagement with the Chinese media had influenced Baswedan in using the Malay terms *totok* (newcomers) and *peranakan* (Indies born) to denote the division between *wuilaiti* and *muwallad* within the Hadhrami community. Furthermore, he was also influenced by Liem who found the Indonesian Chinese Party (Persatuan Tionghoa Indonesia, PTI). The organisation called on Chinese immigrants to consider the Indies their homeland. This later inspired him to form an organisation for *muwallad*.

According to Jonge, Baswedan also engaged in local Indonesian institutions that made him acquainted with other parts of society. For instance, he served as a member of the Preaching Council (*Majelis Tabligh*) of Muhammadiyah in East Java in which he undertook preaching activities. He also became a member of Jong-Islamieten Bond (JIB), an Indonesian Muslim youth organisation. Engaging with local communities, he could hear their criticisms and stereotypes regarding the Hadhrami community, such as Arabs were usurers, misers, and swindlers, which motivated him to correct these negative perceptions (Jonge, 2004, p. 382).

His efforts in emancipating the Arabs through writing led him and his supporters to found a new organisation for the young Hadhrami generation, the PAI. Baswedan actively disseminated his ideas in pro-nationalistic newspapers such as *Sin Tit Po*, *Soeara Umum*, and *Matahari* (Jonge, 1993, p. 87). He attacked the dominant view among the Hadhrami that the Indies was only 'a temporary domicile' and criticises the bad behaviour of *wulaiti* Arabs who were different from *muwallad* (Jonge, 2004, p. 385). Realising that his articles were welcomed by many fellow young Hadhrami, he followed up by visiting Hadhrami communities, both *sayyids* and non-*sayyids*, around Java persuading them to join a conference for establishing the organisation. The conference took place in Semarang in October 1934. There were about 40 young participants, either active supporters of Rabithah or Al-Irsyad (Mobini-Kesheh, 1999, p. 136). To avoid any friction over the use of the *sayyid* title during the conference, it was decided that participants would call each other *saudara* (brother). All participants supported Baswedan's idea for establishing a new organisation, the Union of Indonesian Arabs (PAI). The main goal of this organisation was to promote "the emancipation of the Hadhrami and their integration into the society at large" (Jonge, 2004, p. 387). Among the PAI's main principles were the recognition of Indonesia as the homeland for the *peranakan* Arabs and the need to improve their position in social, political, and economic matters (Mobini-Kesheh, 1999, p. 137). Identifying themselves as Indonesians, members of the PAI considered their organisation to be a nationalist movement like all other nationalist movements in Indonesia, and therefore, they should have the same rights as their fellow Indonesians (Algadri, 1988, p. 120).

The founding of the PAI divided the two Hadhrami generations. On the one hand, the majority of *wulaiti* – who were proud of their pure Arabness and their cultural heritage – felt deeply offended and accused Baswedan and his PAI of trying to persuade Hadhrami to abandon their Arab identity for the sake of assimilation into Indonesia society (Mobini-Kesheh, 1999, p. 143). Furthermore, they accused the PAI of creating a new conflict within the Hadhrami community by dividing children and their parents. Many *wulaiti* wanted to meet Baswedan to debate him and even attack him physically (Haikal, 1986, p. 343). On the other hand, a minority of *muwallad* welcomed such an organisation, and others opposed it, but "the majority preferred to adopt a wait-and-see attitude" (Jonge, 2004, p. 387). They were reluctant to openly express their support for the PAI for fear of insulting their *wulaiti* parents, families, or their employers (Jonge, 2004, p. 387).

After the declaration of Indonesian independence in 1945, the majority of the Hadhrami supported Indonesian nationalism. Some *wulaiti* Hadhrami who opposed PAI apologised to Baswedan realising that his idea was right (Haikal, 1986, p. 441). The new policy under the new government allowed all political parties that were abolished during the Japanese occupation to be reinstated. However, instead of reviving the PAI, Baswedan and his colleagues decided to join Indonesian political parties. This decision was meant to demonstrate their greater assimilation into Indonesia. As a result, former PAI leaders could be found in various political parties from Islamic to communist one (Algadri, 1988, p. 131; Jonge, 2004, p. 394).

Hadhrami after Independence: Towards a Greater Assimilation

Despite the assimilation attempts of Hadhrami communities, especially among PAI leaders, the Hadhrami did not obtain equal treatment from the post-independence governments as indigenous Indonesians. They were categorised as *golongan kecil* (small groups), together with Indo-Chinese and Indo-Europeans (Jonge, 2004, p. 392). This minority status was in contrast to the objective of the PAI which was to achieve full citizenship for Arabs. Several articles of constitution and regulations remained discriminatory, limiting the rights of Hadhrami. Article 58, for instance, stipulated that three parliamentary seats would be allocated to the Arab minority (Algadri, 1988, p. 133). At the societal level, Hadhrami were not allowed the same eligibility for financial support as indigenous entrepreneurs. They also encountered barriers in joining co-operatives and buying land. At work, Hadhrami office workers had to sit behind those who were 'real Indonesians' (Jonge, 2004, p. 393). Thus, it is not surprising that many Hadhrami still felt themselves to be second-class citizens.

26 *Internal Dynamics within Hadhrami Arabs*

As part of a protest against the discrimination of Arabs, former PAI leaders who became parliamentary members refused to run as Arab representatives for the three seats allocated to their community in the first election in 1955 (Jonge, 2004, p. 395). The Hadhrami held a conference in Malang to oppose article 58. The result was the formation of the Board of the Conference for Indonesian Arabs (*Badan Konferensi Bangsa Indonesia Turunan Arab*). One of the objectives of the board was to have 58 removed from the Constitution. Hadhrami parliamentary members in various parties – most notably A.R. Baswedan (Majelis Syuro Muslimin Indonesian, Masyumi), Said Bahreisj (Partai Nasional Indonesia, PNI), Ahmad Bahmid (Nahdlatul Ulama, NU), and Hamid Algadri (Partai Sosialis Indonesia, PSI) – worked actively to make their community's voice heard. In response to the demands of Hadhrami, the government promised to accommodate their aspirations but said it would also need to make broader policies for accommodating other minorities (Algadri, 1988, p. 136). In the 1955 election, Hadhrami gained six seats in the House of Representatives, but as the representatives of Indonesian political parties rather than the representatives of Arab communities. This was confirmed in a book published by the Indonesian Parliamentary Secretary (n.d., pp. 606–620). Unlike the Indo-Chinese and Indo-European parliamentary members who represented their community, the name lists of Hadhrami ones in the 1955 national election were all from national parties and not one single name listed as a 'small minority' respresentative. This became a supporting evidence for the Hadhrami to demand that the government treat them no differently than other 'Indonesians' (Algadri, 1988, p. 136).

Although the unequal treatment of Hadhrami by the government persists to this day, the problem appears to have diminished along with the growing social acceptance of Hadhrami as Indonesians (Jonge, 2004, p. 396). The fight for social acceptance was led by the increasing numbers of Hadhrami who occupied positions in a wide range of institutions, such as the government, the army, foreign service, education, and the arts (Jonge, 2004, p. 396). There have been a few ministers of Hadhrami descent. Ali Alatas, for instance, served as Minister of Foreign Affairs from 1988 to 1999. His position was later taken up by another Hadhrami, Alwi Shihab. The position of Minister of Religious Affairs was also occupied by two Hadhrami, Muhammad Quraish Shihab in 1998 and Said Agil Husin Al-Munawar from 2001 to 2004. Their important government positions notwithstanding, Hadhrami tend to downplay their Arab identities due to 'the ambivalent position of Arabness' in Indonesia (Mandal, 2011, pp. 299–300). In the course of time, Indonesian government and societies have come to see them as indigenous and cannot even recognise their Arabness.

Hadhrami in Contemporary Indonesia: Internal Divisions and Growing Sectarianism

Since the 1980s to present time, the Hadhrami have encountered internal frictions due to the spread of Shi'ism and Salafism in Indonesia. The conversion of younger Hadhrami generations to Shi'ism and Salafism created tension within *sayyid* and

Internal Dynamics within Hadhrami Arabs 27

Irsyadi group. This led to a reassertion of religious identity within each group. The following section will first discuss the relationship between Shia' and Hadhrami *sayyid* and then analyses the forms of doctrinal conflict and their causes within the *sayyid* community. The section ends with an analysis of the current split and its cause within the Al-Irsyad community. I argue that the doctrinal issue has dominated the current conflict within the Hadhrami community.

A Brief Look at Shi'a and the Roles of Hadhrami Sayyids in Indonesia

The negative attitude towards Shi'a is a recent phenomenon within the *sayyid* community considering its close relationship with Shi'ism. The Shi'a tradition encourages reverence to the Prophet and his family (*ahl bayt*), while *sayyid* are descendants of the Prophet who also revere the Prophet and his family. There is no clear account on the religious beliefs of the early Hadhrami *sayyids*, especially those of their ancestor Ahmad b. Isa, who moved from Iraq to Hadhramaut. What is clear is that most Hadhrami *sayyids* have retained their Sunni identity, adhering to the Shafi'i school in legal matters and the Ash'ari school in theology (Bang, 2003, p. 13). The majority of *sayyid* scholars maintain that their ancestor belonged to the Shafi'i school (Alatas, 1999, p. 328). However, there was an account arguing that Ahmad b. Isa was an imam of Shi'a, considering that he was a fourth-generation descendant of Imam Ja'far al-Sadiq. Imam Ja'far was a descendant of the Prophet who was believed to be the sixth Shi'a imam (Alatas 1999, p. 328). According to this account, Ahmad b. Isa concealed his Shi'a beliefs (*taqiyya*) and adopted Shafi'i views, which he then propagated to the population of Hadhramaut since the area was dominated by the Ibadi Muslims who opposed Shi'a. In other words, "Imam Ahmad disseminated the Shafi'i school but had the historical consciousness of the Shi'a" (Alatas, 1999, p. 328). Chiara Formichi offered an interesting view that the Hadhrami-*sayyid* traders contributed to the spread early forms of Shi'im in Southeast Asia. To explain her theory, Formichi borrows the term 'Alid piety' from Marshall Hodgson and 'cultural Shi'ism' from the Indonesian terminology (Formichi, 2014a, p. 5). These terms refer to a condition of 'pre-sectarian differentiation of devotional practice' which is different from the current formal Shi'a practice (Formichi, 2014a, p. 5; Formichi, 2014b, p. 101). In this context, the terms denote devotion to the Prophet and his family (*ahl al-bayt*) through religious and local rituals that were accepted and celebrated by Sunni Muslims (Formichi, 2014a).

In spite of the different views on past Shi'a influences, *sayyids* have played important roles in disseminating Shi'ism in Indonesia. Zulkifli (2013) found that several *sayyids* were of significance in the formation of a Shi'i community both before and after Indonesian independence. From the 19th to the 20th century, there were three eminent Shi'ite leaders from different *sayyid* families in the Netherland East Indies: Sayyid Muhammad b. Ahmad al-Muhdar (1861–1926), Sayyid Ali b. Ahmad Shahab (1865–1944), and Sayyid Aqil b. Zainal Abidin (1870–1952). The first was born in Hadhramaut and migrated to the Netherland East Indies where he engaged in religious teaching and *dakwah*. He contributed to establishing the Jam'iyyah al-Khairiyyah al-Arabiyyah, a sister Arab organisation of Jamiat Khair

28   Internal Dynamics within Hadhrami Arabs

in Batavia (Zulkifli, 2013, p. 17). The second was born in Batavia and became a leading Arab figure in Batavia for his role as a scholar, activist, and successful trader. He was also one of the founders of Jamiat Khair in Batavia. Both, however, only expressed their Shi'sm through writings and confined their Shi'a propagation to their relatives and close associates (Zulkifli, 2013, p. 19). The last mentioned, Sayyid Aqil, was born in Surabaya and spent his time studying in Mecca under Sunni Muslim scholars. It was only after he went to Singapore and learnt under Shi'ite ulama that he converted to Shi'ism. Unlike his predecessors, Sayyid Aqil preferred to propagate Shi'a teaching openly and engaging in debates with Sunni Ulama in Surabaya (Zulkifli, 2013, p. 20).

In the wake of the Iranian revolution in 1979, several Shi'ite *sayyids* with connections to Iran emerged and actively spread Shi'ism in Indonesia through *dakwah* and education. Although there were several leading figures, I will only mention two important *sayyids*. The first is Sayyid Husein al-Habsyi (1921–1994). Zulkifli found that Sayyid Husein al-Habsyi played a prominent role in the development of Shi'ism in Indonesia. Born in Surabaya, he started his formal education at the Madrasah Al-Khairiyyah in Surabaya and went on to study under the leading ulama in Johor, Malaysia, before teaching at the Al-Attas school for a period of time. Afterwards, he studied in Hadhramaut then went to Saudi Arabia for two years. He later moved to Najaf, Iraq to study under several eminent ulama. After returning to Surabaya, Sayyid Husein al-Habsyi began dedicating himself to teaching and scholarship within the Muslim community (Zulkifli, 2013, p. 53). Besides his career in Islamic education, he was also politically active and joined Masyumi (*Majelis Syuro Muslimin Indonesia*), the largest Muslim party during the Soekarno period. After Masyumi was banned in 1960, he returned to Islamic education and *dakwah*. In 1976, he established a *pesantren* called YAPI (*Yayasan Pesantren Islam*, Foundation of Islamic Pesantren) in Bangil. This school went on to become a centre of Shi'a education in Indonesia. Using his connections with Shi'ite leaders in Iran, he sent many of his students to continue their study in Qum. Many of these graduates later became renowned Shi'ite teachers in Indonesia (Zulkifli, 2013, pp. 27, 55–56). From the point of view of Sunni militants, the YAPI *pesantren* is "the factory of Indonesian Shi'ism" (Interview with Achmad Zein Al-Kaff, March 13, 2013).

The second *sayyid* is Husein Shahab. He is currently considered to be the pre-eminent Shi'a teacher (ustadz) in Indonesia. Born in Palembang, South Sumatra, on 27 December 1961, Husein Shahab received his primary and secondary education in his hometown, but completed senior high school at the *pesantren ar-Riyadh* founded by Arabs in Palembang. His engagement with Shi'ite teaching started during his years as a student at *hawza 'ilmiyya* in Qum and *halaqah* in Iran. He studied various Islamic disciplines including *fiqh*, Qur'anic exegesis, and Islamic philosophy and history under a number of renowned Shi'ite ulama and scholars. Between 1991 and 1994, he went to Bandung to join the Muthahari foundation led by a prominent Shi'i intellectual, Jalaluddin Rakhmat, serving as religious teacher. In 1994 he enrolled in a master programme at the International Institute of Islamic Thought and Civilization (ISTAC) in Malaysia. However, his study was

Internal Dynamics within Hadhrami Arabs 29

not completed as he was forced by the Malaysian government to leave due to his Shi'a beliefs (Zulkifli, 2013, pp. 62–64). This was connected to the new fatwa in 1996 by national religious councils to ban Shi'ism as it contradicts the theology of Sunni Islam (Saat, 2014, p. 366). Since 1999, Husein has been living in Jakarta and established himself as an *ustadz* and popular preacher. Having considerable social and cultural capital, he participated in the establishment of Shi'ite institutions such as the Islamic Cultural Centre of Al-Huda (ICC). He also participated in establishing Sufi teaching centres in Jakarta, such as the *Fitrah* Foundation and Forum *Al-Husainy*. Not only is he an active preacher, Husein Shahab has also written and translated several books on the topic of Sufism and Islamic philosophy to disseminate Shi'ism among Indonesian audience (Zulkifli, 2013, pp. 64–66).

The Current Sunni-Shi'a Division within the Sayyid Community

The friction within the Hadhrami-*sayyid* community over the Shi'a issue has occurred at both the leadership and grassroots levels. However, the dispute among *sayyid* leaders receives more exposure in the media than the grassroots conflict. Several *sayyids* told me that the doctrinal tension occurred in the community as a result of the rising Shi'ism in Indonesia in the wake of the Iranian revolution in 1979. The charisma of Ayatollah Khomeini, who is also a *sayyid*, and his success in leading the revolution made him an appealing figure among the *sayyid* community in Indonesia. He was regarded as a brave Muslim scholar and leader who opposed a tyrannical government backed by the US (Interview with Habib Hasan Daliel, January 28, 2013). A popular preacher in Malang, Habib Jamal b. Ba'agil, told me that the conversion of young Hadhrami to Shi'ism was also due to the fact that there was no ulama from Hadhramaut who could inspire Hadhrami-*sayyids* in the 1980s and 1990s (Interview with Habib Jamal b. Ba'agil, March 25, 2013). The severing of ties between Indonesia and Yemen after the Socialist won power in Sana'a from 1967 to 1990 partly explained the conversion of young generations of *sayyids* to Shi'a. The story of Husein Shahab, who went to study in Iran several months after the revolution, is a good example of this trend. Initially, his reason to study in Qum was more educational than doctrinal. In time, though, he converted to Shi'ism (Zulkifli, 2013, pp. 61–62). Conversion to Shi'ism increased among the Hadhrami, and Indonesians in general, after the graduates returned from Iran. Many of them became preachers and writers, and went on to found Shi'ite educational institutions and religious learning centres. As observed by Zulkifli, the majority of students at the Shi'i YAPI *pesantren* in Bangil were predominantly Indonesian Arabs (Zulkifli, 2013, p. 144).

The growing conversion of young *sayyids* to Shi'ism has caused deep concerns in Sunni-Shafi'i Hadhrami community. Some *habaib* told me that the Shi'a issue has led to disputes and splits within *sayyid* families. There have been cases of Sunni parents repudiating their children who converted to Shi'ism. Several divorces also happened when one spouse found the other had converted to Shi'ism (Pers. communication with Syafiq, August 12, 2015; Alwi al-Kaff, August 13, 2015). *Sayyid* families who are tolerant towards Shi'ism or seek to maintain harmony within

30   *Internal Dynamics within Hadhrami Arabs*

their family tend to be silent on the matter if they know that one of their family members is Shi'a. In organisational and educational settings, tension also occurred. The leader of Ahlul Bait Indonesia (ABI), one of the main Shi'ite organisations in Indonesia, Habib Hasan Daliel al-Aydarus, was fascinated with Ayatollah Khomeini when he, along with his Sunni colleague, Habib Rizieq Syihab, studied in the Saudi Arabia. Upon returning to Indonesia, he dedicated himself to teaching at his former school, Jamiat Khair in Jakarta. However, when the school's principal and teachers found that he had 'converted' to Shi'ism he was censured and eventually resigned (Interview with Syauqi, February 2, 2013). Habib Hasan later established ABI together with his Shi'i friends.

Albayyinat and Anti-Shi'a

The vast majority of *sayyid* religious scholars and preachers in Indonesia maintain that their ancestors are Sunni. They emphasise that Sunni Islam has been integral to the identity of Hadhrami-*sayyids* ever since their ancestor's migration to Indonesia and until now. They regard Shi'a a new and disturbing development among *sayyid*. Most preachers I met argue that Shi'a is a deviant sect within Islam. In countering Shi'ism, the majority of Sunni *habaib* choose to focus on peaceful preaching and education rather than public agitation or violent action. Claiming to follow the ethics of the *Tariqa 'Alawiya* ('Alawi spiritual path), most *habaib* also prefer not to mention their Shi'a rivals by name in their sermons. However, some *habaib* do openly oppose Shi'ism in their preaching and writings.

Habaib resistance to Shi'ism took a tangible form with the establishment of Albayyinat in 1988. This movement was founded by several *habaib* in Java including Habib Ahmad b. Zein Al-Kaff of Surabaya, Habib Thohir b. Abdullah Al-Kaff of Tegal, Habib Abdul Qadir Al-Haddad of Malang, and Habib Ahmad Assegaf of Bangil (Interview with Habib Achmad b. Zein Al-Kaff, March 13, 2013). Although it was founded in 1988, its name did not appear in public until after the fall of the New Order. Its website states that the formation of the group was driven by growing development of Shi'ism in Indonesia spreading religious beliefs that 'deviated' from the Prophet's teachings. The group also claimed that Shi'is condemn and insult the Companions of the Prophet (Albayyinat n.d). Albayyinat calls itself the Sunni group that seeks to protect Sunni Muslims from the spread of Shi'ism. Despite the diversity of Shi'ism, Albayyinat regards it as single religion – a false and deviant religion, and therefore an enemy of Islam. The group's activities focus on socialisation and preaching on the danger of Shi'a through publications and internet resources, training courses, seminars, and sermons. The group has also built a collaboration with Muslim organisations, either traditionalist or Salafi, in opposing Shi'ism. Despite their limited activity, Albayyinat is becoming more vocal in the media and has been at times guilty of inciting intolerance and violence towards the Shi'a community.

The chairman of Albayyinat, Habib Achmad b. Zein Al-Kaff, has sharply criticised Shi'as and condemned Muslim leaders who appeared to be tolerant to Shi'ism, including *habaib*. He has been popularly invited by various organisations,

Internal Dynamics within Hadhrami Arabs   31

both traditionalist and reformist, to give anti-Shi'a talks and cadre training. He urges all Sunni Muslims, including the Salafis, to fight against Shi'a as a common enemy. Not only is he attacking the Shi'i leaders and their institutions, he also criticises moderate Muslims who seek to build a harmony with Shia.

Attacking Fellow Habaib

Criticising and denouncing fellow *habaib* publicly is a recent phenomenon among *habaib* in Indonesia. This is largely due to the tension arising from theological issues. Habib Achmad of Albayyinat is an example of this phenomenon. In several public sermons and seminars, Habib Achmad strongly criticised fellow *habaib* who have converted to Shi'ism. He regards their conversion as a blight on the *sayyid* community. He argues that Sunnism has always been the core identity of *habaib* since the times of their earliest ancestor in Yemen, Ahmad b. Isa al-Muhajir. In a seminar entitled 'Why Shi'a are not Muslim' on February 2014 in Surakarta, Habib Achmad stated very clearly that "if there are *habaib* becoming Shi'i, (it means) they have become traitors to their ancestor (the Prophet). If they do not walk along the path of '*Alawiyyin*, they are not *habaib* anymore" (Kiblat, 2014).[1] In my interview with him, he expressed his dissatisfaction with the Rabithah Alawiyah which he accused of not being serious in their efforts to counter Shi'ism, although it bases its religious principles on Sunni Islam. He urged the Rabithah to adopt his anti-Shi'i programme. He also suspects that the reason for Rabithah's failure is that some Rabithah leaders have Shi'a relatives. He mentioned the case of the general chairman of Rabithah Alawiyah, Habib Zen Umar b. Smith, who has a Shi'a brother-in-law, a famous religious singer, Haddad Alwi (Interview with Habib Achmad b. Zein Al-Kaff, March 13, 2013).

One of Habib Achmad's targets is the famous Muslim scholar and the prolific writer Professor Quraish Shihab, who is also a *sayyid*. Quraish is a former rector of the State Institute for Islamic Studies (IAIN) of Jakarta (1992–1998) and a former Minister of Religious Affairs (1998). He pursued Islamic studies at the Al-Azhar University, Egypt, from the undergraduate to the doctoral level. Although Quraish has descent from the Prophet, he avoids using the tittle *habib* and does not wear specific clothing that identifies him as *habib*. Quraish is popularly known as a moderate ulama whose views and works have a wide appeal to many Muslims in Indonesia. He has produced numerous books on Islam and a complete volume of Qur'anic exegesis. Despite his moderate views, aspects of his thought have been criticised by Islamist and conservative groups in Indonesia. One of those is his idea to bridge the distance between Sunnis and Shi'is, as indicated by his book entitled *Sunni-Shi'i Holding Hands: Is it Possible?* The book examines the similarities and differences in terms of theological doctrines between both groups. For Quraish, the difference between the two is not significant, and therefore, he advocates unity and enjoins Indonesian Sunni Muslims to live in harmony with Shi'a. Habib Achmad condemned the idea of bridging the two groups and argued that Shi'as are non-Muslims due to their incorrect theology. He likens Sunni and Shi'a to water and oil that can never mix. The differences between the two in both doctrinal pillars

32 Internal Dynamics within Hadhrami Arabs

(*usul*) and branches (*furu'*) are too great to ignore, according to Habib Achmad. *Usul* is related to pillars of religion, while *furu'* is related to practices of religion. Having different views on the former can lead a Muslim to be judged 'deviant', while having different views on the later has no consequence since it has different interpretations. Habib Achmad suspected that the project of reconciling the two groups is part of a hidden Shi'a agenda aimed at converting the Sunni majority in Indonesia. He also suspected that Quraish was approached and funded by the Shi'is through their generous projects (Interview with Habib Achmad b. Zein Al-Kaff, March 13, 2013).

Another target of Habib Achmad's criticism is the leader (*imam besar*) of Islamic Defenders Front (Front Pembela Islam [FPI]), Habib Muhammad Rizieq b. Syihab. Habib Rizieq, with his FPI, has acquired notoriety as a radical figure who fights against immorality and threats to Islam. He has been very critical of liberal Muslim thinkers, and several groups considered to be deviant such as Ahmadiyah. Despite his militant views and actions, Habib Rizieq still considers Shi'a as a part of Islam. He divides Shi'i into two groups: the just and moderate Shi'i (*mu'tadil*) and the extremist Shi'i (*ghulat*). For Habib Rizieq, despite their high respect for Ali, the former group does not condemn the Companions of the Prophet and his wife, Aisha. They also do not attack Sunni Muslims in public. Moderate Shi'a, for him, are not deviant and are still within the straight path of Islam. However, for the second group, he considers it deviant since they condemn the companions of the Prophet and Aisha and readily attack Sunni Muslims in their sermons (Interview with Habib Muhammad Rizieq b. Syihab, April 4, 2013). Despite Habib Rizieq's criticism of 'extreme' Shi'a, he is still denounced by Habib Achmad, particularly for his attitude regarding the moderate Shi'is and for his willingness to have Shi'i give sermons in his house. He urged Habib Rizieq to be more critical against all Shi'is (Interview with Habib Achmad b. Zein Al-Kaff, March 13, 2013).

Since Albayyinat is only a small group, its radical attitude to Shi'ism does not represent the behaviour of Indonesian *habaib*. The organisation has no headquarters, clear structure, and mass-following. Neither has it any means for systematic mass mobilisation. Its anti-Shi'a campaign is expressed mostly through sermons and books written by Habib Achmad. Although many Sunni *habaib* reject Shi'a, they do not express their rejection though public agitation and violence. They prefer to strengthen the Sunni belief of their community in order to protect them from Shi'a influences. However, Habib Achmad's strong anti-Shi'ism makes him popular among conservative *sayyids* and Islamists.

Despite its organisational limits, the anti-Shi'a campaign has stigmatised and provoked violence against Shi'is. One instance of the anti-Shi'a campaign resulting in violence was the mob attack on Ponpes Darul Sholihin owned by Habib Ali b. Umar al-Habsyi in Jember, East Java, on 11 September 2013. This attack, however, was not mobilised by Albayyinat leaders. It was ignited by the allegation that the *pesantren* had been spreading Shi'ism to its students. Habib Ali clarified that he and his teachers did not spread Shi'ism, but only taught Sufism and undertook healing practice in the *pesantren* (Kontras, 2013; Republika, 2013). The Commission for the Disappearance and Victims of Violence (Kontras) found in the field that the false accusation was driven by competition and envy on the part of several local *ustadz* (religious preachers and teachers) in the area due to the success of Habib Ali in managing the *pesantren* and expanding its building facilities (Kontras, 2013). Sources from Shi'i media, a few blogs, and videos on YouTube claimed that Habib Muhdhor al-Hamid, a vocal anti-Shi'i *habib* from Jember who is affiliated to Albayyinat, was involved in inciting the violence.[2] It was reported that local preachers, who were hostile to Habib Ali, facilitated a public gathering several months before the incident and invited anti-Shi'a *habaib* from Albayyinat including Habib Achmad b. Zein Al-Kaff of Surabaya and Habib Muhdhor al-Hamid of Jember to give sermons on the danger of Shi'a to local Muslims. However, it cannot be proved whether their sermons were the major cause of the mob attack on the *pesantren*. In fact, the masterminds behind the attack were local preachers who invited Albayyinat leaders to give sermons on anti-Shi'ism.

The growing anti-Shi'a campaign by some *habaib* has not led to greater conflict between Sunni and Shi'a within the *sayyid* community. The major reason is that the *sayyid* community have been divided in their response to Shi'ism. The Rabitah Alawiyah itself has not officially declared that it rejects Shi'ism. Shi'a *sayyids* are tolerated and allowed to attend the Rabitah's social and religious events, although none holds a position in the Rabitah. As the minority, the Shi'a leaders and scholars tend to use defensive strategy by clarifying perceived misunderstanding of Shi'ism and put forward the common platform and unity among Muslims. Their attempt has also been supported by moderate Sunni scholars such as Quraish Shihab and former religious leaders from the Nahdlatul Ulama and Muhammadiyah such as Said Aqil Siradj and the late Ahmad Syafii Maarif, respectively.

The Split of Al-Irsyad Al-Islamiyah: A Doctrinal Contest

Over the past decade, Al-Irsyad Al-Islamiyah has been divided into two camps: Al-Irsyad Al-Islamiyah and Perhimpunan Al-Irsyad. The former is the old guard that claims to maintain the original modernist spirit of the organisation, while the latter is the conservative faction, which is influenced by Salafi views that have sought to bring about a purification of Islam and more professional management within the organisation. I argue that while leadership rivalry is the trigger for the division, the root cause of the conflict was the contest for authority between the modernists and the young conservatives as both factions claim to maintain the teachings of the founder, Imam Ahmad Surkati.

The leadership conflict started in the mid-1990s. A group of Irsyadis was dissatisfied with the leadership of Geys Amar who had been chairman three times since 1982. The anti-Geys group wanted to revitalise the organisation through religious purification. At the Al-Irsyad congress in 1996 in Pekalongan, Geys Amar once again ran for the chairmanship. His only rival, Muhammad Bawazir, withdrew from the election in order to avoid conflict. Winning by default, Geys Amar came under pressure from some members of his executive board whom he considered fanatics and troublemakers in the organisation (Interview with Geys Amar, February 11, 2013). In 1998, therefore, Geys purged more than ten executive members,

34 *Internal Dynamics within Hadhrami Arabs*

including his deputy chairman, Muhammad Bawazir. This removal led to the dissident group to hold an extraordinary congress in Tawangmangu, Central Java, in October 1999, resulting in the formation of a new rival Al-Irsyad leadership. The newly elected chairman was Farouk Zein Bajabir. In the following year, the Amar's camp held a 37th congress in Bandung in which Hisyam Thalib was elected as the new leader, while Geys Amar became General Secretary.

There were several attempts by the rival boards at reconciliation through mediation. They agreed to organise a joint congress in Cilacap in 2002. At this congress, the majority of participants voted for Farouk from the conservative group. Greatly chagrined at their defeat, the old guards denounced the congress as unconstitutional and refused to accept the result. Both groups appealed to the high court in East Jakarta to validate their legal status. In 2004, the court ruled in favour of the modernists and declared the 2002 congress in Cilacap invalid. After their defeat, the conservatives established a new organisation called 'Perhimpunan Al-Irsyad' (Al-Irsyad Association) by modifying the name and the flag of the former organisation. The organisation has been registered with the Ministry of Law and Human Rights through a ministerial decision in 2013. There have been attempts from both sides at reconciliation albeit unsuccessfully, to date.

Both the old modernist and the young conservative group share a similar concern regarding Al-Irsyad's stagnation. Compared to another modernist organisation, Muhammadiyah, Al-Irsyad has experienced very little organisational expansion or an increase in the number and quality of its educational institutions. In 2009, Al-Irsyad only had 132 branches across 23 provinces, 8 hospitals in various cities, and 140 educational institutions from kindergarten to high schools (Al-Irsyad, 2009). According to Slama, the limited expansion of Al-Irsyad lies in its failure "in recruiting substantial numbers of Indonesian Muslims from outside the Hadhrami community and is still widely perceived as an 'Arab' organization" (Slama, 2014, p. 121). Besides, Al-Irsyad schools also show poorer performance compared to other Islamic schools due to the lack of human resources, limited support from Hadhrami community, and the lack of Irsyadi orientation in its curriculum (Al-Irsyad, 2006). Despite various indicators of Al-Irsyad's malaise, most Irsyadi leaders in both camps are more inclined to attribute their organisation's decline to the lack of ideological commitment within the organisation and its educational institutions. In other words, Irsyadis organisations and schools do not teach students nor implement the values of 'being Irsyadi' in everyday life.

The two groups have made attempts to revive the golden age of the organisation and its educational institutions as developed by Ahmad Surkati. They believe that Al-irsyad is in crisis, especially in terms of adherence to ideological principles and the mastery of Arabic and Islamic studies. Some leaders told me that many young Irsyadis now no longer implement and nor even understand Al-Irsyad's principles (*mabadi*). Moreover, many young Irsyadis no longer comprehend Arabic and lack Islamic knowledge. Not surprisingly, Irsyadi leaders are anxious to revive the identity and Islamic skills of Irsyadis.

Doctrinal issues are the main source of division. The old Al-Irsyad leaders argue that the big challenge facing the organisation is Salafi-Wahhabi influences upon the

Internal Dynamics within Hadhrami Arabs 35

young generation. They believe that too many Irsyadis are studying in Salafi educational institutions in Jakarta, such as the Institute of the Study of Islam and Arabic (*Lembaga Ilmu Pengetahuan Islam dan Bahasa Arab* [LIPIA]). Some LIPIA graduates would later continue their study in Islamic universities in Saudi Arabia, Yemen, and Afghanistan. At these institutions, they often come under the influence of Salafi-Wahhabi teachings. Geys said in exasperation:

> Those (Irsyadis) who studied in the Middle East, either wittingly or not, were influenced by Wahhabi thought. This could be seen from the way they pray and the style of their clothes and appearance such as wearing trousers right to their ankles (*isbal*), having long beards, and their wives wearing an enveloping black veil. They behave as if the truth is only on their side.
>
> (Gatra 26, May 7, 2009)

Noorhaidi Hasan's study (2006) on the Salafi movement in Indonesia observed that several leading Salafi leaders in Indonesia were Hadhrami Arabs, and some of them were previously educated in Al-Irsyad schools. According to older Al-Irsyad leaders, when these young Hadhrami returned to Indonesia, they became active members and spread conservative views that differ radically from traditional Irsyadi principles. For instance, these youths prefer to use *ru'ya* (sighting moon) instead of *hisab* (modern calculation) on determining the coming day of Ramadhan month. Many of them also insisted on segregating men and women in Al-Irsyad's events. Senior Irsyadi leaders complained that these youths' views and attitudes were puritanical and contrary to Irsyadi principles that teach adapting to modernity; these views contained seeds of radicalism and possibly even terrorism (Interview with Said Sungkar and Zeyd Al-Hiyed, April 16, 2013). Geys Amar claimed that the conservative group tried to inject their Wahhabi teachings into young Irsyadis and to hijack the organisation by running for leadership positions. The reason he dismissed more than ten executive members in 1998 was that he believed they were causing problems in the organisation (Interview with Geys Amar, February 11, 2013).

The old camp leaders saw that the penetration of Wahhabism in the organisation has been caused by both external and internal factors. The external factor is the expansion of Salafism in Indonesia through generous Saudi funding. According to Geys Amar, the Wahhabi infiltration came through Saudi donation that was channelled through the Religious Attaché in the Saudi Arabia embassy in Jakarta. Donations were delivered to schools, *pesantren*, and mosques owned by Al-Irsyad. They also provided scholarships to those wanting to study Arabic courses and Islamic studies in Indonesia, such as LIPIA, and to those who want to study in Saudi Arabia (Gatra 26, May 7, 2009). I observed that several Irsyadis who studied in Saudi-funded institutions have become prominent preachers within the Salafi community in Indonesia. They include Yusuf Usman Baisa (the current chairman of the Perhimpunan Al-Irsyad), Farid Ahmad Okbah (the former member of Perhimpunan Al-Irsyad),[3] and Ja'far Umar Thalib (the former principal of Al-Irsyad school in Tengaran and the founder of Laskar Jihad).

36   Internal Dynamics within Hadhrami Arabs

The second factor is related to the reformist nature of the organisation and the lack of Irsyadi identity. One Irsyadi leader, Said Sungkar, said that it is understandable why Irsyadis easily moved to Wahhabi groups as both have similar ideals of religious reformism (i.e. returning to the Qur'an and Hadith). The difference is that the Salafi are heavily reliant on religious texts, and thus rigid and textual, while Irsyadis also take into account external factors such as social reality and science in understanding texts. He mentioned the case of slavery as an example; Salafis view slavery as justified by texts (Interview with Said Sungkar, April 16, 2013). Furthermore, the organisation's identity and established ideology fail to attract younger Irsyadis. Since Indonesian independence, the government has demanded that all schools, including Al-Irsyad, use Indonesian language as the primary language in learning activities. This affected Al-Irsyad schools which used Arabic as their main language. The problem was exacerbated by the fact that the founder of the organisation, Ahmad Surkati, did not leave obvious works that could become a doctrinal foundation. Unlike the reformist organisation Muhammadiyah, Al-Irsyad schools do not offer a particular subject related to the ideological principles that can serve as a point of reference in their religious views and practices. Moreover, the 'secular' subjects are now more dominant than religious subjects because of the need to meet national guidelines (Interview with Said Sungkar and Zeyd Al-Hiyed, April 16, 2013). In dealing with this situation, Al-Irsyad Al-Islamiyah has recently published a manual containing the organisation's principles and their explanation for Irsyadis aiming at strengthening their identity. The principles include the source of Islamic law, *akidah/tauhid* (theology), *ibadah* (religious devotion), *akhlak* (ethics), egalitarianism (*al-musawa*), knowledge, and modernity (PP. Al-Irsyad al-Islamiyyah, 2012). To illustrate their approach to asserting their ideology, the chairman of Al-Irsyad Al-Islamiyah, Abdullah Jaidi, stated in his foreword of the book:

> Today, foreign thoughts have infiltrated the environment of Al-Irsyad. The thoughts seem not in line with our *mabadi'* (principles) that we hold. This infiltration takes form in two big streams. The first wave brings us to a conservative condition (*jumud*) in which people only rely on the past and use *taqlid* (blind following), while the second wave is liberal thought that could uproot us from our values of religion and history…Therefore, as the central leaders of Al-Irsyad Al-Islamiyyah consider that it is important to revive the identity (*jati diri*) of the followers of al-Irsyad by enhancing their understanding of *mabadi'*, which serves as ideology of organisation, and their understanding of Islam that is adaptive and in line with the development of history and situation.
>
> (PP. Al-Irsyad Al-Islamiyyah, 2012, pp. 9–10)

Such statements indicate the concern and suspicion of old Al-Irsyad leaders towards new thoughts which they perceive as a challenge to the religious identity of Irsyadis. Interestingly, the foreign thoughts are coming from Muslim groups. Abdullah mentioned two streams of thoughts: conservatism and liberalism. Although Abdullah did not clearly state which groups he meant, we can infer that he was

Internal Dynamics within Hadhrami Arabs 37

talking about Salafism and liberal Islam. The book was published partly to prevent young Irsyadis from becoming once again influenced by Saudi Salafism. In terms of his rejection of liberal Islam, Abdullah holds the same view as the young Al-Irsyad, although his camp was accused as liberal. Both camps see liberal Islam using rationality over doctrines in understanding Islam. In their view, this could lead Muslims to adopt secularism and abandon their Islamic values. By publishing the *mabadi'*, Abdullah hopes that it could become a guideline for Irsyadis in grasping the Al-Irsyad ideological principles and protecting them from foreign influences.

The rival executive board, Perhimpunan Al-Irsyad, emphasised leadership and doctrinal problem as the cause of the conflict. The leadership problem, in their view, lay with the style of leadership of Geys Amar, who was too dominant and not accommodative to young Irsyadi aspirations. As Geys had occupied four periods of leadership from 1982 to 2000, he was seen as resistant to organisational regeneration and innovation. The Perhimpunan group sees itself as idealists who have fought to improve the organisation through more professional management and the maintenance of Irsyadi basic principles (*mabadi'*) (Interview with Yusuf Usman Baisa and Husin Maskati, July 4, 2013; Muhammad Bawazir, September 11, 2013). Before the conflict, the Chairman Deputy, Muhammad Bawazir, and several executive members proposed to improve the organisation through the adoption of standard operating procedures and spelling out the authority and rights of chairman and other members. Geys approved this idea but later reneged, believing that the new rules limited his leadership. He felt under pressure and later removed several executive members. The Perhimpunan camp considered the reshuffle as the way for Geys to secure his position from internal threats (Interview with Muhammad Bawazir, September 11, 2013).

Besides leadership issues, the Perhimpunan group also objects to the doctrine of the main Al-Irsyad's camp. They reject the accusation that they are Wahhabis who have radical understanding of Islam. They regard such accusation as slanderous and a vilification of their group. They fought back by stating that the old group is too slack in upholding and implementing religion (Gatra 26, May 7, 2009). Yusuf suspected that the former camp was influenced by the ideas of liberalism and pluralism. This is due to their consideration in adapting social reality and modernity in interpreting the texts. In Yusuf's view, the former group leaders tend to favour hedonism (*hura-hura*) by mixing the interaction of men and women in Al-Irsyad's programme activities and wedding parties. For the Perhimpunan camp, this contradicts with the Qur'an and Hadith. The Perhimpunan group, therefore, has sought to revive religious purification in the organisation. In so doing, they seek to remind Irsyadis to uncompromisingly uphold the Qur'an and Hadith through education and *dakwah*. Yusuf regards the spirit of purification as the important principle of Al-Irsyad Al-Islamiyah laid down by the founder Ahmad Surkati. He sees the common platform between Al-Irsyad and Salafis in terms of ideology (Interview with Yusuf Usman Baisa, July 4, 2013).

Yusuf's puritanical views and his close connection to Salafi group indicate that he is a Salafi. A Salafi means that he follows the puritanical doctrines of Salafism. There are several indications of this. Firstly, he follows the conservative views of

38 *Internal Dynamics within Hadhrami Arabs*

Salafi in several aspects. One of them is the strict segregation between men and women in public activities. I observed that he and several members of Perhimpunan also follow Salafi style of clothing such as wearing trousers right to their ankles (*isbal*). What is more, he regarded Al-Irsyad as a Salafi in spirit. He even suggested me to listen to Rodja Radio and TV, the most important Salafi media in Indonesia, in order to know more about Al-Irsyad's views. Secondly, the clear evidence of his connection to Salafi group could be seen from his important roles in Salafi communities where he is often invited as speaker and preacher. Yusuf himself did not object to being called a Salafi, yet he did not like to be called a 'Wahhabi'. This might be because the Salafi term sounds positive, while Wahhabi, which means 'followers of Muhammad b. 'Abd al-Wahhab', is now viewed negatively and linked to Islamic radicalism and terrorism.

Yusuf's arguments indicate that he misunderstood the modernist principles of Al-Irsyad as laid down by Ahmad Surkati. His Salafi outlook led him to pick up only the purification aspects of Al-Irsyad and neglect its modernity aspects such as upholding egalitarianism and the compatibility between Islam and modern development. His failure in understanding Al-Irsyad's modernity led him to label Geys and his camp as liberal. Geys's views seem to follow the teachings of Imam Surkati. He and the old camp still uphold religious purification as an important part of Irsyadi identity. The recent manual of the old camp even regards Islamic liberalism as the challenge facing Al-Irsyad besides conservative Salafism. However, the major problem with Geys is his lengthy leadership and his failure to accommodate young Irsyadis' aspirations for a modern and successful organisation. Instead, he exaggerated the danger of Salafi-influenced Irsyadis and blamed them as the source of the organisation's decline.

Conclusion

This chapter has examined the internal dynamics within the Hadhrami community from the colonial era till modern-day Indonesia. It concludes that the conflicts within the Hadhrami community shifted from Hadhrami traditional stratification to Islamic doctrine. The coming of a new religious belief that challenges the privilege and authority of religious elites can lead to tension and division between groups. However, the changing political and social contexts have also influenced the way Hadhrami maintain their authority and status. In colonial times, the Hadhrami community united in an attempt to gain equality and modern education (Hadhrami awakening) in the Netherland East Indies. This was inspired by the Chinese awakening embodied in the establishment of modern associations and schools. It was also a response to the discriminatory policy of the colonial government which categorised Arabs as the second class after Europeans. According to the Hadhrami tradition, *sayyid* was a privileged group who was at the top of traditional hierarchy in their homeland. As the inheritors of the Prophet and the intercessors, they enjoyed special treatment and received signs of respect from other Hadhrami groups and local Muslims, such as hand-kissing. However, the coming of the teacher

Internal Dynamics within Hadhrami Arabs 39

from Mecca, Syekh Ahmad Surkati, who spread views of Islamic reformism, challenged the privileged position of the *sayyid* group. The reformist idea, which was adopted from Egypt thinkers, called for egalitarianism (*musawa*) among Muslims irrespective of their nationalities, class, and lineages. The challenge against Hadhrami social stratification eventually divided the community into two organisations: Jamiat Khair and Al-Irsyad. Most of the non-*sayyids* who favour Islamic reformism joined the latter group. However, the Indies-born Hadhrami, fed up with the conflict between their parents, sought to unite the Hadhrami from different groups, and appealed to them to consider Indonesia as their motherland. Their movement gained momentum with the foundation of the PAI whoese members were mostly *muwallad* (diaspora-born). This movement created yet another division among the Hadhrami, especially between the *wulaiti* and *muwallad* members of the PAI. This division, however, ended after the independence of Indonesia.

In post-independence Indonesia, especially after the 1980s, the two Hadhrami groups faced a new challenge. Globalisation has facilitated the flow of ideas and funding from the Middle East to Indonesia. The ideas of transnational Islamic movements such as Salafism and Shi'ism have been spreading among university students since the 1980s and later culminated in the formation of various organisations after the fall of Soeharto. Like other Indonesian Muslims, large numbers of young Hadhrami became interested in and joined these movements. The charisma of Khomeini and his successful revolution attracted young *sayyids* to study in Iran and later converted to Shi'ism. The conversion of young Hadhrami had a negative impact on the *sayyid* community, which generally follows Sunni theology and Shafi'i legal school. Several conservative *habaib* emerged and directed criticism at both Shi'a *sayyids* and moderate scholars, including *habaib*, who tried to promote dialogue between the two groups. They asserted that Sunnism was the identity of *sayyids* and Indonesian Muslims. In this respect, traditional Sunnism becomes the binding ideology among *sayyids*.

In the case of Al-Irsyad Al-Islamiyah, the conflict took place at the organisational level, driven by doctrinal contestation between old modernist and young conservative camp. The conflict was triggered by the reshuffle of several executive members by the long-time leader Geys Amar in 1998. Amar regarded the executive members he ousted from the organisation as Salafi intruders who were spreading conservatism among the Irsyadis. The conflict eventually divided the organisation into two: Al-Irsyad Al-Islamiyah and Perhimpunan Al-Irsyad. The former group claims to defend Al-Irsyad from conservative Salafi influences, while the latter vows to restore the organisation to its former glory through more assertive religious observance and more professional management. The leaders of the second group were educated in the Saudi-funded Salafi educational institutions and were largely influenced by Salafism. They are cast as a Wahhabi group trying to bring radical Islam into the organisation. In the meantime, the conservative camp views the old modernist as liberal and pluralist, and hence deviated from the true principle of Al-Irsyad (*mabadi'*). The two groups have competed for Irsyadi authority by reasserting the doctrinal principles of Al-Irsyad.

Notes

1 Habib Achmad's talks and interviews on Shi'ism are often exposed by conservative on-line media such as www.kiblat.net, www.voa-islam.com, www.arrahmah.com, www.hidayatullah.com, www.eramuslim.com, and www.antiliberalnews.com.
2 See for instance http://www.tvshia.com/indonesia/index.php/news/299-kronologi-kejadian-penyerangan-pp-darus-sholihin-dalam-rangka-peringatan-maulid-nabi-saw-ke-28 (accessed on 14 July 2015).
3 Okbah actively promotes anti-Shi'ism through *dakwah* and urges Indonesian Muslims to join jihad in Syiria against the Assad regime. According to Sidney Jones, Okbah is an ex-member of Jemaah Islamiyah and Afghan veteran. See Jones (2013), IPAC Report 2 December, p. 4.

3 Defending Traditional Islam

Habaib and Anti-Salafism

Introduction

Preaching (*dakwah*) to defend traditionalist Islam has become a widespread activity among *habaib* and traditionalist Muslim preachers in contemporary Indonesia. The aim of their *dakwah* is to promote traditionalist Sunni Islam and to challenge Salafism as well as other perceived 'deviant' groups. The emergence of this kind of *dakwah* in public was a response to the expansion of global Islamic movements such as Salafism, Shi'ism, and Hizbut Tahrir. While many scholars have studied these movements in an attempt to understand what they perceive as a threat to Indonesian democracy and pluralism, only a few have studied the traditionalist *dakwah* and its various forms in post-New Order Indonesia (see, for instance, Alatas, 2009; Woodward et al., 2012; Zamhari and Howell, 2012). One gap in the existing studies is analysis of Sunni tradition and doctrines. This chapter finds that some traditionalist preachers and activists have worked together in reasserting traditional Sunni Islam or what they call '*aswaja*' (the abbreviation of *ahl sunna wa al-jama'a*). Their *dakwah* movement seeks to reassert traditionalist Sunni orthodoxy while promoting anti-Salafism through various media such as sermon groups, books, print and electronic media, and internet.

The aim of this chapter is to analyse the religious factor that has paved a way for the emergence of the traditionalist *dakwah* in contemporary Indonesia. It argues that the emergence of the *aswaja dakwah* and its call for unity has been a response to the threats from internal and external forces that are seen as challenging the established religious doctrine and practice of traditional Islam. While Salafism is the primary perceived 'threat', some other Muslim movements, such as Shi'ism, Ahmadiya, Hizbut Tahrir, and Liberal Islam, are also deemed deviant.

The first part of this chapter discusses the general concept of Sunni Islam and its particular meaning for traditionalist Muslims in the Indonesian context. The second part examines the social and political context of the post-Soeharto era that gave rise to *aswaja dakwah* and the campaign of anti-Salafism among traditionalist Muslims. The third part analyses the variants of *aswaja dakwah* and its characteristics in contemporary Indonesia.

DOI: 10.4324/9781003358558-3

42   *Defending Traditional Islam*

Sunni and Traditional Islam in Indonesia

The term 'Sunni' refers to *ahl sunna wa al-jama'a*, meaning 'the people of the Prophetic tradition' (*sunna*) and 'community' (*jama'a*). Historically, the group emerged as a middle way out of the conflicts and controversies between two early opposing traditions after the death of the Prophet: Kharijism and Shi'ism (Newby, 2002, p. 187; Campo, 2009, p. 646). Disputes over legitimate leadership raised questions that divided Muslims into theological factions. The Kharijite were considered to be an extreme group since it declared that the sinners could not be regarded as Muslim. Shi'i refers to Ali's loyalists who believed that authority derives only from *ahl bayt* (family of the prophet) (Newby, 2002, p. 198; Campo, 2009, p. 646). In the current development, the label of Sunni is contrasted with Shi'a. Sunnism constitutes the largest branch of Islam in the world; however, Sunni Muslims are subdivided into various groups and organisations with different legal schools (*mazhab*) and different social and cultural centres (Newby, 2002, p. 198). In Indonesia, for instance, there are numerous Muslim organisations which claim to be Sunni, regardless of whether they are traditionalist or reformist in their religious orientation. Each group promotes Sunni Islam based on their own version of interpretation.

In an Indonesian context, traditionalist Muslims uses the distinctive abbreviation '*aswaja*' to identify their particular Sunni group. The term refers to the particular characteristics of Sunni traditionalists that are culturally linked to the largest Islamic mass organisation, Nahdlatul Ulama (NU; the Revival of the Islamic Scholars) (Burhani, 2012, p. 572). The term was used by NU members to distinguish themselves from the modernists, such as Muhammadiyah, Al-Irsyad, and Persis. In contemporary Indonesia, it also becomes a distinguishing identity from transnational Islamic movements such as Salafism, Shi'ism, and the Muslim Brotherhood. Among these groups, the reformist and Salafi movements have become a major concern for the traditionalists since they have challenged the doctrinal and traditional practices of traditionalist Muslims, especially for traditional religious leaders such as *kiai* and *habaib* who have enjoyed a privileged status and economic rewards from Muslim societies.

Any discussion of traditional Islam in Indonesia would be incomplete without considering the emergence of NU – the country's largest traditionalist Muslim organisation. The NU was established on 31 January 1926 in Surabaya by a number of religious scholars and businessmen from East Java (Bruinessen, 1994, p. 17; Fealy & Barton, 1996, p. xx). The aim was to "represent and foster traditional Islam in the Netherlands Indies" (Fealy, 1998, p. 17). The NU views itself as Sunni Islam and adheres to the concept of *ahl sunna wal-jama'a* or what they popularly called *aswaja*. For the NU, *aswaja* has three basic doctrines: adopting al-Ash'ari and al-Maturidi in Islamic theology; following one of the four legal Islamic schools (Hanafite, Malikite, Shafiite, and Hanbalite), especially Shafi'ite in *fiqh*; and following Sufi schools of al-Ghazali and al-Baghdady (Dhofier, 1982, p. 158; Haidar, 1994, p. 74; Burhani, 2012, p. 573). In general, the traditionalist ulama adopted a tolerant view towards non-Islamic local cultures. They understood that such local customs can serve as a means for spreading Islam more widely; therefore, the incorporation of various local customs has appeared in religious ceremonies popular among NU members, such as marriage, circumcision, *maulid* (the celebration of the Prophet's birthday), and *ziarah* (visiting the saint's tombs to obtain blessing and intercession) (Fealy, 1998, p. 20; Saleh, 2001, p. 70). Islamic rituals containing local customs have received criticism from the reformist groups, which regard them as non-Islamic and therefore an unlawful innovation (*bid'ah*).

The founding of NU in colonial Indonesia was a response to the growing challenge of Islamic modernism in the 20th century. The transmission of reformist ideas from the Middle East to Indonesia was accelerated by Indonesian leaders who went on pilgrimage to Mecca (Saleh, 2001, p. 71). The ideas of Egyptian reformers – Jamal al-Din al-Afghani (1838–1897), Muhammad 'Abduh (1849–1905), and Rashid Rida (1865–1935), to name but a few – inspired the creation of reformist organisations such as Muhammadiyah, Al-Irsyad, and Persis. The common platform of these reformist movements was to encourage people to purify their Islamic faith by returning to the fundamental sources of Islamic doctrine, the Qur'an and Hadith, and to reject local customs that contain heresy, superstition, and idolatry (Noer, 1980, p. 109; Saleh, 2001, p. 71). The reformists urged people to adopt independent reasoning (*ijtihad*) in their understanding of Islam rather than 'blindly' following the ulama's ideas from medieval times (*taqlid*). Not surprisingly, Muslim reformists were highly critical of the religious practices and customs of traditionalist Muslims that they considered to be *bid'ah*, such as reciting prayer's intention (*usalli*) with a loud voice, addressing prayers to the dead (*talqin*), commemorating the death of important figures through annual celebrations (*haul*), and holding feasts (*kenduri*) for the dead. According to the reformists, these rituals were not practiced by the Prophet during his lifetime. Given the challenge of Muslim reformists at that time, some scholars have argued that the establishment of the NU was the Muslim traditionalists' reaction to reformist movements that were increasingly gaining influence in Java (Chumaidy, 1976; Noer, 1980; Jones, 1984). Another scholar, Martin van Bruinessen, also found that the long dispute between modernists and traditionalists had an important impact; however, he argued that developments in the Middle East were the direct cause leading to the founding of the NU (Bruinessen, 1994, pp. 17–34). One such development was the occupation of Mecca by the Wahhabi under Ibn Sa'ud in the wake of the abolition of caliphate in 1924. The traditionalists were concerned that the occupation could lead to the ban of the Shafi'i-based religious rituals within and around Mecca, such as *ziarah* (grave's visitation) and Sufi activities, and the destruction of the graves of the Prophet and his companions. Failing to make their voice heard at several Islamic congresses in Indonesia, the traditionalists then formed the *Komite Hijaz* that enabled them to send their own delegates to Mecca. They also agreed to establish an organisation called 'Nahdlatul Ulama' to represent traditional Islam. The short-term goal of the NU was to enhance the authority of the Komite delegation, while the longer term was to "create an institution capable of coordinating and developing traditionalist responses to the modernist threat" (Fealy, 1998, p. 27; see also Bruinessen, 1994,

44 *Defending Traditional Islam*

p. 34). Thus, it can be said that the foundation of the NU was a response to both the reformist movements in Indonesia and the rise of Salafi-Wahhabism in Mecca.

From the 1920s to the mid-1930s, Muslim traditionalists and modernists engaged in heated debates. Tension arose not only in Java but also in Sumatra (Noer, 1980, pp. 237–241). However, since the mid-1930s, there has been a growing awareness in both groups to reconcile and forge unity. The modernists came to realise that they could not eradicate *bid'ah* in a short space of time, while the traditionalists accepted that they had to co-exist with the modernists (Noer, 1980, p. 260). Furthermore, the discriminatory actions of the Dutch government caused discontent among Muslim groups that led to non-cooperation with the colonial administration. The reconciliation between the two groups was evident through the joint establishment of MIAI (Majlis Islam A'laa Indonesia or Supreme Council of Indonesian Muslims) on 21 September 1937 in Surabaya. The purpose of this federation was to promote unity and cooperation between Muslims (Fealy, 1998, p. 39; Bush, 2009, p. 41).

Since the foundation of the Indonesian nation state, there has been no significant doctrinal dispute between traditionalists and modernists; however, in the years after independence, the NU engaged in politics that led them to a compromise with the state. The NU's political activity was at its height especially after it separated from Masyumi and became a political party in 1952. Between the 1950s and the 1970s, NU leaders came to a compromise with Soekarno's restrictive Guided Democracy administration and Soeharto's authoritarian New Order regime (Fealy, 2007, p. 154). In 1984, however, NU withdrew itself from party politics and decided to return to *Khittah 1926* (the original platform of the organisation). The period from the 1980s to the 1990s was the era of growing intellectualism for the NU. Many progressive intellectuals and activists emerged and established various institutions such as NGOs and study centres for promoting pluralism and tolerance (Bush, 2009, p. 90). Despite these developments, NU leaders remained active in Indonesian politics. Their return to formal politics was marked by the foundation of four NU-based parties in 1998. The largest surviving party is PKB (Partai Kebangsaan Bangsa; National Awakening Party). Given the rising activity of leading NU intellectuals and leaders in business and politics in post-Soeharto era, NU is no longer "a major force for reform or religious and social liberalization" (Fealy, 2007, p. 165).

Aswaja Dakwah and Anti-Salafism in the Post-New Order Era

A Glance of Indonesian Salafism

The reforms that followed the fall of Soeharto paved the way for freedom of expression in the public sphere. Several Islamic parties emerged and Islamic movements proliferated (Zada, 2002; Azra, 2004; Jamhari & Jahroni, 2004). The ideas of political Islam that had been suppressed by the state were revived and came into public debates (Hasan, 2006, p. 14).

Defending Traditional Islam   45

Islamic movements that went underground in the New Order era – Salafism, Tarbiyah (Indonesian version of Muslim Brotherhood), Hizbut Tahrir, and Tablighi Jamaat, to name but a few – took the opportunity of the new freedom to conduct Islamic activities in public and urge people to support their missionary work. Polemics between Muslim groups articulating different views were expressed through periodicals, books, websites, and public discussions (Meuleman, 2011, p. 246). Salafi movement is the most active one in propagating puritanical Islam in Indonesia. Salafis call on Muslims to return to the original ways of Islam by emulating the Prophet and early Muslim generations (Meijer, 2009, pp. 3–4). Their puritanical Islam was reflected in their concerns with "matters of creed and morality, such as strict monotheism, divine attributes, purifying Islam from accretions, and anti-Sufism, as well as typical Arab-style dress, exclusivist tendencies and rigid ritual practices" (Hasan, 2010, p. 677). Moreover, the Salafi activists also criticise local Muslim practices that they regard as 'unlawful innovation' (*bid'ah*).

The active propagation of Salafi doctrine in Indonesia has been a part of the Saudi global campaign for spreading the Wahhabi version of Islam to the Muslim world (Hasan, 2010, p. 675). The goal of the Saudi government was to counter both the expansion of Arab socialist Nationalism in Egypt in the 1960s and the influence of the Iranian revolution which erupted in 1979 (Hasan, 2007, p. 87; Wahid, 2014, p. 5). Those influences were regarded as threats to the Saudi Kingdom. Thanks to the oil boom in the 1970s, the Saudi has become active in exporting Salafism to Muslim countries through Muslim organisations that it set up such as Rabitat al-' Alam al-Islami (the Muslim World League) (Hasan, 2005, p. 30; Gause III, 2011, p. 20). Through Rabitat, the Saudi distributed financial funds for building Islamic schools, mosques, and social and *dakwah* facilities, and granting scholarships to Indonesians to study at Saudi universities (Hasan, 2005, p. 30; Wahid, 2014, p. 5). In Indonesia, the first channel for spreading Saudi Salafism was the Dewan Dakwah Islamiyah Indonesia (DDII; Indonesian Council for Islamic Propagation), an organisation created for Islamic propagation (*dakwah*) in Indonesia's rural areas (Wahid, 2014, p. 5). The first and main educational institution, which was established in Jakarta in 1980 with Saudi funding, was Lembaga Ilmu Pengetahuan Islam dan Bahasa Arab (LIPIA; Institute of the Study of Islam and Arabic). Hundreds of its graduates went on to study in Saudi Arabia; upon their return to Indonesia, many of these graduates became important Salafi teachers and preachers (Hasan, 2005, p. 43). Along with the growing Salafi communities, a number of Salafi leaders have established their own foundations in order to obtain financial support from Saudi Arabia, Kuwait, and other Arab countries (Hasan, 2007, p. 91).

With the financial support from Saudi Arabia and the Gulf countries, Salafi communities have established an increasing number of *pesantrens* in various provinces in Indonesia. The International Crisis Group (ICG) report in 2004 mentioned that there were no less than 29 *pesantrens*. While the exact number of *pesantrens* is unknown, Din Wahid (2014) assumes that their number has increased probably to 50 *pesantrens*. After gaining significant followers, the Salafis establish *pesantren* as a means for producing new Salafi preachers and teachers who will spread their

46 *Defending Traditional Islam*

knowledge to other Muslims (Wahid, 2014, p. 151). The Salafis actively conduct preaching around Muslim communities by delivering sermons in public mosques in the area where their *pesantren* is based. In some cases, the Salafis even took over the mosque resulting in conflict with the existing committees of the mosque. In his study, Wahid discusses the case of Dewan Da'wah al-Furqan Mosque in Central Jakarta where its officials drove out the Salafis (Wahid, 2014, pp. 98–99).

The proliferation of Salafi media technology is another indicator of the Salafi expansion. Starting from publishing Salafi periodicals in the 1990s, the Salafi has moved to expand their *dakwah* through media technologies after the 2000s. Their motivation was to defend the Muslim belief and morality from the existing electronic media, which they believed has been controlled by non-Muslims "wishing to destroy Islamic values, to turn Muslims away from shari'a and lead Muslims to a false *akidah* (belief)" (Wahid, 2014, pp. 102–103). Among Salafi radio stations in Indonesia, Rodja is the most popular one. The Salafi started establishing Rodja as an FM radio community in 2005, which was later formally launched as AM radio station in 2007. Rodja then expanded its wing to launch TV through streaming internet in 2009 and then through satellites in 2011 (Profil Radio Rodja dan Rodja TV). By using radio and TV, Salafis have made their Islamic propagation accessible to a wider audience in several regions in Indonesia and worldwide.

The Aswaja Response

The increasing *dakwah* expansion of Salafi prompted a critical reaction from the traditionalist Muslims. This is mainly due to the contents of their messages which attack traditionalist doctrines and practices. Several research reports indicated that the presence of Salafi groups in traditionalist majority areas have triggered conflicts with local Muslims. Nuhrison's research (2009) in West Lombok found that the puritanical approach of Salafis and their attacks on local beliefs and practices was the root cause of the conflict. The Salafis, for instance, condemned the celebration of the Prophet's birthday (*maulid*) by the local community in Lombok and judged it as a part of the Hindu heritage. A similar account was shared by many traditionalist preachers and leaders whom I met in Java and Jakarta. Concerned that the increasing expansion of Salafi would diminish their beliefs and traditions, traditionalist Muslim leaders, scholars, and activists have spoken out and written against the Salafi movement.

The *Aswaja dakwah* takes various forms ranging from public preaching to new media (books, magazines, radio, TV, and internet). Traditionalist religious leaders and preachers who engage with local communities include *habaib* and *kiai*, and teachers and activists graduated from *pesantrens* and traditional institutions in the Middle East who are dedicated to guarding their fellow traditionalist community. Many of them have stated that their mission is to protect *aswaja* Islam from the 'viruses of Wahhabism'. According to the traditionalist preachers, the Salafi *dakwah* has spread widely through the use of modern technologies and has even started to penetrate NU communities. Some *habaib* and traditionalist preachers mentioned the Rodja Radio and Rodja TV as two of the most important media for propagating

Defending Traditional Islam 47

the Salafi ideology. They claim that the Salafi have used these media to actively propagate Salafism and openly criticise the doctrines and religious practices of traditionalist Muslims considered to be *bid'ah*.

The majority of anti-Salafi preachers come from Java, especially in East and Central Java. Their concern regarding Salafism has led them to strengthen the traditionalist *dakwah* by forming a network among *aswaja* advocates. Their shared mission is apparent in their various *dakwah* groups through *majelis taklim*, publications, or radio and online media. According to the former General Chairman of the Central Board of NU (Pengurus Besar Nahdlatul Ulama, PBNU) Said Aqil Siradj, the traditionalists organised *aswaja dakwah* movements on their own initiative without any mobilisation and financial assistance from PBNU. He said that the *aswaja* had arisen because traditionalists felt that their long established tradition had been disturbed by the Salafi-Wahhabi preaching (Interview with Said Aqil Siradj, October 1, 2013). This reason was also given by several *aswaja* preachers whom I met in Jakarta and Java.

Aswaja Defenders

Currently, the most vocal *aswaja* advocates are local preachers and religious teachers. To capture their diversity, I classify them into three groups: popular preachers, NU scholars, and online media activists. This classification, however, is not absolute as some preachers are also NU scholars and owning media network. In the discussion below, I discuss some of the prominent persons in the campaign to counter Salafism.

1   Popular Preachers: The Case of Habib Noval b. Muhammad Alaydrus

The *dakwah* for strengthening *aswaja* has become a common platform among young preachers, especially *habaib*. Some *habaib* use various media in undertaking their *dakwah* ranging from public preaching, books, magazines, radio to internet. In this category, I locate Habib Noval as an example of a young *habib* who actively defends *aswaja* and promote it through public preaching and publications to the wider public audience. Habib Noval is among the popular preachers in Solo, along with Habib Syekh b. Abdul Qadir Assegaf, and has thousands of followers. He was born in 1975 into an Arab *sayyid* family in Solo. He received his basic education in secular schools but actively attended religious learning activities such as public sermon and *ratib* chanting in Ar-Riyadh Mosque, Solo. He also studied at the Pondok Pesantren Darul Lughah wad Dakwah (Dalwa), Pasuruan, in East Java for seven months. Returning to Solo, he avidly attended public sermons by the charismatic scholar, Habib Anis b. Alwi Al-Habsyi, from whom he received a deepening understanding of religious knowledge. In 2009, he established a sermon group (*majelis taklim*) in his mother's house where he gave sermon regularly. At the beginning, the participants of his *majelis* numbered only about 30 people but later increased to 200; the group grew so large that many people had to sit outside. Two years later, he bought a plot of land for building his *majelis ta'lim*. He said that

48   *Defending Traditional Islam*

in his new building, the number of participants increased to around 1,500 people (Interview with Noval Alaydrus, September 2, 2013). When I met him for interview, his *majelis* building was being renovated and expanded to two floors with additional spaces at the back of the house.

Guarding *aswaja* Islam has become a motto for Habib Noval's *dakwah* activities. His concern about the growing influence of what he sees as 'deviant Islamic movements', such as Salafism, motivated him to expand his *dakwah* through peripatetic preaching and utilising modern media technologies. For Habib Noval, Salafi-Wahhabism is an extreme ideology that can cause people to become radical and intolerant towards other groups. He argues that the strategic way to counter such groups is through strengthening *aswaja* teachings and traditions so that Muslims themselves can resist the movement. With this objective in mind, besides regularly running his sermon group and attending sermon invitations, he has promoted *aswaja* through his *majelis*' official website 'Majelis Dzikir and Ilmu Ar-Raudhah' at www.ar-raudhah.info/. The website contains his profile and his *majelis*, live streaming, sermon video and mp3 records, and advertisements of his books and religious merchandises produced by his *majelis*. It is also through the website that Habib Noval seeks funding to support his *majelis* by providing a list of four bank accounts to which supporters can donate. Furthermore, the website also has information links to its YouTube and social media (Official Facebook and Twitter).

Habib Noval has been also productive in writing books to defend the beliefs of *aswaja*. He asserted that his *dakwah* style is more scientific in orientation than merely advising people and religious chanting. His books are usually displayed and sold by his crew in the front yard of the *majelis* where the public sermon is going to be held. His books reflect the content of his regular preaching as the topics of the books are also the topics discussed at his *majelis*. Most of his books contain the ulama's arguments and doctrines on traditionalist rituals. One of his current books is entitled *Ahlul Bid'ah Hasanah: Jawaban Untuk Mereka Yang Mempersoalkan Amalan Para Wali* (The Doers of Good Innovation: The Answers for those who question the practices of saints). Through this book, Habib Noval seeks to 'correct' the Salafi's 'misconception' that *bid'ah* (innovation) is identical with a bad or heretical thing. He argues that there are good innovations (*bid'ah hasanah*) in religion such as what traditionalist Muslims have been practising. His books are aimed at traditionalist Muslims so that they can equip themselves with insight on *aswaja* doctrines in order to argue against the Salafis if they are being approached or criticised. Furthermore, he also has produced T-shirts that contain various images and remarks that promote *aswaja* rituals.

2   *NU Scholars: The Case of Muhammad Idrus Ramli*

Idrus is an example of a young NU local scholar who actively defends *aswaja* through books, seminars, and training courses. He was born on 1 July 1975 in Jember, one of the main bases of traditionalist Muslims in East Java. Idrus did most of his schooling at the Pondok Pesantren Sidogiri in Pasuruan, East Java, from primary school to senior high school (1986–2004). After graduation, he dedicated himself to teaching in various *pesantrens* in Madura, Kalimantan, and later returned to teach in his hometown, Jember. During his studies and teaching, he was active in the local NU division of *Lembaga Bahtsul Masail* (a body for discussing contemporary problems in relation to Islamic law) in Pasuruan and Jember. His current position is now that of chairman of NU's *Lembaga Bahtsul Masail* (LBM) in Jember. Besides, Idrus has also been active in managing magazines and publications serving as editor-in-chief of media in pesantren and local NU. Since 1998, Idrus has been active as a trainer and speaker in *aswaja* training courses and seminars hosted by local NU branches (Galeri Kitab Kuning, 2021). His skills in presentation and debates have made him popular as a vocal defender of traditionalist Islam against other Muslim groups such as Salafism and Shi'ism.

Idrus represents a conservative faction within the NU that strives to revive Sunni orthodoxy. His preaching activities are a response to various Islamic groups that, in his view, challenge even the NU's doctrines of *aswaja*. Idrus also joined the Forum Kiai Muda Jawa Timur (Forum of Young Kiais in East Java) which criticised the PBNU chairman Said Agiel Siradj and the NU liberal Muslim thinker Ulil Abshar Abdallah for their progressive thoughts deemed to deviate from the *aswaja* principles. In 2009, the Forum Kiai Muda invited Said Agiel Siradj and Ulil Abshar Abdallah to give clarification (*tabayyun*) on their controversial thoughts. In the forum where Said became a speaker, several young *kiais*, including Idrus, criticised Said for his reference to Shi'ite and Mu'tazilite sources that he claimed was a part of

Figure 3.1 Front Covers of Habib Noval's books

50 *Defending Traditional Islam*

aswaja teaching. Likewise, the young *kiais* also criticised Ulil for his controversial ideas, especially with regard to his doubt about the facts of stories in the Qur'an and his attempt to analyse them using human logic and historical assessment.[1]

Idrus opposes Shi'ism and Hizbut Tahrir but sees Salafism as the most dangerous since it actively attacks traditionalist Muslims' beliefs and practices. His books all have confronting titles such as *A Smart Guide on How to Argue against Wahhabi*, *The Guide for Ahl Sunna wa al-Jama'a in Facing Salafi-Wahhabis*, and *Open Debates: Sunnism versus Wahhabism in al-Haram Mosque*. His sharp criticism has offended the Salafis especially in online media. Judging by their tittles, Idrus's books aim at not only fighting back the Salafis but also providing literatures for traditionalist Muslims to rely on in defending their doctrines and instructing them on how to argue with the Salafis. To advance his mission, Idrus also actively organises *aswaja* training courses for students, religious teachers, and activists, especially those who are linked to the NU such as PMII cadres and local NU's members in various regions in Indonesia (Galeri Kitab Kuning, 2021).

3   *The* Aswaja *Online Media Activists: The Case of The Grave Scholars (Sarjana Kuburan_Sarkub)*

One of the most innovative and colourful sites is the Sarkub. Sarkub is an online network of traditionalist Muslim activists whose main concern is to spread *aswaja* and defend it from the Salafi and other groups' attacks. Founded in Semarang on 30 September 2010, Sarkub also has an official website which was launched on 16 October 2011 at the Ponpes Salafiyah Sladi Kejayaan, Pasuruan, East Java (Sarkub, 2014). According to Sarkub members, the reason for establishing the Sarkub network was similar to that of several social media users who actively countered the spread of Salafism on the internet: growing anxiety about the rapid Salafi expansion (Interview with Thobary Syadzily, October 20, 2013; Dian Kusumaningrum, November 20, 2013). Due to criticism from some Salafis, who often refer to them 'penyembah kuburan' and 'quburiyyun' (grave worshippers), they have decided to call their network 'Thariqat Sarkubiyah' (the Spiritual Path of Grave Scholars), popularly known as 'Sarkub' (*Sarjana Kuburan*, Grave Scholars). This naming is a direct rejection of Salafi teachings on visiting Saints' graves (*ziarah*). Since Sarkub is an online network, some activists have not met their peers within the network and only meet when they organise a 'hanging out meeting' (*kopi darat*) or attend particular religious events (Interview with Mas'ud, October 20, 2013). The network has connected numerous links of *aswaja dakwah* on the internet from either websites, blogs, social media, or radio.

In its fight against Salafism, Sarkub's approach is more relaxed than other *aswaja* advocates. Its website and community groups in social media use a distinctive way of *dakwah* by combining a combative style and the use of humor in attacking Salafits. Rather than using serious and deep explanations in their *dakwah*, Sarkub uses irreverent, mocking, and 'fun' approach to Salafis. Some Sarkub members in social media often create humorous posters and images of their traditionalist identity and their rival. In an image spreading through the social media, for instance,

Defending Traditional Islam   51

the Sarkub team call themselves as 'Hunters of Wahhabi'. Such image implies that Salafi-Wahhabi is a deviant and dangerous group that needs to be eliminated from Indonesia.

Thobary Syadzily is a founder and the leader of the Sarkub network. He has been called the guardian of *aswaja* in cyberspace by some Islamic magazines (*alKisah*, 2013; *Tabloid Media Ummat*, 2013). Besides serving as the head of the Pondok Pesantren Al-Husna in Tangerang, Banten, Thobary is also a chairman of the Department of Astronomy (*Lajnah Falakiyah*) of the local NU board in Banten and a member of Majelis Ulama Indonesia (MUI) in Tangerang. He claims to be a descendant of the great ulama of Banten, i.e. Shaikh Nawawi Al-Bantani and Shaikh Abdul Karim. He has been conducting a regular Islamic study group (*pengajian*) in his house, countering Salafism by analysing the classical religious books (*kitab kuning*) that have been distorted by the Salafis. He also relies on classical books in posting a religious opinion on the internet or in delivering his sermons in public. Thobary encourages traditionalists to preserve classical sources by scanning them and using them as teaching materials for Islamic education for younger generations so that they are armed with knowledge to counter the *dakwah* of Salafi (Interview with Thobary Syadzily, October 20, 2014).

Thobary and his Sarkub are popular among traditionalist Muslim activists and scholars as well as his Salafi opponents due to his active *dakwah* in cyberspace. The Easy Counter site reported that in March 2016, for instance, his Sarkub website was visited by about 868 daily visitors, 94 percent of whom were from Indonesia.[2] The number of visitors usually increases when a controversy erupts between Salafis and traditionalists in Indonesia. With his special team, what he calls 'Densus 99 Antiterror Akidah' (Special Detachment 99 for Anti-terror of Traditionalist Doctrines), Thobary often visits and debates with the Salafi authors whose books have criticised the NU's doctrines and rituals. Moreover, Thobary with Sarkub members also actively attend seminars or discussions in which the speakers are from the Salafis. In these events, he often raises questions and debates with the speakers. The results of the visits and debates are posted on their website with photos to show that they have debated with the Salafi scholars and discovered flaws in their opponents' arguments. For instance, as posted on the Sarkub website, the Sarkub team attended a book discussion on *The Sacred Graves in Archipelago* (*Kuburan-kuburan Keramat di Nusantara*) by a Salafi author, Hartono Ahmad Jaiz, at the book fair in Jakarta in 2011. In some parts of the book, Hartono states that a visit to the saints' graves to seek their blessings (*ngalap berkah*) is not a tradition of Islam but a tradition of Hinduism and therefore whoever follows this tradition could be judged as infidel (*mushrik*). According to Thobary, he came forward to raise a critical comment during the question session. Quoting from classical book *Tarikh al-Baghdady*, he rejected Hartono's opinion and argued that some classical ulamas did allow the practice of seeking blessings at the saints' graves (Sarkub, 2014).

The most quoted event that increased Thobary's profile is when he accompanied Muhammad Idrus Ramli as a speaker representing the *aswaja* group in a debate against the representative of Salafis, namely Firanda and Zainal Abidin, on 28 December 2013 in Batam.[3] This event was hosted by the local ministry of religious

52 *Defending Traditional Islam*

affairs of Batam. The major issue of debate concerned the position of *bid'ah* (unlawful innovation) in Islam. While the Salafi group affirmed their stand on any innovation related to religious practice, the *aswaja* group defended their position as traditionalist by arguing that good innovations (*bid'ah hasanah*) are acceptable in Islam. Both camps presented doctrinal arguments and ulama's opinions in justifying their position. The Sarkub team judged the *aswaja* camp as more convincing in the debate and proudly posted the video link on social media (Sarkub, 2014).

New Conservatism

Buttressing Aswaja and Opposing 'Deviancy'

NU has a reputation as one of the largest moderate Muslim organisations in Indonesia. Throughout the Indonesian history, the NU has had a number of leaders, scholars, and activists who raised progressive ideas in terms of Islamic thought, Islamic law (*fiqh*), and culture as the embodiment of the middle path of NU (Qomar, 2002; Ida, 2004). One example is the idea of redefinition of *aswaja* by Said Agil Siradj in 1995 when he had just returned from his study in Saudi Arabia. Said questioned the established notion of *aswaja* that had been identified as a religious school (*madzhab*). Instead, he defined *aswaja* as

> a method of religious thinking that covers various aspects of life and stands on the virtues of balance (*tawazun*), the middle path (*tawassuth*), and neutrality in adhering to the faith (*akidah*), being a mediator and glue in the social interaction, and justice and tolerance in politics.
>
> (Qomar 2002, p. 190)

In this regard, it is apparent that Said views *aswaja* as a method of thinking (*manhaj al-fikr*) rather than a product as his predecessors have emphasised. Through this idea, Said tries to widen the concept of *aswaja* to cover all Muslims so that there are no more dichotomies between Shia and Sunni or between Mu'tazila and Sunni, and so forth (Qomar, 2002, p. 190; Feener, 2007, p. 156). Said's liberal ideas, especially with regard to his efforts in bridging Sunni and Shi'a, have sparked criticism not only from Islamist groups but also from conservative wing within the NU. Besides Said, there have been several senior NU progressive thinkers such as the late Abdurrahman Wahid (Gus Dur), the late Muhammad Sahal Mahfudh, Ali Yafie, and Masdar Farid Mas'udi. More liberal ideas have also been promoted by young NU activists such as Ulil Abshar Abdallah, Marzuki Wahid, Jadul Maula, Rumadi, Zuhairi Misrawi, and Ahmad Baso. Those activists continue the ideas of Gus Dur, especially the idea of the 'indigenisation' of Islam (*pribumisasi Islam*) in the Indonesian context; they have also adopted progressive Islamic thoughts from the Middle Eastern thinkers and critical discourses from Western philosophers. Some of these young NU activists call themselves the proponents of 'Post-Tradisionalisme Islam' (Islamic Post-Traditionalism) or 'Postra' in short. This kind of thought was the result of eclectic ideas taken from Mohammad Arkoun, Abid Al-Jabiri, and

Defending Traditional Islam   53

Nasr Hamid Abu Zayd (see Rumadi, 2008; Kersten, 2015). Like Gus Dur, they oppose the formalisation of Islam and push for the protection of minority rights and Indonesian local traditions.

The new traditionalist group, however, does not engage in progressive debates of the NU. In fact, it opposes Islamic post-traditionalism as a part of the liberal ideas imported from the West. Most of them tend to revive the classical orthodoxy of Sunnism that has been preserved by conservative *kiais* and *habaib*. The orthodoxy includes the adherence to Ash'arite and Maturidite in Islamic theology, the acceptance of Sufism, and the adoption of Shafi'ite from the four schools in Islamic law. Rather than offering new thinking, the group is more concerned with propagating the established traditional Sunni doctrines, its rituals and practices, and responding to the criticisms that have been posed by the Salafi group. In general, the group emphasises that NU practices and rituals (*amaliah* NU) have doctrinal basis (Qur'anic verses, Prophet's practices, and authoritative ulama's opinions) and need to be preserved by Muslims.

The new *aswaja* advocates show a contradiction in their religious orientation. It is complicated if one uses two fronts: moderate vs. radical Islam in explaining the *dakwah* groups. On the one hand, the *aswaja* resists Islamist movements such as the Salafi and Hizbut Tahrir and regards them as extremists, but, on the other hand, it also rejects so-called 'deviant sects' such as Shi'a, liberal Islam, and Ahmadiyah.[4] It seems they have redefined 'moderate' into a narrower concept. Habib Noval b. Muhammad Alaydrus is a good example. Considered to be a moderate habib in Solo, Habib Noval has been active in reviving *aswaja* teachings as a way of countering Salafism. He is also close to *habaib*, *kiais*, and Sufi movements and has been invited by the Tarekat Naqshabandi Haqqani to give a sermon in Jakarta. However, when I asked his opinion on Shi'ism and liberal Islam, he answered without hesitation that those groups were definitely deviant and Muslims should have no tolerance for them. However, as he said, he prefers using a peaceful *dakwah* in opposing these movements. Furthermore, he has a sympathetic view of the leader of militant Islamic movement in Jakarta, Habib Rizieq Syihab, and considers him to be a brave figure who has fought to eradicate iniquity (*maksiat*) in Indonesia. He blames the Indonesian media for not being objective in delivering news on Habib Rizieq and his movement (Interview with Noval Alaydarus, September 2, 2013).

While the new *aswaja* advocates generally show opposition to Salafism, Shi'ism, and liberal Islam, they have adopted very different responses.[5] Habib Rizieq, for instance, states that he only opposes extreme Shi'ism and Salafism and not all their variants. He suggested that Muslims need to be objective about these movements. In the case of Salafis for instance, he said that some Salafis are *mu'tadil* (fair and just), i.e. they appreciate various religious strands within Islam, including the *aswaja* group. For these Wahhabis, he urges Muslim to show respect and engage in dialogue with them. Yet, he opposes *takfiri* Salafis who openly criticise *aswaja* and label *kafir* (unbeliever) as those who have different views and religious practices. During my fieldwork, I observed Habib Rizieq delivering a sermon on the characteristics of Sunni Islam (*Ciri-ciri Ahlus Sunnah wal-Jama'ah*) in which he described the differences between Sunnism and Salafism. In his sermon,

54 *Defending Traditional Islam*

he criticised 'extreme' Salafis who apostatised other Muslims as infidels (*kafir*) and accused *aswaja* Muslims as guilty of *bid'ah* (unlawful innovation). A similar case holds also for Shi'ism. Although many *habaib* preachers judge all Shi'ism as deviant, Habib Rizieq only denounces 'extreme' subgroup within Shi'a. The deviant Shi'ism for him is the fanatics (*ghulat*) who regard Ali as God and denounce the companions of the Prophet (Interview with Rizieq Syihab, April 3, 2013). Similarly, in one of his sermons, which is available on DVD, he stated that some Shi'is respect the companions of the Prophet and avoid criticising Sunni believers. He added that some transmitters of Prophetic tradition (hadith) are Shi'ite ulama, and if people reject Shi'ism, it means Sunni Muslims will need to reject the authoritative collection of hadith collected by Bukhari and Muslim. Because of his objective opinion on this issue, several Wahhabi media have accused Habib Rizieq of being Shi'a.

The emphatic opposition to Shi'ism has been expressed by a few *aswaja habaib*. The interesting case of this anti-shi'a *dakwah* is the late Habib Ahmad b. Zein Al-Kaff with his organisation Albayyinat in Surabaya. While most *aswaja dakwah* oppose Salafism, Habib Ahmad had focused his struggle against the spread of Shi'ism in Indonesia. Habib Ahmad states that Albayyinat is a *dakwah* movement based on *aswaja* teaching. He founded the organisation in 1988 in Surabaya together with Habib Thohir b. Abdullah Al-Kaff of Tegal, Habib Abdul Qadir al-Haddad of Malang, and Habib Ahmad Assegaf of Bangil (Interview with Ahmad b. Zein Al-Kaff, March 13, 2013). As stated on his website, the reason for opposing Shi'ism is that

> Shi'ism has deviated from the 'true' teachings of the Prophet and they have condemned Muslim leaders who helped the Prophet in spreading Islam. As a consequence, Shi'ism has created anxiety and conflict within society and ruined the stability and security guarded by the government
>
> (Albayyinat, n.d)

Habib Ahmad claims that the organisation has spread in several parts of Indonesia, and its activities include providing information to the public on the truth of *aswaja* teaching and the danger of Shi'ism through either publications, book translation, preaching, or training (*kaderisasi*). Albayyinat also has appealed to the government and Muslim organisations to work together in banning the Shi'a movements. Based on my observations and conversations with several informants, Habib Ahmad had been invited to several *majelis taklim* of *habaib* and *kiais* and usually talked about the danger of Shi'a. Habib Ahmad criticised Muslim leaders and intellectuals such as Said Agiel Siradj and Quraish Shihab who have tried to bridge the Sunni-and-Shi'a divide in Indonesia. He even suspected that Shi'a leaders have paid Muslim elites to stop attacking Shi'a Muslims. Furthermore, he also attacked Habib Rizieq for tolerating Shi'a (Interview with Ahmad b. Zein Al-Kaff, March 13, 2013).

Despite this variation in *aswaja dakwah*, there has been cooperation among *aswaja* defenders to strengthen their Islamic doctrine against external forces. It can be said that the challenge from Islamist movements, most notably Salafism, has created the anxiety that their religious practices will be wiped out. Habib Rizieq

Defending Traditional Islam 55

contends that he and other *aswaja* preachers began speaking out against Salafism only recently in the post-Soeharto years due to the fact that many of the Salafi preachers and their media have been publicly criticising Muslim traditionalists (Interview with Rizieq b. Syihab, April 4, 2013). Some preachers have built media network among *aswaja*. Habib Noval of Solo, for instance, arranged IT training for *majelis taklim* members to make them media savvy and able to spread their own *dakwah* in cyberspace. Similarly, Idrus Ramli has actively organised *aswaja* training for Muslim youths, including university students, to strengthen *aswaja* doctrine and provide them with the skills to counter Salafism and other rival movements. By doing these activities, they are also sending messages to their rivals that the *aswaja* Muslims are powerful and represent a majority in Indonesia.

Contesting the 'True' Sunni Authority

Both *aswaja* and its rival, Salafism, claim to be following Sunnism or the path of *ahl sunna wa al-jama'a*. The attachment to *ahl sunna wa al-jama'a* is significant for Sunni Muslims as it is related to the idea of salvation in the hereafter. This is based on some traditions of the Prophet (*hadith*) saying that after his own age has passed, Muslims would split into 73 groups, all of which would go to hell except one. The single saved group would be those who have constantly observed the Sunna of the Prophet and his Companions (Saleh, 2001, p. 63). The Salafis claim that their method of understanding and practicing Islam is in accord with the method of *ahl sunna wa al-jama'a*. They assert that to be Sunni, "Muslims should consistently follow the instructions prescribed by the Prophet Muhammad and his Companions and join a community that practices his Sunna consistently" (Hasan, 2006, p. 135). The Salafis, as could be seen from various websites, enjoin Muslims to refer to the basic sources of Islam (the Qur'an and Hadith) and to follow the path of the pious forefathers (*al-salaf al-salih*). Based on their teachings in religious purification and their opposition to *bid'ah* (unlawful innovation), the Salafis claim their Sunnism is more authentic than the traditionalist variants. They criticise the traditionalists for adopting practices outside the teachings of *ahl sunna wa al-jama'a* (Hasan, 2006, p. 136).

In responding to the Salafi challenge, the new *aswaja* groups have advanced various arguments to show that they are the more authentic Sunnis. The first and main argument to maintain their Sunni authority is through textual reasoning. This is carried out through the reference to classical texts of ulama who support their position. Some *aswaja* authors, for instance, refer to classical ulama's writings, such as those of al-Imam al-Murtada al-Zabidi (1732–1790 CE) who defined *ahl sunna wa al-jama'a* as based on the Ash'arite and Maturidite thinking. In Islamic theology, both schools represent Sunni orthodoxy (Halverson, 2010, p. 30). Al-Zabidi stated that Sunnism consists of *ahl hadith* (followers of hadith), Sufis, and followers of the Ash'arite and Maturidite (Alaydrus 2011, p. 39). Idrus, on his website, states that one of the characteristics of *aswaja* is the adoption of one among four schools of Islamic law (*madzahib*), i.e. Hanafite, Malikite, Shafi'ite, or Hanbalite, for everyday religious practice. He argues that, by referring to al-Imam Shah

56 *Defending Traditional Islam*

Waliyullah al-Dahlawi (1699–1769), following one particular school (*madzhab*) has been a general practice of the majority of Muslims since the times of the pious predecessors (the first three generations of Islam). This tradition, however, was challenged by the Salafi-Wahhabi movement emerging in the 18th century in Saudi Arabia, which called on Muslims to abandon schools of law and return to the Qur'an and Sunna. For Idrus, Salafi injunctions are erroneous because they assume the founders of *madzahib* did not base their interpretations and opinions on the principles of the Qur'an and Sunna (Ramli, 2013). Hence, according to Idrus, Salafism is not a part of Sunnism but the Kharijite. The Kharijite is the first extreme sect in the early history of Islam that rebelled against the ruling power. Idrus rejects Salafism as their teaching justifies *takfir* (accusing one as unbeliever) and the spilling of blood of Muslims whose opinion is different from theirs. Idrus supports his view by displaying several texts of the founder of Salafi-Wahhabism, Muhammad b. 'Abd al-Wahhab, who endorsed the use of violence (Ramli, 2010, p. 42).

Similarly, in defending the religious practices deemed by Salafis to be *bid'ah*, the *aswaja* preachers and authors resort to authoritative texts of Islam and opinions of the Middle Eastern ulama. In the eyes of *aswaja* preachers, the Salafis have a narrow and rigid understanding of *bid'ah* that leads them to castigate and lead astray their fellow Muslims. As stated in the Qur'an, God commands Muslims to consult with knowledgeable persons (*ahl dhikr*) on a religious problem. In this case, Habib Noval cites several ulama's definition of *bid'ah*. He quotes Imam Shafi'i's opinion, which divides *bid'ah* into two types: *bid'ah mahmudah* (lawful innovation) and *bid'ah madzmumah* (unlawful innovation). The former is in line with the Qur'an and Sunna, while the latter is not (Alaydrus, 2011, p. 11). Habib Noval refutes the Salafi's insistence that all *bid'ah* are deviant. He also quotes various Qur'anic verses and other ulamas' opinions in the defence of lawful *bid'ah*. For Muslim traditionalists, lawful *bid'ah* includes *tahlilan, maulidan, salawatan, yasinan, tabarruk, ziarah,* and so forth. Like other *aswaja* books, Habib Noval provides a doctrinal basis for each practice. In the case of visiting the saints' graves, for instance, he contends that it is part of the Prophetic tradition that has been exemplified by his Companion and the pious predecessors (*salaf salihin*). For him, visiting the saints' graves has a very useful impact on both visitors and the dead. He refers to a hadith, stating that the Prophet allowed Muslims to visit saints' graves since such practice can induce visitors to *renounce worldly pleasures* (*zuhud*) and to remember God (Alaydrus, 2011, p. 121). He also refers to some *salaf* ulamas such as Ibn Hajar Al-Haitsami, Imam Fakhrur Razi, and Muhammad Sa'id Ramadan al-Buthi to support his argument that visiting saints' graves is a cherished practice (*amal yang disukai*) and visitors could obtain grace (*rahmat*) from doing so (Alaydrus, 2011, pp. 133–136).

The *aswaja* defenders also use historical and factual account to uphold their own authority and to reject Salafism. Echoing the general reasoning of the NU scholars, the *aswaja* group argues that traditional Islam has long been established in the archipelago, thanks to the roles of Sufi ulama, especially the nine saints (*wali songo*). Most *habaib* commonly told me that most of the nine saints were in fact the descendants of the Prophet (*sayyids*) from Hadhramaut who introduced

Defending Traditional Islam 57

Islam to Southeast Asia in the earlier phase of Islamisation.[6] Rather than attacking the local customs, the saints adopted local cultures as a medium of Islamisation, provided that they did not go against the principles of Islam. Such argument aims to prove that *aswaja* Islam was rooted in the Indonesian history. For the *aswaja* defenders, the Salafi and other 'deviant' groups came later in the 18th century onwards and have destabilised the long established beliefs and practices of *aswaja* as well as the peaceful nature of Indonesian Islam. A late popular preacher in Jakarta, Habib Munzir, contended that Salafism is misleading (*mengkufurkan*) Sunni Muslims who practice *tawassul, ziarah kubur, maulid,* and so forth. Habib Munzir stated that in the history of Islam, the followers of Muhammad Abdul Wahhab, who were driven by misguided attempt to purify of Islam, destroyed various sacred sites of Islam such as the grave of the grandson of the Prophet Husein b. Abi Talib in Iraq, the dome where the Prophet was born, and the domes on the Companions' graves. For the Salafis, such sacred sites were a potential source of veneration and idolatry for Muslims due to a large number of visitors to the sites (Guntur & Tim MR, 2013, pp. 73–76). Habib Munzir also stated that the Salafis had killed thousands of Muslims in Hijaz (now Saudi Arabia) around 1805 under the pretext of eradicating *bid'ah* (Guntur & Tim MR, 2013, p. 79).

The *aswaja* preachers have also accused the Salafis of attacking their beliefs in Indonesia. While the Salafi media are the main concern, there are some cases of mainstream media's religious programme that have worried the attention of *aswaja* preachers and activists. One instance in 2013 was the involvement of national TV channel TRANS7, through its Islamic programme called *Khazanah*, in depicting traditionalist rituals such as visiting the saints' graves as idolatry (*kemusyrikan*). The programme was criticised by the traditionalist Muslims, especially from *majelis taklim*, who asserted that the TRANS7 had become a tool of Salafi propagation (Sarkub, 2013). The Sarkub team and Islamic Defenders Front were among *aswaja* representatives who came to the TRANS7 office demanding clarification and rectification.

Considering the challenges to *aswaja* community, several sermon groups have raised special topics in countering Salafism. In Solo, for instance, Habib Noval has organised a special public preaching (*tablig akbar*) in April 2013 with the theme of 'Strengthening Your Faith-Let's Return to the Muslim Saints' Teaching'. The opening sentences of Habib Noval in his public sermon below better illustrated how he responded to Salafi challenges:

> Today is the revival era for *ahl sunna wa al-jama'a*, let's revive the true *aswaja*, let's revive the groups of *la ilaha illa-llah* (*tahlilan*), let's revive the groups of *sallal-lahu 'ala Muhammad* (*salawatan*), let's revive the groups of *khatmil qur'an* (Qur'anic reciting), let's revive *majelis yasinan*, let's revive visiting the graves, which is recently criticized by TRANS7's Khazanah Program. I urge *aswaja* social organisations to criticise the program so that it could be reviewed or stopped as it offends *aswaja* by stating that those who visit the graves are unbelievers (*mushrik*). They now dare to use TV to attack NU, to attack *habaib*, to attack *kiais*. Therefore, I ask *kiais* and *habaib* to

58 *Defending Traditional Islam*

convey their protest to broadcasting committee since the TV breaks the law of broadcasting…I urge you to say 'say no to Wahhabi, say no to Salafi' (in English), say no to anti-*tahlilan*, anti-*yasinan*, and anti-*maulidan*…the faith issue (*akidah*) is number one, therefore our priority is to strengthen the faith of *ahl sunna wa al-jama'a*.

Popularising Traditional Islamic Authority

In the face of Salafi attacks, the *aswaja* groups have attempted to strengthen their legitimacy by emphasising the traditional authority. One form of reviving such authority is though the revitalisation of knowledge connectedness that was historically used in Islamic education before the coming of the modern educational system. William A. Graham calls this particular transmission of knowledge in the Muslim world as *isnad paradigm* (Graham, 1993). It links transmitters of knowledge from the current generation back to those in the past through face-to-face learning for authentication (Graham, 1993, p. 502; Robinson 2008, pp. 266–267). In this case, the position of descendants of the Prophet is special as they have blood connection to the Prophet and therefore inherit His blessing. This is one of the reasons that make traditionalist Muslims rely more on the religious authority of *habaib* or *kiais*.

The *aswaja* group calls for efforts to revive the importance of *sanad* for the transmission of Islamic knowledge. The lineage of teachers (*sanad*) is usually mentioned in the *ijazah* (certificate) system written by a teacher to his students who have learned a particular subject or text. The *ijazah* is the authorisation to teach a certain discipline of Islamic knowledge or book text in either oral or written form (Graham, 1993, p. 511). Although the modern educational institutions provide a formal certificate, the students also receive a special *ijazah* from individual teachers. Some *habaib* narrated that they continued their study in traditional religious centres such as the ribath of Sayyid Muhammad Alwi Al-Maliki in Mecca and Dar al-Mustafa in Hadhramaut although some of them have already obtained degrees in Indonesia. A popular preacher in Makassar Habib Mahmud b. Umar Al-Hamid, for instance, spent ten years studying in the Middle East moving from one traditional school to another just to receive a *sanad* and blessing from charismatic scholars without formal certification. For him, the blessing (*baraka*) he gained from his participation in his study as well his service (*khidmah*) to his teacher is more important than the degree (Interview with Mahmud Al-Hamid, April 28, 2013). The list of well-known teachers (*sanad*) is important for the preachers as they can mention their teachers to their students or public audience as a way of raising their religious authority.

Given the authority of *sanad*, some *habaib* have criticised the Salafis for the lack of *sanad*. Habib Munzir, for instance, stated on his website that the traditionalist ulamas, when they talk about the Prophetic tradition (*hadith*), have list of transmitters to the six authoritative collections of hadith (*al-kutub al-sitta*). Hence, he said "no knowledge without *sanad*, so the fatwa without *sanad* is false (*batil*)" (Majelis Rasulullah, 2013). Habib Munzir criticised the Salafi scholars for their lack of *sanad*, and therefore, their Islamic knowledge should be questioned. He

Defending Traditional Islam 59

views Shaikh Muhammad Nasiruddin al-Albani (1914–1999) as an example of a Salafi scholar who has become authoritative ulama in *hadith* within Salafis but in fact had no strong *sanad* to the Prophet. In response to this, Salafis, represented by Firanda Andirja Abidin, refuted Habib Munzir's statements, and said it was a false accusation against the Salafi teachers. Firanda accuses Habib Munzir of not being knowledgeable in *hadith* and trying to fool Muslims in Indonesia (Abidin, 2012).

Conclusion

The competition for Sunni religious authority in Indonesia has allowed the emergence of a new traditionalist movement that aims at defending traditional Sunnism (*aswaja*) from the growing challenge of Salafism and other groups. The way the *aswaja* group responded to Salafis replicates the way their predecessors responded to reformist Muslim challenge in the 1920s and 1930s. Although the *aswaja* group has helped to reassert traditional Islam in Indonesia, it also works to revive conservatism within traditional Islam. In this case, it has redefined traditional Islam to be conservative and exclusive such as has been held by NU's conservative wing. The conservative tendency of *aswaja* includes the assertions of being the 'true' Sunnism, opposition to Salafism and other perceived 'deviant' Muslim groups, and the growing attempt to popularise *aswaja* beliefs and rituals among the wider Muslim population. The group also opposes progressive NU leaders and scholars who have redefined Sunnism to be more inclusive. Within this conservative atmosphere, there emerged a growing need for charismatic and traditional leaders, scholars, and preachers such as *habaib* and *kiais*, who are able to provide not only 'authoritative' traditional Islamic knowledge but also pietistic identity and *baraka* (blessing) for their followers.

I have classified the current *aswaja* defenders into three groups: popular preachers, NU scholars, and online media activists. These *aswaja* defenders mostly come from popular preachers and local NU scholars who share a concern regarding the protection of traditional Islam. The three groups have been active in defending and reasserting traditional Islam through Islamic education, preaching, and new media. Not only have they defended traditional Islam, they have also moved to challenge Salafism and other groups by revealing their rivals' doctrinal weakness and extreme actions, which are considered not in line with the 'true' Sunni teaching. Furthermore, they have built and consolidated *aswaja* networks to help Muslims resist the internal and external forces that have the potential to challenge traditional Islam. These developments suggest that traditionalist Muslims tend to unite when there is a perceived threat to their community.

Notes

1 The debates and discussion in this forum could be seen in 'Dialog Terbuka FKM Jatim vs KH. Said Aqil Siradj' from https://www.youtube.com/watch?v=cC3lJxuFJHI&t=1001s (accessed on 17 March 2022).
2 For detailed information, see http://www.easycounter.com/report/sarkub.com (accessed on 17 March 2016).

60 *Defending Traditional Islam*

3 The video is available at https://www.youtube.com/watch?v=HkCIfDrQqUU (accessed on 10 August 2021).
4 See, for example, the vision and mission of Sarkub at http://www.sarkub.com/about/ (accessed on 15 October 2014).
5 This is based on my interviews with a number of popular *habaib* preachers in several cities in Indonesia.
6 This narrative can also be found in *al-Kisah*, 24 February 2008.

4 Performing Arab Saints and Marketing the Prophet

Introduction

Post-Soeharto Indonesia has witnessed the proliferation of young *habaib* preachers along with their sermon groups (*majelis taklim* and *majelis dzikir*). The *habaib* wear white turbans (*imamah*) and long robes (*jubah*), and they hold a walking stick in their hand emulating the Prophet's appearance. They usually deliver sermons on stage with a number of other *habaib* and local preachers accompanied by a group of traditional Arab musical performers (*hadhrah*). Popular preachers such as the late Habib Munzir b. Fuad Al-Musawa, Habib Hasan b. Ja'far Assegaf, Habib Syech b. Abdul Qadir Assegaf, and Habib Noval b. Muhammad Alaydrus have gained a high profile among traditionalist Muslims in urban areas, most notably in Jakarta, Central Java, and East Java. Their public sermons usually attract thousands and frequently create traffic jams as people and vendors of religious merchandises crowd onto nearby streets. This phenomenon indicates two important aspects: the popularity of Arab-*sayyid* culture in public preaching and the rising demand for public preaching among Indonesian Muslims.

The increasing number of celebrity preachers with their own distinctive styles has accelerated Islamic commodification in Indonesia. Many preachers such as Abdullah Gymnastiar (Aa Gym), the late Jefrie al-Buchori (Uje), Yusuf Mansur, the late Arifin Ilham, Achmad Ikhsan (Ustaz Cepot), and Maulana Nur have turned into celebrities due to their roles on national television. Due to the demands for entertainment and information, many TV stations offer more opportunities for preachers who have media literacy and good mass communication skills (Muzakki, 2008, p. 210). Each celebrity preacher has their own trademark of religious entrepreneurship: Aa Gym uses simple everyday language in his preaching concentrating on 'heart development' or what he called '*manajemen Qalbu*'; the late Arifin Ilham had a skill in leading mass gatherings reciting prayer and invoking crying; Yusuf Mansur has a preaching style that promotes the power of philanthropy, especially alms giving (*sedekah*) for achieving prosperity; the late Uje was skilled in using 'street talk' (*bahasa gaul*) and singing Islamic songs (Fealy, 2008, pp. 25–26), while other preachers such as Maulana Nur and Achmad Ikhsan employ comedy in their preaching. A study by Hew Wai Weng also points to the rise of Chinese

DOI: 10.4324/9781003358558-4

62   *Arab Saints and the Prophet*

preachers who capitalise on their Chineseness while using a mixture of different performing styles to lift their popularity (Wai Weng, 2012, pp. 178–199).

Several scholars have studied the shift of religious authority from the traditionally trained preachers to lay preachers who have created what Hoesterey calls "innovative claims of religious authority" (Hoesterey, 2008, p. 97). According to Julian Millie, the rising Muslim televangelists in Indonesia, most of whom lack formal religious qualifications, "break the mold of the classic or old-style religious scholars (*ulama*)" (Millie, 2012, p. 123). While most scholars have focused their attention on the new preachers who broke away from tradition, this study discusses new preachers who style themselves as traditionalist ulama and saints (*wali*). In recent years, there has been a resurgence of traditionalist preachers in urban areas, especially in Jakarta, thanks to a variety new media technologies and marketing strategies. Focusing on two *habaib* preachers and their *majelis*, I will analyse how they have emerged as popular preachers by examining their profiles and autobiographies, sermons, *dakwah* performance style, and their religious branding. This chapter argues that *habaib* rely more on performance and entertainment than oratorical competence in attracting followers. Their appeal lies in their distinctive appearance, which combines symbols of traditionalism, sainthood, and Arabness. The *habaib* perform as traditionalist scholars and Arab saints, a classical style that makes them look charismatic and authoritative to audiences. This study confirms Hilary Kalmbach's analysis of new religious intellectuals in Egypt that "performance plays a key role in the legitimation of Islamic authority" (Kalmbach, 2015, p. 163). This notion implies that having a traditionalist education and religious capital (as *habaib*) is not sufficient to gain popularity; preachers also need to perform as traditionalist scholars and saints to meet the expectation of their audiences.

The first part of this chapter discusses the profiles of Habib Hasan b. Ja'far Assegaf and Habib Munzir b. Fuad Al-Musawa along with their respective sermon group in Jakarta. It analyses how they founded and developed their sermon group as well as popularised their *dakwah* among Jakartan Muslims. The second part looks at the growing popularity of *habaib* along with their *majelis* by underlining three aspects of their commodification: the performative aspect of sainthood and Arab ethnicity, the role of new media and musicality in popularising their *dakwah*, and the reference to the Prophetic symbols in their branding.

Habib Hasan b. Ja'far Assegaf and His Nurul Musthofa

Habib Hasan, founder of the Majelis Nurul Mustafa (The Council of the Light of the Chosen One), was born in Bogor, West Java, in 1977. He grew up in a *sayyid* family that attached great importance to their children's religious practice and education. Habib Hasan has a genealogical connection to a charismatic *sayyid* ulama in Bogor, Habib Abdullah b. Muhsin Al-Attas, through his mother Syarifah Fatmah b. Hasan. He spent his childhood in the village of Keramat Empang where the grave of his grandfather, Habib Abdullah, is located. The grave has been venerated and visited by many ulama from both Indonesia and other countries because Habib Abdullah is revered as a *wali* (saint) (Mauladdawilah & Mauladdawilah, 2010, p. 38).

Most of Habib Hasan's education was shaped by Indonesian ulama, both Hadhrami and non-Hadhrami. He received his early education from his father, Habib Ja'far b. Umar Assegaf, who was familiar with the practices and rituals of *tariqa Alawiya* (the spiritual path of Alawi ancestors). Habib Hasan also studied with local Hadhrami ulama such as Shaikh Usman Baraja, Abdul Qadir Basalamah, and Shaikh Ahmad Bafadhal (Mauladdawilah & Mauladdawilah, 2010, p. 39).

Habib Hasan spent his formal education in traditional religious schools (*pesantren*) in Malang, East Java, starting with the Pesantren of Darul Hadith Al-Faqihiyyah, a traditional school established by Habib Abdul Qadir b. Ahmad bil-Faqih. Many *habaib* and *kiai* sent their children to the *pesantren* because of the high reputation of its founder who was well known for his expertise in Islamic studies, especially in *ulum al-hadith* (Science of Prophetic Tradition). After two years, Habib Hasan transferred to Pesantren Darut Tauhid in Malang, a *pesantren* that was also established and run by an Indonesian Arab Syeikh Abdullah b. Awadh Abdun (*alKisah*, February 24, 2008). He also had the opportunity to study at the Tarbiyah Faculty of the State Institute of Islamic Studies (IAIN) Sunan Ampel (now State Islamic University of Malang) (Zamhari and Howell, 2012, p. 56). After two years in Darut Tauhid, Habib Hasan returned to Bogor to accept his grandfather's offer to send him to study in Hadhramaut. Sadly, this plan came to nothing when his grandfather died. Instead of travelling to Hadhramaut, he continued to gain Islamic knowledge through informal study clubs (*majelis taklim*) of *habaib* in Jakarta, such as the *majelis taklim* of Habib Abdurrahman b. Ahmad Assegaf and of Habib Ali b. Abdurrahman Assegaf. Besides, he also studied with local *kyais* such as KH. Syafii Hadzami, KH. Dimyati in Banten, KH. Maman Satibi in Cianjur, KH. Buya Yahya in Bandung, KH. Muallim Shaleh in Bogor, and other ulama in Jakarta (Mauladdawilah & Mauladdawilah, 2010, p. 48).

Habib Hasan started his religious teaching and preaching activities in Bogor in 1998 after gaining inspiration from what he claimed were his 'spiritual experiences'. When staying in Bogor, Habib Hasan isolated himself from social life, a phase which he called '*uzlah*' (self-seclusion from people). He claimed that for a year and three months, he spent all his time on three main acts of religious devotion: regular visits to the grave of his grandfather, Habib Abdullah b. Muhsin Al-Attas; conducting congregational prayers in a nearby mosque; and regular contemplation and *wirid* (reciting passages of praise and prayers to God). He recalled that it was through these acts of devotion that he gained inspiration and guidance (*bisyarah*) to undertake religious teaching and preaching to Muslims (Mauladdawilah & Mauladdawilah, 2010, p. 53). With the request from his father and support from local *kyai* and *ustadz*, Habib Hasan began religious teaching and preaching by moving from one village to another until he could set up a *majelis taklim* in his parents' house. The *majelis*, which he named Al-Irfan (wisdom), suceeded in drawing about 200 attendees. However, his father, Habib Ja'far Assegaf, opposed Habib Hasan's *majelis* being based in the regency where his grandfather had been famous. He suggested that Habib Hasan should establish his *majelis* in another regency where he could build his own reputation (Mauladdawilah & Mauladdawilah, 2010, pp. 53–54). Following a visit to the grave of the charismatic ulama Habib Ahmad b. Alwi

64   *Arab Saints and the Prophet*

Al-Haddad (well known as Habib Kuncung) in South Jakarta, Habib Hasan had a dream in which Habib Kuncung asked him to move to the capital in order to continue his religious preaching (Zamhari and Howell, 2012, p. 57).

Moving to South Jakarta, Habib Hasan started his *dakwah* among a small congregation of followers (*jemaah*). As a new preacher in the area, he visited local *kyais* and local figures to gain support for his *majelis*. Initially, the preaching activity took place in the houses of his students. As the number of participants began to increase to hundreds of people, however, Habib Hasan was forced to move his *majelis* to several mosques in Cilandak, South Jakarta (*alKisah*, February 24, 2008). Soon the number of participants grew too large even for the mosques; therefore, Habib Hasan decided to hold public preaching in open areas such as roads and fields (Mauladdawilah & Mauladdawilah, 2010, p. 91).

As the *majelis* gained more participants, Habib Hasan changed the name of his *majelis* from Al-Irfan (wisdom) to Majelis Nurul Musthofa (the Light of the Chosen man) in 2001, following a consultation with two charismatic *habaib*, Habib Umar b. Hafiz of Tarim, Yemen, and Habib Anis b. Alwi Al-Habsyi of Solo, Central Java, who made a visit to the *majelis* that year (Mauladdawilah & Mauladdawilah, 2010, pp. 91, 96, 97). The term 'Musthofa' (the Chosen One) refers to a name of the Prophet Muhammad, with the evidence that the *majelis* was using the Prophet as their symbol. This name change was considered to be a kind of 'spiritual authorisation' (*ijazah*) for Hasan to lead his *majelis* (Mauladdawilah & Mauladdawilah, 2010, p. 97; Zamhari & Howell, 2012, p. 58).

To promote his *majelis*, Habib Hasan formed a management team in 2002. The crew's main task was to help Habib Hasan in managing and promoting the *majelis* to a wider audience and, more importantly, creating new strategies for attracting young Muslims (*alKisah*, February 24, 2008, p. 125). To that end, Habib Hasan and his crew have employed a wide variety of publicity strategies. Several days before the *majelis*, for instance, the crew would erect long banners, billboards, and flags of their *majelis* along the streets near the advertised location of the coming event. The photos of Habib Hasan with his brothers and guest preachers featured prominently in the advertisement. The crew was also in charge of the production of religious merchandise such as jackets, key holders, stickers, posters, DVDs, and books with the *majelis* logo or Habib Hasan's photo on them. On the day, a convoy of vehicles and motorcyclists would be organised to escort Habib Hasan to the location of the *majelis*. Habib Hasan would be riding at the front in a sedan guarded by police officers on motorcycles. There would also be fireworks to entertain young participants.

The leadership of the Majelis Nurul Musthofa rests with Habib Hasan and his brothers. Previously, Habib Hasan was the sole leader of the *majelis*, yet after his three brothers completed their studies, he called on them to play a greater role in the *majelis*. His brothers are Habib Abdullah b. Ja'far Assegaf, Habib Musthofa b. Ja'far Assegaf, and Habib Qasim b. Ja'far Assegaf. Habib Abdullah completed his senior high school in the Pesantren Darul Lughah wa al-*Dakwah* (Dalwa) in Pasuruan, while the other brothers studied for some years in Hadhramaut. The presence of two of Habib Hasan's brothers who graduated from Hadhramaut has strengthened the religious authority of the *majelis* by connecting it to the centre

Arab Saints and the Prophet   65

of saints (*wali*) in Hadhramaut, Yemen. The growing demands of public preaching prompted Habib Hasan to divide the *dakwah* areas among his brothers. Their *dakwah* areas are known collectively as Jabodetabek (Jakarta, Bogor, Depok, Tangerang, and Bekasi). Habib Abdullah, for instance, is assigned to help Habib Hasan in South Jakarta; Habib Musthofa is assigned to be the leader of the *majelis* in Bogor, Ciawi, and Cibinong, while Habib Qasim is responsible for East Jakarta and surrounding areas such as Bekasi and Pondok Gede (Interview with Habib Abdullah Assegaf, June 13, 2013). Habib Hasan regularly invites local senior preachers such as KH. Abdul Hayyie Na'im, KH. Abdul Rasyid Abdullah Syafi'i, Habib Ali b. Abdurrahman Assegaf, Habib Muhammad Rizieq b. Syihab, Ustadz Adnan Idris, KH. Abdul Rasyid Harris, the late Ustadz Jeffrie Al-Bukhari, and Ustadz Imam Wahyudi (Mauladdawilah & Mauladdawilah, 2010, p. 90). The presence of these popular preachers adds variety and entertainment to performances that often last for three hours. Habib Hasan sometimes invites guest speakers from Hadhramaut who happen to be visiting Indonesia at the time. Preaching in the Arab language, these guest speakers help to enhance the image of the *majelis* through their connection to the Middle East – the origin of Islam – as well as providing the *majelis* with religious legitimacy.

Nurul Musthofa has established itself as one of the biggest *majelis* with a large following among Muslim youth. In 2005, the *majelis* was transformed into *yayasan* (foundation) and was formally registered as 'Majelis Shalawat and Zikir Nurul Musthofa' with the Ministry of Religious Affairs of the Republic of Indonesia. The foundation is headed by Habib Hasan's brother, Habib Abdullah. Nurul Musthofa focuses on public preaching that takes place almost every night. Based on my observation, the public preaching of the *majelis* can attract tens of thousands of participants, and in some occasions, especially at National Monuments, it can draw up to 50,000 people. The *majelis* now has its own permanent building that functions as a centre of organisational operations as well as a place for regular preaching and praying. It is located behind the house of Habib Hasan in Ciganjur, South Jakarta. All equipment such as musical instruments, loud speakers, audio system tools, and banners are kept in that building. Some staff members live in that building and make all necessary preparations for the *majelis*.

Habib Munzir b. Fuad Al-Musawa and His Majelis Rasulullah

Habib Munzir was the founder of the Majelis Rasulullah (MR). He was born in 1973 in Cianjur, West Java, and died of asthma and encephalitis in Jakarta on September 15, 2013. He was the fourth of five siblings. Unlike other *habaib* preachers, he came from a secular educational background. His late father, Fuad b. Abdurrahman al-Musawa, obtained a Bachelor in Journalism from The New York University in the US and later worked as a journalist in *Berita Yudha* newspaper. All Habib Munzir's siblings also received a secular education (Guntur & Tim MR, 2013, p. 2). Habib Munzir spent his primary and secondary education in Cianjur. However, he did not complete senior high school due to his asthma problem; helping to manage his father's motel also took up much of his time (Al-Musawa, 2014, p. 5).

66 *Arab Saints and the Prophet*

Habib Munzir's early Islamic education was shaped by informal learning sessions at *majelis taklim* and in *pesantren*. His interest in learning Islam was inspired by stories of his ancestors' pursuit of knowledge and adherence to *habaib* traditions. Since an early age, he became active in attending sermon groups and visiting the graves of Muslim saints in Bogor and Jakarta (Al-Musawa, 2014, pp. 8–12). He began studying *shari'a* (Islamic law) at the Madrasah Al-Thaqafah Al-Islamiyah of Habib Abdurrahman Assegaf in Bukit Duri, South Jakarta. After only two months at the Madrasah, he took an Arabic course at Lembaga Pendidikan Bahasa Arab (LPBA) Assalafy, led by Habib Bagir Alatas in East Jakarta. Habib Munzir then deepened his Islamic knowledge at Pesantren Al-Khairat owned by Habib Hamid Nagib b. Syeikh Abu Bakar in East Bekasi. It was during this time that he met the renowned Yemeni ulama Habib 'Umar b. Hafiz who was visiting the Pesantren in 1994 as part of his outreach (*alKisah*, October 13, 2013, pp. 45–46). 'Umar's visit to Indonesia was at the invitation of a senior ulama in Solo, Habib Anis b. Alwi Al-Habsyi, who was trying to rebuild the intellectual connection between Indonesia and Hadhramaut by sending sons of leading *habaib* and *kiais* to study in Hadhramaut. Habib Munzir was one of 30 young Indonesian Muslims selected by Habib 'Umar to study in Hadhramaut (Alatas, 2009, p. 96).[1] He spent four years studying traditional Islamic sciences in Dar al-Mustafa, a religious educational institution founded and led by Habib 'Umar.

After completing his studies in Yemen, Habib Munzir returned to Indonesia and commenced his *dakwah* activities in 1998. He began his Islamic outreach in his hometown Cianjur but was not as successful as he had hoped. He then moved to Jakarta and began to go from house to house to conduct *pengajian* (Islamic learning) with a particular focus on basic Islamic law (*fiqh*). At first, only six followers agreed to let Habib Munzir use their homes for *pengajian*; they also provided him with a place to stay as he travelled back and forth from Cianjur to Jakarta. Upon the suggestion of his followers, Habib Munzir established a *majelis taklim* and chose Monday night as the time for *majelis* activities. He also named his *majelis* Majelis Rasulullah (The Assembly of the Prophet) as most of his sermons were related to the messages of the Prophet. As the number of participants increased and soon exceeded the capacity of private houses, Habib Munzir changed the venue to several large mosques while still basing their Monday night's *majelis* at the Mosque Al-Munawwar in Pasar Minggu, South Jakarta (*alKisah*, October 13, 2013, p. 49).

The growth and successful development of Habib Munzir's congregation was due to the change in his preaching material at the early stage. As he admitted on his *majelis*'s official website, when he was teaching *fiqh* he discovered that followers were not so enthusiastic about listening to his sermons. Learning from this experience, he left out the *fiqh* materials and, instead, raised ethical matters from the Qur'an and Hadith and began to deliver sermons in a more accessible style. All his messages called on people to make the Prophet the role model in their lives (Majelis Rasulullah, 2013). Based on my observation, Habib Munzir regularly used hadith text from Imam Bukhari's and Imam Muslim's collections as a basis for his preaching. Printed on a small piece of paper, the hadith text would be handed out to participants by his team of volunteers before the *majelis* started. His preaching,

Arab Saints and the Prophet   67

for the most part, emphasised the ethics (*akhlak*) of the Prophet, such as his love, tolerance, and respect for human beings (Guntur & Tim MR, 2013, p. 22). Clearly, the shift of focus from Islamic law to ethical matters contributed to the growing number of his followers.

Habib Munzir established his headquarters in a rented two-storey house in Pancoran, South Jakarta, and made it the centre of *dakwah* operations. Habib Munzir appointed several staff members and built an outlet for his Islamic merchandise. These staff members lived in the house and were responsible for a whole host of duties including scheduling sermons, maintaining IT and the websites, publishing books, and welcoming guests. Some staff were also authorised to give religious instruction to Habib Munzir's followers. The staff was employed professionally and received a disbursement called 'infaq', the amount of which could change depending on the income of the *majelis*. There were also staff members working in Kios Nabawi outlet (the Prophet's Kiosk) to produce and sell the *majelis*' merchandise such as jackets, shirts, books, DVDs, and prayer equipments. Besides the salaried staff, there was also a team of volunteers who dealt with technical operations of the *majelis* in the field such as installing billboards and banners, directing traffics, and looking after the congregation (Interview with IT Team, October 5, 2013).

Habib Munzir's preaching strategy included the use of new media and religious merchandise. The internet was significant for Habib Munzir in promoting his *majelis*' profile and its *dakwah* activities. Staff regularly updated the website with preaching schedules for the coming month. There is a special section of discussion forum in which Habib Munzir addressed questions from followers in relation to religious matters. The followers of Habib Munzir often refer to the website in order to be well informed on the *majelis* activities. They can also watch the video live streaming and recorded video of the past preaching events. Some followers of the *majelis* voluntarily create communities or fan groups in social media informing forthcoming activities of the *majelis* and providing online spaces for their fellows to interact and discuss. The new media also promotes religious merchandise of the *majelis* by displaying product images and their prices. The photo of Habib Munzir and the logo of MR are printed onto many products. Products like black jackets with MR logo at the back has been the most marketable with large numbers of orders from outside of Jakarta. Most of the buyers of this jacket are Muslim youths who actively participate in *habaib*'s *majelis* even though they are not linked to the MR. In this regard, the MR logo on the jacket symbolises the connection of a traditionalist Muslim identity with *habaib*.

Starting from Jakarta, Habib Munzir's outreach expanded to other parts of Indonesia and even to several other Southeast countries. His *majelis* has established a network with many mosques in Jakarta. Habib Munzir expanded his outreach in several areas in Central Java, Western Java, Bali, Sunda Islands, and Papua. He also preached in Singapore, Johor, and Kuala Lumpur. However, due to poor health and after consultation with his spiritual teacher Habib 'Umar, he focused his outreach only around Jakarta, limiting visits outside the city to once a year (Majelis Rasulullah, 2013). In spite of the limited mobility of Habib Munzir, he kept two venues as the central basis for his *majelis*: the first is the Mosque Al-Munawwar located

68 *Arab Saints and the Prophet*

in Pasar Minggu for Monday nights and the second is Dalailul Khairat, a building located in Cidodol, South Jakarta, for Thursday nights. The latter is a two-storey building owned by Habib Muhsin Al-Hamid, a wealthy businessman who now serves as the chairman of *majelis syura* (consultative body) of MR. Both buildings have wide front yards where most participants sit and watch the big screen that displays speakers delivering sermons inside. Several vendors of religious products, both legal and pirated, occupy the nearby pavements and help to create the atmosphere of a crowded night market. In both places, the number of young participants can be up to 5,000 crowding around the *majelis* sites. On special occasions such as the celebration of the Prophet's birthday, the *majelis* is convened in the public spaces of National Monument (Monas), attracting about 50–100,000 participants. Senior state officials such as President Soesilo Bambang Yudhoyono and government ministers often attend the event. The MR media claim that their celebration of the Prophet's birthday (*maulid*) is the largest *maulid* event in the world.

The death of Habib Munzir in September 2013 shocked his followers who idolised him. Habib Munzir died in a hospital in Jakarta after suffering complication from encephalitis and asthma. Thousands of MR followers flocked to the Mosque of Al-Munawwar to pray for him and attended his funeral at the Habib Kuncung Cemetery in South Jakarta. Based on my observation, the number of his followers remained stable even months after his death. It seems the loss of the main figure in the *majelis* did not affect the size of the followers. Several staff and followers stated that Habib Munzir was irreplaceable, yet they feel a moral obligation to continue what he had fought for, namely to transform Jakarta into what they call 'the Prophet's city' (*Kota Nabawi*).

After Habib Munzir's death, the new leadership of MR was organised into formal structures. Traditionally, the leadership of *majelis* belongs to the family of the preacher and ideally to one of his descendants. However, Habib Munzir's two sons are too young to lead the *majelis*. According to some MR staff, the oldest son of Habib Munzir, Sayyid Muhammad b. Munzir, is expected to assume the mantle of leadership in the future. They said that Sayyid Muhammad, together with his brother, Sayyid Hasan, is now studying under Habib 'Umar in Hadhramaut and is being prepared to lead the *majelis* when he is old enough. In 2013, the MR advisors consulted with Habib 'Umar and asked for his approval to appoint the next leader, Habib Ahmad b. Novel, who was also a graduate of Dar al-Mustafa. They also proposed forming a new structure for MR and limiting the period of leadership. The reason for this idea is to avoid central leadership on one figure. Habib Nabiel Al-Musawa stated that this policy aims at training (*kaderisasi*) the graduates of Dar al-Mustafa by providing them with leadership roles. The *majelis* is now organised into two bodies: the consultative body (*majelis syura*) and the executive body. The executive body consists of a daily committee (*pengurus harian*) and a teaching team (*dewan guru*). The consultative body consists of Habib Muhsin al-Hamid, Habib Nabiel Al-Musawa, and Habib Ahmad Al-Bahar. According to Habib Nabiel Al-Musawa, all important decisions of MR are made by the consultative body with the approval from Habib 'Umar. He emphasised that there is no general chairman position for the executive body since it consists of two leaders for two different tasks. The daily committee is headed by Habib Muhammad al-Bagir b. Yahya, while the teaching team is headed by Habib Ja'far b. Muhammad Al-Bagir Al-Attash (Pers. communication with Habib Nabiel Al-Musawa, September 17, 2015; Habib Muhammad Alwi Al-Kaff, September 19, 2015).

The new *majelis* structure seems to depersonalise the leadership model, which used to centre on one single figure. In Weber's term (1978), this transformation is a form of 'routinization of charisma'. It refers to the process where a religious institution is weakened after the death of its charismatic leader. By adopting traditional mechanism and bureaucracy, the next leaders could maintain the mission of the institution. This process is used to maintain the commitment of followers to MR although the founding figure has passed away. There was a concern among *majelis* stakeholders that the number of followers would diminish because there is no figure that could replace the appeal of Habib Munzir. The new structure seems to be a transition before Habib Munzir's son is old enough to lead the *majelis*. The new leaders and staff, therefore, often remind followers to remain committed to pursuing the religious mission and dreams of their past leader.

Majelis Taklim, **Religious Market, and New Media**

Majelis taklim is a popular venue for Indonesian Muslims to receive Islamic knowledge by listening to a single preacher or several preachers. Abaza defines it as "a meeting, sitting or council where the process of *ta'lim* (education) takes place" (Abaza, 2004, p. 179). *Majelis taklim* is often associated with Islamic study groups, religious learning forums, preaching gatherings, private gatherings for religious teaching, and as salon-style religious discussion groups (Winn, 2012). In the Muslim world, *majelis taklim* is quite similar with *halaqah*, a common term for Islamic study circle. However, the term and form of *majelis taklim* is distinctive and only found in Indonesia. While it is informal and open to the public, *majelis* are usually convened in mosques, houses, meeting rooms in hotels or offices, or public areas. Many preachers or organisers of *majelis taklim* usually provide a special large room in their houses with mats on the floor (Abaza, 2004, p. 179). There is no clear history on the origin of the *majelis* in Indonesia, yet some *habaib* refer to the Majelis Taklim Habib Ali Kwitang in Jakarta as the pioneering *majelis* in Indonesia. The *majelis* was founded by Habib Ali b. Abdurrahman al-Habsyi (popularly called Habib Ali Kwitang) at the end of the 19th century and has been continued by his descendants up to the present. Many local *kiais* and large number of participants attended the *majelis* throughout the history. In the past, *majelis taklim* such as Majelis Habib Ali Kwitang was led by a senior *habib* whose religious knowledge was acknowledged by local communities. Their popularity with the Muslim public was apparently due to their charisma and their mastery of traditional Islamic knowledge.

Majelis taklim became increasingly popular in Indonesia from the 1990s onwards (Winn, 2012) at the time when Islamic revival shaped the social and cultural spaces of Muslims. It has been more popular among middle-aged and married Muslim women who want not only to study Islam but also to spend time with their

70   *Arab Saints and the Prophet*

friends and neighbours. According to Phillip Winn (2012), "participation in *majelis taklim* attracted considerable legitimacy as a vehicle for religiously engaged contemporary Muslim women to contribute to national life". Due to its popularity, *majelis* spread in many provinces. According to the directorate of Islamic education, there were 153,357 *majelis taklim* in Indonesia in 2006 (Winn, 2012). As the number of participants increased, 732 *majelis taklim* agreed to establish the Body for Contacts among *majelis taklim* (*Badan Kontak Majelis Taklim* [BKMT]) in Jakarta in 1981. It was chaired by the late Professor Tutty Alawiyah (1942–2016), a daughter of the late Jakartan ulama, K.H. Abdullah Syafi'i (1910–1985). According to its website, the BKMT aims to enhance the quality of learning within the *majelis taklim.* This is achieved by establishing a collaborative forum for communication among fellow *majelis taklim* in Indonesia (BKMT, "History of BKMT").[2]

Although in its development *majelis taklim* was largely associated with the domain of Muslim women, there were a few *majelis taklim* which had male-only followers or mixed-sex meetings. The oldest *habaib majelis* in Jakarta, Majelis Habib Ali Kwitang, for instance, consists of male and female audiences who are segregated during the sermon. Another old *majelis*, such as *Al-Kifahi Al-Tsaqafi*, in Bukit Duri, Jakarta, also has followers from both men and women, but each of the group has a different schedule. The common characteristic of *majelis* audiences in the past is that they consisted predominantly of older people and very few youths and teenagers.

The booming popularity of young *habaib*-led *majelis taklim* among young Muslims has become a new phenomenon in post-Soeharto Indonesia. While the older generation of *habaib* prefers to keep a low profile, the new generation actively promotes themselves. There are several points that distinguish them from earlier generations of *habaib* preachers. Firstly, most of the new preachers are young, ranging from 20 to 30 years at the start of their preaching career. Many of them graduated from Hadhramaut, Yemen, while some graduated from traditional Islamic schools (*pesantren*) in Java. Secondly, the new preachers tend to establish their own *majelis taklim*, becoming the pivotal figure in their organisation and utilising advertising and the internet to promote their sermons. The newly established *majelis* often have a logo or brand, flags, a headquarters, an official website, and a religious merchandise. They also have a multimedia team, young staff members, and volunteers to help organise their events. Thirdly, many young *habaib* preachers emphasise their distinctive status by wearing white turban (*imamah*), long white dress (*jubah*), and a shawl (mostly green) on their shoulders. Finally, most of the participants in this type of *majelis* are young people, both men and women, ranging from 12 to 30 years and mostly coming from the traditionalist Muslim families. Participants usually wear the uniform jackets of the *majelis* showing their commitment and their linked identity to the *majelis*.

The resurgence of *habaib dakwah* cannot be isolated from the context of competing authority among Muslim groups. In the evolving public sphere and increasingly deregulated market, we have witnessed the rapid expansion of various Muslim groups that compete for followers (Meuleman, 2011). They actively organise public activities, sell religious products, and spread their religious messages

Arab Saints and the Prophet   71

through the new media. Various interpretations of religious messages, ranging from puritanical to liberal ones, have been disseminated in print media and the internet. The advanced development in technology and communication as well as globalisation has allowed the flow of ideas from overseas. Several new Muslim movements rooted in the Middle East have expanded their ideology through *dakwah* and education in Indonesia. As I established in the Chapter 3, among the new Islamic movements, Salafi groups are prominent in preaching Islamic purification through sermons and new media. They also denounce the beliefs and rituals of traditionalist Muslims which they regarded as unlawful innovation (*bid'ah*). Traditionalist Muslims, who constitute the Muslim majority in Indonesia, believed that Salafi *dakwah* was a challenge to their tradition. The community became increasingly concerned when several incidents appeared to threaten their position, such as the taking over of traditionalist mosques, the denouncing of unlawful innovation (*bid'ah*) in their religious practices, and Salafi 'penetration' into Muslim organisations. On the other hand, they also viewed that the propagation of Shi'a and liberal Islam, deemed as deviant, had exerted a negative influence on their young generation.

In a situation where traditionalist Muslims were under the perceived 'threat' of Salafi and other new Muslim groups, there was a growing demand for *dakwah* and religious marketing within the traditionalist community. Religious marketing in this sense refers to "a competition for followers who can be captured on the basis of strong public presence and seducing and convincing rhetoric, performance, and imagery" (de Witte et al., 2015, p. 120). In this sense, *dakwah* and religious markets are a medium for preachers and religious groups to attract followers. This resonates with Pattana Kitiarsa's view (2008 and 2010) which counters secularisation theory emphasising the triumph of market over religion. He contends that "market and media make religions more accessible to the public and convert religions into popular cultural practice in modern societies…" (Kitiarsa, 2010, p. 579). This point of view is adopted by the majority of *habaib* preachers who seek to popularise their traditionalist Islam through new media and markets. Realising the growing demand for *dakwah* from traditionalist communities, *habaib* have responded by conducting *dakwah* through sermon groups (*majelis taklim*) in urban areas. They called on Muslims to strengthen their Sunni belief through regular participation in *majelis taklim* so that they can protect themselves from the influence of Salafi and other 'deviant' groups.

The increasing competition for followers led *habaib* to creatively brand their traditionalist *dakwah* and fashion it in order to meet the aspirations of urban Muslim youth. *Habaib* are determined to establish sermon groups (*majelis taklim*) that are totally different from conventional ones. The new sermon groups are structured in such a way as to offer young Muslims a venue to express their aspirations through *dakwah* activism and identity expressions. The *habaib* fashioned their *majelis taklim* to be like a public performance and entertainment that give followers active roles. As the result, the *majelis* is no longer seen as a serious place for religious learning, but rather a pleasurable place for socialising, chanting, and singing praises of the Prophet accompanied by traditional musical performance. The following section discusses strategies used by *habaib* to attract young followers.

72   *Arab Saints and the Prophet*

Performing Arab Saints (*Wali*)

One distinctive aspect of the *dakwah* of new *habaib* is the promotion of sainthood (*kewalian*). Both *sayyid* status and the Arab ethnicity are expressed in the performance of a *habib* preacher. Sayyidness here refers to the genealogical link to the Prophet marked by the title '*habib*' (beloved) attached to the name of the preacher. In addition, particular clothing and visual attributes also represent outward marks of a *habib*. Their appearance also expresses their Arabness as they originated in Hadhramaut, Yemen. Many of their followers also remark favourably upon what they see as typical Arab traits, such as long sharp noses, beards, and dark complexion. Besides, several *majelis* use Arabic words on their banner on the stage.

The lineage to the Prophet endows the *habaib* with a special position in the Muslim community. Several books and posters sold in the *majelis taklim* as well as the stories told by the *habaib* preachers describe the *sayyid* ulama in Indonesia's past as Muslim saints (*wali*) who not only played a major role in Islamisation but also possessed extraordinary spiritual powers. The *wali*'s graves are considered *keramat* (sacred) by many and have the power to give blessings to their visitors. According to Sumit Mandal, calling a specific burial place *keramat* is a form of respect from the community for the deceased because of "his outstanding spiritual piety, learning, historical accomplishments or some other notable distinctions" (Mandal, 2012, p. 357). During my fieldwork in Jakarta and Java, I visited several *keramat sayyid* graves that attracted many visitors. The graves of popular saints in Jakarta, for instance, include those of Habib Ali b. Abdulrahman Al-Habsyi in Kwitang Jakarta, Habib Hasan b. Muhammad Al-Haddad and Habib Husein b. Abubakar Alaydrus in North Jakarta, and Habib Ahmad Al-Haddad in Kalibata South Jakarta. These graves have become popular destinations for young *habaib* preachers who include saint veneration in their *majelis*' regular programme. Their visit is meant to bring blessings (*baraka*) from the dead saint and the hope that their prayers are answered by God, thanks to the mediating role of the saints.

For traditionalist Muslims, *habaib* are considered as having inherited blessings (*baraka*) through their blood connection to the Prophet. The *baraka* for traditionalist Muslims can bring success and happiness or a way out of the problems in their lives. It is therefore not surprising to see Muslim participants in the *majelis* stand up when they meet a *habib* and flock to shake and kiss his hand hoping to get blessings from him. Some participants also bring a bottle of water and request the *habib* to recite prayers that would give the water healing powers or the power to solve any problem that might be troubling the participant.

A clear indication of descent from the Prophet is the attribution of title '*habib*' or '*al-habib*' before the name. In colonial times and early independence, the title '*sayyid*' (lord) was more popularly used in print rather than '*habib*'. This is based on my reading of old newspapers and internal publications of Majelis Habib Ali Kwitang in Jakarta. Several *habaib* told me the usage of *habib* title is now more popular than *sayyid* in Hadhramaut and Indonesia. According to the chairman of Rabithah Alawiyah, Sayyid Zein b. Smith, the tittle of *habib* cannot be attributed to all descendants of the Prophet. He stated that every *habib* is *sayyid*, but not all

Arab Saints and the Prophet 73

s*ayyids* can become *habib*. The recognition of *habib* has to come from a community with several requirements. To be a *habib*, a *sayyid* needs to be of mature age, erudite, and learned in Islamic knowledge, implementing religious knowledge in practice, showing sincerity, fearing God (*takwa*), and applying Islamic ethics (*akhlak*). However, as mentioned above, the title is now increasingly used by many young *sayyids* for doing *dakwah* despite their limited knowledge of Islam and their lack of ethical qualities (*Republika*, October 11, 2014). This suggests that the new preachers realise the marketing value of the title in enhancing their authority. This is also the case with the title '*kiai*' which is now routinely attributed to new preachers. The commodification of *habib*'s title is clearly apparent from the advertisement media and websites that promote a new preacher figure of *majelis taklim*.

The *sayyid* communities have a family organisation, Rabithah Alawiyah (the Alawi Union), that issues a genealogical passport (*buku nasab*) for their members. Founded in 1928, the organisation serves to strengthen solidarity among *sayyids* with a primary concern for improving education and *dakwa*. One of its roles is to maintain genealogical records and formally issue a genealogical certificate (Anggaran Dasar/Anggaran Rumah Tangga Rabithah Alawiyah). For those who want to obtain an official certificate of *sayyid/sharifa*, they need to apply to the Rabithah office and bring proof of their family connection in the line of their father. Some Rabithah staff worry that the booming popularity of *habaib* preachers leads to the commodification of *habib* status. They remark that some preachers in Jakarta and South Kalimantan use fake titles in order to promote themselves in the preaching market. However, they have not taken any action against this. Instead, they call on the *sayyid* community to preserve their cultural and religious tradition. One of the ways is to apply for genealogical passport through Rabithah office. By having the passport, the *sayyids* can show the proof of their lineage. This is important especially for maintaining the *kafa'ah* (equality in marriage) tradition within the *sayyid* community, in which a female *sayyid* (*sharifa*) is required to marry a *sayyid* man who can prove his sayyidness through genealogical passport.

Given the importance of genealogy for building religious legitimacy, many *habaib* preachers display the poster of genealogy prominently in their houses or offices. The poster shows the names of male family descendants back to the Prophet Muhammad. Most *habaib* preachers I met claim they are the 38th–40th generation descendants of the Prophet. According to Alwe Al-Mashoor, the family names of Alawiyin total about 180, and those also reflect their *sayyid* identity (Al-Mashoor, 2011, p. 175). Several family names of popular preachers in Indonesia include Al-Aththas, Al-Saqqaf, Shihab, Al-Habsyi, Al-Aydarus, Al-Kaff, b. Jindan, Al-Musawa, b. Yahya, Jamalullail, and Al-Jufri.

Apart from the title and family name, dress is also important in expressing sayyidness. The *habaib*'s clothes follow the old style of traditional ulama and saints (*wali* or *sunan*) in Indonesia. *Habaib* preachers often wear those as identity markers. Moreover, some preachers also bring *siwak* (tooth-cleaning stick made from tree twigs) in their pockets and use them before conducting a prayer. *Habaib* consider their style of clothing as imitating clothes worn by the Prophet during his lifetime. I observed a popular *habib* in Malang who suggested that his male followers

74 *Arab Saints and the Prophet*

should wear turbans as a symbol piety. He argued that the Prophet, his companions, and many ulama in the past wore turbans during their lifetimes.

The traditional dress of *habaib* also replicates the appearance of Muslim saints who are respected and venerated among Muslim traditionalists. The famous Muslim saints in Java were called 'the nine saints' (*wali songo*) who are credited with spreading Islam in Java. While there are various versions of the origin of the saints, most *habaib* and a few Hadhami scholars (Alatas, 1997; Shihab, 2001) claim that the nine saints were originally from Hadhramaut and migrated to Southeast Asia for religious proselytising and trade. The tendency to claim sayyidness for 'the nine saints' is popularised in *habaib*-owned magazines, most notably the *alKisah* magazine, and also in sermons. The *habaib* preachers often narrate their ancestor's struggles in Islamisation, their ethical principles, their spiritual exercises, and miracles. By connecting with the past, the *habaib* seek to emphasise the important roles of their ancestors and their spiritual qualities to the congregation. On some occasions, preachers recounted their dreams to their followers describing how they meet the Prophet and dead saints and receive messages and advice from them. The story of Habib Munzir's dream, for instance, is widely circulated among his followers after his death in 2013. Long before his death, Habib Munzir had told his followers that he saw the Prophet in a dream. In the dream, the Prophet suggested Habib Munzir take a rest from *dakwah* and promised that he would meet the Prophet at the age of 40. This dream was later interpreted as a prediction of Habib Munzir's death at the age of 40. This story was often related with pride by his brother, Habib Nabiel b. Fuad al-Musawa, and other *habaib* preachers, alluding to the miracle (*karama*) of Habib Munzir. Miraculous stories like this are common in the Sufi literature, which bestows special status on Muslim saints. The dream narratives have been used by several preachers as a way of building their spiritual authority with Muslim followers.

Mediating Spirituality with Musicality

Many young *habaib* preachers have used new communication technology as an instrument in promoting their *majelis* and disseminating their messages to a wider audience. The use of new media, especially the internet, and advertising was started by the two largest *majelis* in Jakarta, namely the MR and the Majelis Nurul Musthofa. Both *majelis* began their *dakwah* expansion in 1998 in Jakarta. The *majelis* website is critical in promoting the *habib* leader or main preacher and his *majelis*. The home page of the MR website, for instance, shows images of the *habib* appearing pious in traditionalist costume, praying, or preaching to the congregation. The page provides various options such as a *majelis* profile, *majelis* schedules, religious programmes, discussion forums, reports on *dakwah* trips, the Prophet's kiosks, donation, and live streaming. The options not only give information on *majelis* and religious messages but also encourage audiences to engage in and support their *dakwah* through donations. On the website, the sermons of *habaib* are accessible and people can watch live-streamed preaching and listen to musical prayers. Besides, it provides online spaces for Muslim audience to follow

Arab Saints and the Prophet 75

the ongoing activities of the *majelis* and take part in online discussion forum (*forum tanya jawab*), in which audiences can ask questions about matters related to Islamic law and theology. Habib Munzir personally answered all the questions and posted them in the forum.

The new media has enabled the creation of informal networks that link the followers of *majelis taklim*. The most popular media for young followers are mailing list, online communities in social media, and chat groups through smartphone. Some *habaib* fans have created community pages in social media to strengthen the bond among followers. Through online communities, followers can discuss and share their stories and impressions of their *habib* as well as sharing information on the forthcoming activities of the *majelis*. Moreover, they can mobilise their peers to attend *majelis* religious programmes or social gathering. The followers of MR, for instance, have mobilised their fellows to attend public preaching or to organise solidarity meetings called 'Kopi Darat' (Meet to know each other) in the house of their fellow volunteers. For the latter activity, they often invite the second rank *habib* and some staff of the MR to give a sermon at their own gatherings. The host of the meeting feels blessed due to the presence of an *habib* and believes that the recital of the Prophet's praises in their house can bring them more good fortune and prosperity.

The young *habaib majelis* emphasises ethical improvement and practical Sufi practices rather than black and white legal doctrine. This is very different from global Muslim movements, most notably Salafi, which emphasises a strict set of Islamic theology and Islamic law in their study groups. *Habaib* preachers in most events appeal to people to be pious through religious rituals and good deeds and avoiding sins. Their *majelis* provide more ritualistic activities than serious learning of particular religious texts (*kitab*). Many informants feel that they obtain tranquillity and peace when attending the *majelis*. One female follower of Majelis Nurul Musthofa stated:

> I don't know why I was attracted to the *majelis* at first. The main thing is that when I come to the *majelis*, I feel peaceful and secure. I also feel free from any burdens and problems that I face in my life. What is more, when I join singing *salawatan* (sending praises to the Prophet), my tears cannot stop dropping.
>
> (Interview with Siska, February 13, 2013)

The distinctive part of the young *habaib*'s *majelis* is the recital of *dzikir* (remembrance of God) and *salawat* (praises to the Prophet) that can constitute up to half of the sermon activity. It is common for the participants to recite the prayers with great emotion, and some of them are moved to tears. During the recital, participants usually hold in their hands the *majelis*' booklet containing a series of hagiographies of the Prophet, *dzikr* and *salawat*, that are to be read during the preaching activity. Each *majelis* has produced its own recital booklet with their preacher's photo and logo on it. The MR uses the hagiographic text written by the Yemeni Habib 'Umar b. Hafiz entitled *al-Dhiya al-Lamiy* (the Shimmering Light), while

76   *Arab Saints and the Prophet*

the Nurul Musthofa uses the text by the late Habib Ali b. Muhammad Al-Habsyi entitled *Simth al-Durar* (Chains of Pearls).

Arab traditional music (*hadhrah*) accompanies the chanting and preaching activities. The *majelis* has crew members assigned for chanting *dzikir, salawat, maulid* texts, and singing Islamic songs. In Nurul Musthofa, the sermon is alternated with musical performance in order to avoid boring the congregation. The crew at the back play traditional musical instruments, such as tambourines and drums, with several vocalists singing the prayers and songs. The musical performance has become an important attraction for young participants to *majelis*. The leader of Nurul Musthofa has composed a number of religious songs which he modified from popular Indonesian songs. The music has created an extravaganza that stimulates emotion and excites the crowd. During the performance, some young followers wave their *majelis'* flags or swing their hands to the right and left while singing and enjoying the music as if they are in a music concert.

The leaders of *majelis taklim* have become superstars for Muslim youth due to the effect of their own media, advertisements, and performance. Self-promotion through websites, books, billboards, and merchandises have helped to bolster the profile of *habaib* among their audience and the general public who access such medium. The participants, who engage with *habaib* and are awed by their performance, religious messages, and pleasing personality, help to spread their image to the wider community. Some participants relate their experiences to friends and family in the social media, and this helps to spread the *habaib*'s fame. Many followers of the *majelis* depict their preachers as holy men (saints), humble, pious, but also cool (*keren*). 'Coolness' in this sense means that *habaib*, although wearing traditional garb, understand youth slangs and fancy style of speech and dress. Habib Hasan and his brothers in the Nurul Musthofa, for instance, often fascinate young participants by using the local dialect of Jakarta and slangs. The *sayyid* status, self-promotion, and stylish performance have turned young *habaib* preachers into new idols for Muslim youths.

Marketing the Prophet

Young *habaib* have created a niche within the growing *dakwah* movements in Indonesia by identifying their movements as serving devotees of the Prophet Muhammad. Many of them have named their *majelis taklim* to emphasise the link with the Prophet: Majelis Rasulullah (The Assembly of the Prophet), Nurul Musthofa (The Light of the Chosen One), Ahbabul Musthofa (The Lovers of the Chosen One), and Waratsatul Musthofa (The Inheritor of the Chosen One), to name but a few. The MR and Waratsatul Musthofa use the image of the Prophet's grave for their logo. They declare that their main concern of *dakwah* is to invite people to love the Prophet. They argue that in order to make people commit to the faith, young Muslims must first recognise and love the Prophet. To attract people to their religious sermon, *habaib* try to introduce Muhammad as a man through stories and Islamic songs instead of preaching about serious religious matters. By introducing and preaching about Muhammad the Man, *habaib* hope that the congregation will

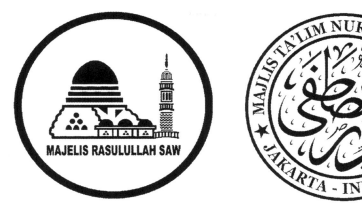

Figure 4.1 Logo of the MR and the Nurul Musthofa
Source: www.majelisrasulullah.org and www.nurulmusthofa.org.

make the Prophet the role model in their earthly lives. This missionary method resembles the new evangelical churches in the US which preach discipleship of Jesus by following His teachings and examples (Stassen, 2012, p. 51).

The love of the Prophet in *habaib*'s *majelis* is expressed in religious rituals and festivities that serve for remembering and sending praises to the prophet. The religious rituals associated with the Muslim traditionalists such as reciting praises to the Prophet (*salawatan*), celebrating the Prophet's birthday (*maulid*), and visiting saints' graves (*ziarah*) are framed as prophetic practices. This is different from reformist and Salafi groups which insist on the strict emulation of the Prophet in terms of religious practice and oppose unlawful innovations (*bid'ah*) that venerate the Prophet in the forms of *mawlid* festivals and reciting praising texts to the Prophet. In several *majelis taklim*, the ritual of reading the *maulid* texts usually precedes the preaching activities. Each *majelis* often celebrates the festivity of *maulid* in an open area with thousands of participants. For *habaib* preachers, the *maulid* rituals are seen as a means to pleasing the Prophet. Some *habaib* and participants believe that the Prophet's spirit is present when *maulid* texts are recited. By reciting the praises of the Prophet, the congregation believe that they will get blessings for them and their families as well as gaining special help (*Syafa'at*) from the Prophet in the hereafter regardless of their numerous sins.

Habaib use the symbols of the Prophet as branding in their religious marketing. According to Mara Einstein (2008), branding is about making meaning that creates a kind of individual thinking and feeling to the consumers on a product beyond its physical attributes. In Indonesia, various preachers and spiritual trainers have referred to the specific stories and sayings of the Prophet "in ways that resonate with the civic concerns, consumerist desires, and aspirational piety of the Muslim middle class" (Hoesterey, 2012, pp. 38–61). Aa Gym, for instance, when giving seminars and training on entrepreneurship, framed the Prophet as the role model of ethical entrepreneur who exemplified piety, trustworthiness, and initiative for

78 *Arab Saints and the Prophet*

achieving prosperity. This frame sought to show the Prophet as the measure of Muslim cosmopolitanism (Hoesterey, 2012, p. 46). The *habaib,* however, brand their products as avenues for recognising and imitating the Prophet's personality and appearance. They argue that recognising the Prophet will lead people to deepen Islam and carry out its teachings. The religious products with various prophetic symbols (*nabawi*) are attractive to the followers of *habaib*. The retail outlet of MR calls itself 'Kios Nabawi' (the Prophet's Kiosk). It sells books on how to follow the Prophet's ethics and prayers. There are also several books by Hadhrami scholars on *maulid* texts containing poems and praise to the Prophet. The MR staff argue that the marketing of the merchandise is a form of *dakwah*, and the income is used for supporting the circle of *majelis* activities. By consuming these products, people identify themselves as the followers of *habaib* (*muhibbin*) and pious Muslims who help to ensure the survival of the Prophet's *dakwah*.

Considering that *habaib* are the family of the Prophet, the Prophetic branding can enhance the authority of *habaib* preachers. Therefore, it is not surprising that many of the *habaib*'s sermons are related to the Prophet Muhammad. Many *habaib* draw attention to the compassion and moral virtues of the Prophet. By connecting the Prophet to their *dakwah*, *habaib* send the message that they are closer to the Prophet and that they are the legitimate heirs of the Prophet in preaching Islam. To strengthen their legitimacy before the *umma*, some *habaib* declare that they have met and received guidance from the Prophet through dreams and visions.

In the growing competitive market of *habaib*'s *dakwah*, each *majelis* competes to provide a distinctive product that attracts young Muslim consumers. Habib Munzir of the MR, for instance, was a charismatic preacher who used literary, heartfelt, and heart-rending style (*dari hati ke hati*) in his sermons. His *majelis* is also the largest in terms of merchandising. Many followers claim that they have received knowledge and enlightenment after attending Habib Munzir's sermon. His experience of studying in Yemen and his attachment to Habib 'Umar of Yemen enhanced his authority among audiences. In the case of Habib Hasan of Nurul Musthofa, his strength lies in his accommodation of young people's aspirations and their strong liking for entertainment. The chanting and prayer singing of the lyrics composed by Habib Hasan are appealing to young followers, especially teenagers. Habib Hasan usually modifies Indonesian popular songs by changing their lyrics into religious ones. For his followers, the musical performance in the midst of sermons is more colourful and helps them avoid boredom when listening to preachers. Therefore, it is no wonder that many of his young followers are more amazed by the variety of fun and entertainment in the *majelis* than its sermons.[3]

Habaib preachers sometimes invite guest preachers, especially Yemeni-Hadhrami ulama, who can lend authority and novelty to their programme. The educational background and the network of *habaib* preachers are important in linking them with 'international' ulama. The advertisements are used to inform the public of the guest preachers' attendance and appearance. Among *habaib* preachers in Indonesia, Habib Munzir was the most active in presenting Yemeni ulama in his preaching events. As a Hadhramaut graduate, Habib Munzir benefitted from his close relationship with his former teachers and fellow graduates from the Middle

Arab Saints and the Prophet 79

East. For big events, he occasionally invited them to give sermons. If the preachers use Arabic, Habib Munzir and his fellow preachers translate it into Indonesian. The guest speakers, who are often introduced as traditionalist Sunni ulama, frequently acknowledged and endorsed the *majelis* as an important pillar of Sunni *dakwah* in Indonesia. The presence of the Middle Eastern ulama serves to enhance the authenticity and authority of MR to the audience.

Unlike Habib Munzir, Habib Hasan, who lacks a Yemeni network, prefers to invite popular local senior preachers and celebrity preachers in Jakarta. The presence of celebrity preachers in the *majelis* could attract a large audience, thereby spreading the fame of his *majelis* to the wider public.

The popularity of *majelis* has enabled their leaders to develop a mutual interest with the state officials and politicians. Having a connection with the state officials is part of the social capital that *habaib* use in maintaining and advancing their *majelis*. On the one hand, the cooperation between the *majelis* and the state officials and politicians helps funding and facilitating the activities of the *majelis* as well as enhancing its image for Muslim audiences. *Majelis* staff admitted that there have been donations from various politicians and businessmen. The donations include money, cars for *habaib* and *majelis* operations, and rent payments for *majelis* headquarters (Interview with Syukron Makmun, October 9, 2013). Both the MR and the Nurul Musthofa included former President Susilo Bambang Yudhoyono (SBY) and other government officials as advisory board members in the *majelis*. SBY himself established a *majelis taklim*, called Majelis Dzikir Nurussalam (The Light of Peace), which worked as a political venue for building his religious credentials among the *umma*. His own *majelis* also connected him to the networks of *majelis taklim* in Indonesia. During his presidency, his *majelis* often conducted a joint public preaching with *habaib majelis*, especially the Nurul Musthofa. The Nurul Musthofa staff stated that the joint activity with SBY's *majelis* was needed in order to gain support from the state in obtaining permission for public preaching as well as funding assistance for the development of the *majelis*. They claimed that their close connection to the state officials and local government has resulted in easy access to public areas, especially the Monas area, for organising particular events. Moreover, due to such a close relationship, the Nurul Musthofa often received invitations from SBY to deliver sermons or recite prayers in both his palace in Jakarta and his house in Cikeas, West Java. The closeness of *habaib* with the President and some ministers was also used by *habaib* to promote their *majelis'* name. For example, the pictures of important political figures often appear in the *majelis'* profile and banners.

On the other hand, the state officials and politicians use these events as a means to polish their religious image, especially before an election. Borrowing Kertzer's perspective on ritual, politics, and power, religious events serve as a ritual for "aspiring political leaders…to assert their right to rule, incumbent power holders seek to bolster their authorities" (Kertzer, 1988, p. 1). Former President SBY often attended and delivered a speech at the Prophet's birthday festivals (*maulid*) held at the national monument in Jakarta. His attendance reinforced the image of a president who cared about Muslim aspirations. Apart from SBY, some ministers, politicians,

80 *Arab Saints and the Prophet*

and presidential candidates also attended the *habaib's majelis taklim*. During the 2014 presidential election, many presidential candidates, such as Aburizal Bakrie (Golongan Karya), Hatta Rajasa (Partai Amanat Nasional) and Muhaimin Iskandar (Partai Kebangkitan Bangsa), tried to woo Muslim voters who constitute the largest majority in Indonesia by attending *majelis* in Monas quarter in 2013. In the religious events, *habaib* usually mentioned their guests' names, praised their attendance, and asked the congregation to pray for their success in their political career. Although *habaib* did not declare their political support for any particular candidate, the *habaib's* prayers and good wishes during the religious events were interpreted by their audience as political support.

The growing demand for public preaching in urban areas and the high financial rewards have benefitted religious preachers. Several studies have confirmed the success of preachers and trainers in capitalising their Islamic knowledge in big cities (Hoesterey, 2008, 2016; Howell, 2008; Muzakki, 2008; Rudnyckyj, 2010; Kailani, 2015). As the centre of business and national media, Jakarta has enabled the creation of overnight celebrity preachers. Although all preachers claim their work is for the sake of *dakwah*, they have enjoyed financial rewards from the *umma*. Based on my observation and interviews in Jakarta, there are four sources of income of *habaib* in *dakwah*: honoraria from hosts, donations from the participants during public preaching, funding assistance from state officials and generous donators, and the income from selling their merchandise. Staff of the MR and the Nurul Musthofa said that they charge about $600–900 USD for public preaching for local areas (Jakarta) and more than that amount for areas outside Jakarta. They argue that this money is used for paying the preachers, *hadhrah* players, and staff, as well as for providing the stage, speakers, musical instruments, and advertisements such as banners and billboards. Habib Abdullah of the Nurul Musthofa claims that in one *dakwah* performance he often get about 40–90 USD, an amount that he considered small after being shared with his three brothers and staff members. He rejected the rumours that their *majelis* requires tens of millions for *dakwah* (Interview with Habib Abdullah Assegaf, June 13, 2013). Despite this claim, his *dakwah* performance in the Nurul Musthofa has made him popular among Jakartan Muslims. This popularity renders him many personal invitations (outside his formal *majelis*) to give sermons at events in Jakarta such as wedding ceremonies, *pengajian* (religious study gathering), and other religious events.

In public preaching, it is a common phenomenon in Jakarta to see staff and volunteers of *majelis* with donation sacks walking around congregations. Several staff members also distribute a leaflet containing the schedule of sermons. At the bottom of the leaflet, there are details of the *majelis's* website and bank account for those who wish to send donations. Staff said that they sometimes receive assistance from donators in the form of rent payment for their headquarters, cars for operation, and so forth. With regard to merchandise, they said that the market demand is growing among congregations who attend the public preaching. The MR jackets, for instance, are among the bestselling products. They promote and sell their products online, especially through social media, and have sent products not only to Indonesia but also to Malaysia and Singapore.

Conclusion

This chapter has discussed two sermon groups of young *habaib* as a new religious market in contemporary Indonesia. Focusing on the cases of the MR and the Nurul Musthofa, it has analysed the approaches *habaib* use in marketing tradition within the burgeoning Islamic preaching industries in urban areas. While the emerging trend shows that most preachers use public speaking skills in religious markets, *habaib* also utilise performance in enhancing their religious authority and marketability. Their performance expresses a combination of traditionalism, sainthood, and Arabness. Using the internet and popular culture, the *habaib* promote themselves as living saints by capitalising on their *sayyid* status and emphasising their ancestor's roles in Islamisation. In this regard, the using of *habib* titles, distinctive dress, and family names are of significance in expressing their status and Arab ethnicity. By branding their *majelis* as the devotees of the Prophet, *habaib* have offered a new model of traditionalist piety among Muslim youths. Such branding implies that their *dakwah* is closer to the Prophet's mission and is therefore more authentic and authoritative than other *dakwah* groups.

The case of *habaib* preachers suggests that tradition can be mediated and marketed in urban areas. This complements previous studies that largely focused on the modern *dakwah* expression within urban settings. The urban *dakwah* is usually tailored to appeal to a broad Muslim constituency. Furthermore, it tends to accommodate the modern tastes of the Muslim middle class and minimise traditionalist appearance and rituals. The *habaib dakwah*, however, is different and confronts this general pattern. Instead of being accommodative, their *dakwah* is targeted at a particular Muslim group. It promotes traditionalist Islam (*aswaja*) that only appeals to traditionalist Muslim communities culturally linked to the Nadhlatul Ulama. The *habaib dakwah* emerged at the 'right' time when there was a growing demand from traditionalist communities. *Habaib* have identified a market gap and moved into it, promoting devotional practices which meet the needs and aspirations of urban traditionalists. By using new media and religious markets, *habaib* not only succeed in popularising tradition but also gain elevated religious standing, fame, and financial rewards from the *umma*.

Notes

1 There is a different version on Indonesian student's number for the first cohort. Alatas stated that there were 40 students. However, several graduates of Dar al-Mustafa's whom I met, such as Habib Jindan b. Novel, confirmed that there were 30 students.
2 See more details in https://bkmt.or.id/wp/sejarah-berdirinya-bkmt/ (accessed on 26 August 2023).
3 More detailed narration of *majelis* followers are discussed in Chapter 6.

5 Reviving Yemeni Traditionalist Networks

The Assertion of Authenticity and Authority

Introduction

Over the past decade, Indonesian Muslim public has witnessed the proliferation of *habaib's dakwah* groups that promote traditional Sunni Islam (*aswaja*). Many of these groups also promote the Hadhramaut of Yemen as the land of Muslim saints and introduce Yemeni Hadhrami ulama and their religious educational institutions to Indonesia Muslims. They publish the profiles of Yemeni ulama and their translated books and sell them to Indonesian Muslim communities. Moreover, they regularly invite and host charismatic Yemeni ulama to give sermons at major public events. Some of the Yemeni ulama such as Habib 'Umar b. Hafiz, popularly known as Habib 'Umar, have become popular, and their sermons have been followed by thousands of participants. Habib 'Umar's picture is sold and hung on the walls of traditionalist Muslims' houses across the country. Given this development, this chapter asks: How to explain the intensity of traditional Sunni-Hadhramaut connection?

This chapter analyses transnational factors that contribute to the growing influence of *habaib* in contemporary Indonesia. It argues that the reconnection between Indonesia and Hadhramaut in the sphere of traditionalist Islamic education and preaching (*dakwah*) has contributed to the growing authority of *habaib* in Indonesia. The networks have fostered the sending of Indonesian Muslim youths, either *sayyid* or non-*sayyid*, to traditionalist Islamic colleges in Hadhramaut and the building of *dakwah* networks among them. By linking themselves to Yemeni-Hadhrami scholars and their religious seminaries, as well as to sacred places in Hadhramaut, the Indonesian *habaib* are enhancing their authority and presenting their version of Sunni Islam as more authentic than other variants of Islam. Examining the forms of this new connection, this chapter pays particular attention to Habib 'Umar of Yemen, his influence, and his educational and *dakwah* networks in contemporary Indonesia. Habib 'Umar is arguably the most important figure among Yemeni *habaib*; he has played a major role in reconnecting Indonesia and Hadhramaut through education and preaching movements from the 1990s to the present.

The first part of this chapter discusses the Hadhrami diaspora and re-establishing of Indonesia and Yemen ties following Yemen's unification in 1990. The second

DOI: 10.4324/9781003358558-5

part analyses new forms of reconnection, especially in the sphere of traditionalist education and *dakwah*. The last part analyses the ways *habaib* and returnee graduates promote Hadhramaut as a land of saints and Sunni educational centres in the Middle East. Furthermore, it analyses how they promote the rising *sayyid* scholars from Hadhramaut and other parts in the Middle East.

Hadhrami Diaspora and New Connection

Hadhrami Arabs have a long history of migration to regions around the Indian Ocean. The Hadhrami migration began several centuries before the 19th century (Mobini-Kesheh, 1999, p. 17; Boxberger, 2002, p. 39). The wave of migration intensified especially from the 19th to th early 20th century because of increasing political instability in Hadhramaut created by the struggle for power between the Qu'ayti and Kathiri sultanates (Boxberger, 2002, p. 4). The political unrest exacerbated existing hardships in the region due to drought and poverty. The increasing migration in the 19th century was also supported by advances in transportation and communication. The opening of the Suez Canal and the rapid expansion of steamship travel between Arabia and the Indies facilitated Hadhrami migration to other regions in search of work and trading opportunities (Mobini-Kesheh, 1999, p. 21; Boxberger, 2002, p. 40). It was reported that due to the massive migration, 30 percent of the Hadhrami population in 1930 lived outside Hadhramaut (Boxberger, 2002, p. 41).

Hadhrami diaspora communities maintained a connection to their hometown (Freitag and Clarence-Smith, 1997; Ho, 2006; Abushouk and Ibrahim, 2009). Material and emotional links are expressed, among other things, through remittances –

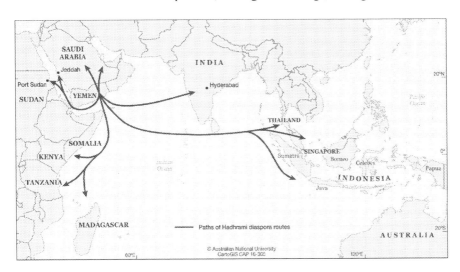

Map 5.1 Paths of Hadhrami diaspora routes. Source: CartoGIS CAP-ANU.

Source: Adapted and modified from Manger, 2010.

84 *Reviving Yemeni Traditionalist Networks*

money that migrants send back to their homeland. Wealthy Hadhrami in Singapore during colonial times sent generous amounts of remittances for the improvement of caravan routes and the construction of roads in Hadhramaut (Lekon, 1997, p. 274). In 1878, wealthy Hadhrami in Batavia also sent donations to the leading Sufi scholar Sayyid Ali b. Muhammad b. Husayn al-Habsyi (1824–1914) to support the founding of a mosque and his traditional learning institution (*ribath*) in Say'un, which served as the centre of religious teaching and Sufi activities (Freitag, 2003, p. 280).

Another form of connecting to the hometown was through religious education. A Dutch scholar, Van den Berg, who researched Hadhrami immigrants in the Dutch East Indies from 1884 to 1886, found that it was a tradition for Hadhrami migrants to send their children to study their religion and culture in their homeland. This tradition was beleived to provide a better education to their children who were isolated from their original language and their culture as they were born and raised overseas (Berg, 1989, p. 141). By living in Hadhramaut, the Hadhrami children could learn and speak Arabic without distraction and immerse themselves in the culture of their ancestors. The Hadhrami viewed Hadhramaut as an ideal place for their children since its stark environment and lack of entertainment supported religious learning and pious practices (Berg, 1989, p. 142). Furthermore, the Hadhrami-*sayyids* saw their homeland as the spiritual land, while Java was the 'damned one' (Alatas, 2005, pp. 142–158). They desired to visit Hadhramaut to receive "spiritual benedictions from the scholars who lived and were buried there" (Alatas, 2005, p. 151). This tradition, however, was interrupted during the Cold War and the civil war that broke out between the pro-Soviet communist South and anti-communist forces in the North, which made travel and communication between Indonesia and South Yemen difficult. That the Soeharto regime strongly discouraged any interaction with South Yemen also hindered the connection to Hadhramaut (Slama, 2005, p. 80).

The Rise of *Sayyids* in Yemen after Unification

The unification of North and South Yemen in 1990 and the weakening of the socialist control allowed a relaxed atmosphere for religious debate among different Islamic groups in the new state. This new political freedom gave rise to many different religious groups that became actively engaged in public debates. Salafi and Sufi *sayyids* are two such groups. Since the 1980s, Salafi have expanded to several regions in North Yemen and become one of the popular destinations for Salafi education in the Middle East.[1] Southern Yemen, however, is largely populated by peasant farmers who follow the Sunni-Shafi'i religious school (Knysh, 2001, p. 402). In Hadhramaut, *sayyids* are key leaders and teachers in religious learning and rituals. Prior to unification, the North Yemeni government supported the Salafi movements as "a fifth column to subvert the southern socialist government" (Ho, 2006, p. 316). Under the socialist regime, the *sayyids* in South Yemen experienced marginalisation, humiliation, and physical persecution from the state apparatus. Moreover, the traditional customs and expressions of devotion to the *sayyid* group were outlawed (Knysh, 2001, p. 408). As a result of unification, the *sayyid* groups are once again free to express their religious views and practise their old customs.

Reviving Yemeni Traditionalist Networks 85

The major challenge has been coming from the Salafi group that denounces the Sufi group for conducting what they regard as unlawful innovations (*bid'ah*). On some occasions, the Salafi activists tried to disrupt traditionalist rituals and even attacked their participants. The tension between the two groups has led to violence and bloodshed (Knysh, 2001, p. 405).

In view of the increasing religious rivalry between Salafi and Sufi *sayyids*, a movement to preserve the ancestral tradition and reassert Hadhrami religious identity emerged. The most influential and charismatic *sayyid* figure in this movement was Habib 'Umar. He was born in 1963 into the *sayyid* family of Shaikh Abu Bakr b. Salim in Hadhramaut. His father went missing in the political turmoil and is believed to have been killed by the socialist regime's secret police. Habib 'Umar studied under several leading scholars in Hadhramaut and started teaching and conducting *dakwah* from the age of 15 (Profile of Habib 'Umar: n.d.). Due to the increasing pressure from the totalitarian regime at that time, Habib 'Umar moved to the city of Bayda', Yemen, where he spent his time on religious learning and preaching. Habib 'Umar later travelled to Saudi Arabia where he spent about ten years receiving religious education under traditionalist teachers (Profile of Habib 'Umar). After the Yemen unification in 1990, Habib 'Umar returned to Hadhramaut and established a religious college called 'Dar al-Mustafa' (the House of the Chosen One) at Tarim. This college has received hundreds of students from various countries, but mainly from Southeast Asia and especially Indonesia.

Habib 'Umar became a leading advocate of Yemeni traditional Islam in Hadhramaut by reviving old religious customs and modifying them to suit modern conditions. These customs include pilgrimage to the shrines of local saints, celebrations of the Prophet's birthday, and collective recitations of Sufi poetry accompanied by traditional musical instruments. In the words of Knysh, "Habib 'Umar and his followers are deliberately reviving sacred geography and pilgrimage calendar of the region, which fell into disuse under the Socialist regime" (Knysh, 2001, p. 408). One important feature of the *sayyids'* religious outlook is their great adoration to the Prophet and His descendants (Knysh, 2001, p. 408). Therefore, the resurgence of these customs has worked to revive the special authority of *sayyids* as religious leaders.

The salient feature of Habib 'Umar's religious movement and educational institution lies in his enthusiasm for religious outreach (*dakwah*). According to my informants, when they studied at the Dar al-Mustafa, they were required to spend up to a month in the remote villages and hamlets of Yemen to conduct religious sermons and preach to the local population. While interacting with Habib 'Umar's students in Tarim, Knysh had the impression that the students regard Habib 'Umar's teaching as the 'true' version of Islam; they also considered themselves the disseminators of his beliefs to ignorant Muslims and non-Muslims. In spreading *dakwah*, Habib 'Umar and his group have utilised proselytisation techniques and multimedia technologies such as publications, video cassettes and DVDs, and the internet (Knysh, 2001, pp. 409, 414).

When Habib 'Umar delivered sermon in Jakarta in 2013, I could directly observed the style of his preaching and his followers' reverence of him. On the stage, he was calm, humble, and wise in appearance and preaching style. He

86   Reviving Yemeni Traditionalist Networks

talked systematically and eloquently and often referred to Qur'anic verses and the Prophet's messages. His speaking style was unmodulated and devoid of humour; however, his speech was usually rhetorical enlivened by colourful words and rhythmically repeated key sentences that sounded like a poem. He reiterated the peaceful and ethical messages (*akhlak*) of the Prophet, reminding audiences to remember God and to resist the material temptations of earthly life. He often stressed the need to attend *majelis* as a way to remember God and comprehend the 'true' teaching of Sunni Islam.

The Majelis Rasulullah's staff and followers showed great respect and admiration for Habib 'Umar. When talking about their teacher, they often referred to him as the 'true' Sunni ulama and praised his perfect character that follows the Prophet's model. It seems Habib 'Umar's *dakwah*, which centres on the Prophet, has made his followers believe that he is replicating the Prophet's character and way of life. His former students from Dar al-Mustafa often praise and extol his ethical virtues and spiritual powers. In the last section of this chapter, I will discuss followers' perception and glorification of Indonesian *habaib*.

Rebuilding New Connection

Reopening Traditionalist Seminaries

Unification and restoration of peace in Yemen led some senior *habaib* from Indonesia and Saudi Arabia to reconnect with Hadhramaut. Several *habaib* told me that the idea to reconnect Hadhramaut and Indonesia came from three senior *habaib*: the late Habib Abdul Qadir b. Ahmad Assegaf, the late Habib Muhammad b. Abdullah al-Haddar (both originally came from Hadhramaut but lived in Saudi Arabia), and the late Habib Anis b. Alwi from Solo, Indonesia. According to Mauladdawilah, the idea of reconnection was precipitated by the complaint of Habib Anis to Habib Abdul Qadir regarding the lamentable condition of *sayyids* in Indonesia who had increasingly been uprooted from their traditional culture and religion (Mauladdawilah & Mauladdawilah, 2009, p. 16). As a response, Habib Abdul Qadir and Habib Muhammad instructed their student Habib 'Umar to travel to Indonesia in order to revive the link. Habib 'Umar visited leading *habaib* in various places in Indonesia in 1993 and selected 30 Indonesian students, mostly *sayyids*, to study in Hadhramaut, Yemen (Alatas, 2009, p. 96). The coming of the Indonesian students to Hadhramaut marked the start of Habib 'Umar's new religious school, Dar al-Mustafa.

The tolerant political atmosphere following Yemen's unification prompted the reopening and establishment of traditionalist schools and colleges in an effort to revive *sayyid* tradition associated with Sufism. Most of the educational institutions are located in Tarim. There are three main institutions that have attracted large numbers of international students, especially from Indonesia: Dar al-Mustafa and its sister institute for women, Dar al-Zahra; Rubat Tarim; and al-Ahgaff University (Bubalo et al., 2011, p. 33). These institutes, which are predominantly led by *sayyid* scholars, follow the Sunni theology and Shafi'i schools of Islamic jurisprudence.

Their doctrines and references are in line with those of traditionalist *pesantren* in Indonesia. The institutes have become popular among *sayyids* and traditionalists in Indonesia because of their high reputation and the excellence of returning graduates in Islamic knowledge and learning. Some *sayyids* and their institutions have facilitated preparation courses and the travel of Indonesian students to Hadhramaut.

However, it is worth mentioning that the growing links between Indonesia and Yemen have been disrupted again due to political crisis as a result of the renewed civil war in Yemen since the late 2014. The Houthi rebel movement from the North has occupied the Yemeni capital city, Sana'a, which forced the Yemeni government into exile in March 2015. The Saudi-led coalition has intervened by launching air strikes on Houthi military positions in Sana'a. This unstable situation has led hundreds of Indonesian students to be evacuated to Indonesia. Some students, however, remained since they feel that Hadhramaut is relatively safer than Sana'a (Pers. communication with Fahmi, April 5, 2015).

In the following section, I will elaborate on the history and character of the three main schools attended by Indonesian students.

Dar al-Mustafa

The religious school was founded in Tarim in 1994 as the result of Habib 'Umar's visit to Indonesia. Instead of sending Indonesian students to the old schools in Hadhramaut, such as Rubat Tarim, Habib 'Umar preferred to run his own school in order to establish himself as a Muslim scholar. At the outset, there was no permanent building for the school. The first cohort of students stayed at the Rubat al-Mustafa located in the city of Sihr, then later moved to the Mosque of Maula Aidid in Tarim. When the new building was completed in 1997, students moved back to Hadhramaut (Imron & Hary, n.d., p. 112). The school was officially opened on 6 May 1997 (Profile of Habib 'Umar). With the passage of time, the numbers of students in the Dar al-Mustafa have increased; the majority of foreign students studying at the school hail from Indonesia. According to a report, the Indonesian students at the Dar al-Mustafa numbered around 300–400 in 2009 and 600 in 2010 (Bubalo et al., 2011, p. 34). Indonesian students who study at the school are those who come from not only Hadhrami background but also non-Hadhrami who graduated from traditionalist schools (*pesantren*) in Indonesia, especially from Java and Kalimantan (Interview with Syarif, March 3, 2013).

Three core objectives of the Dar al-Mustafa define the traditionalist characteristics of the school. Many returnee graduates told me that the school resembles a *pesantren* in Indonesia in which students could study Islamic laws and Sufi teachings which are based on Shafi'i school and Sunni theology. The three objectives include:

1 Learning sacred law (sharia) and related sciences from those who are authoritative to impart them with connected chains of transmission.
2 Purifying the soul and refining one's character.
3 Conveying beneficial knowledge and calling to Allah (*dakwah*) (Web of Habib 'Umar).

88 *Reviving Yemeni Traditionalist Networks*

The first objective is realised by studying a number of books (*kitab*) on topics such as Islamic law (*fiqh*), Islamic theology (*akidah*), and Arabic grammar (*nahw*). Several of these books are familiar to *pesantren* students in Indonesia, such as *risala al-jami'a, safina al-najah, al-muqaddima al-hadhramiya,* and *umdah al-salikin* (Imron & Hary, n.d., p. 115). The second objective indicates that Sufism is part of the core teaching in the Dar al-Mustafa. The students are required to purge themselves of bad behaviour and follow the Prophet's example in terms of attitude and practices. They are also required to participate regularly in congregational religious chanting (*dzikir and wirid*) after prayers. This practice constitutes part of *tariqa alawiya*'s teaching. The *ratib al-haddad* is among the religious litanies chanted after each prayer session (Interview with Habib Jindan b. Novel, April 8, 2013). Habib 'Umar also instructed his students to read his book entitled *khulasah al-madad al-nabawi* (The short version of Prophetic Help), which contains *dzikir* and *wirid*. The last objective points to the school's emphasis on religious propagation (*dakwah*) to the broader society, whether Muslim or non-Muslim. The school has a schedule for their students to go out to conduct weekly *dakwah*, namely from Thursday to Friday, and yearly *dakwah* that takes 40 days (Imron & Hary, n.d., p. 114). The emphasis on *dakwah* has made the graduates of the school highly skilled in preaching. In the Indonesian context, the school's graduates have established a number of sermon groups, Islamic media (electronic and print), and *pesantren* as venues for spreading their version of the faith.

Rubat Tarim

Rubat Tarim is the oldest educational institution for traditional Islamic studies in Tarim. The institution was formed in 1886 as a result of reformism to the old education system that took place in various study circles, mosques, and teacher's place (Boxberger, 2002, p. 167). The concern of the institute's founders, who were leading *sayyids* in Tarim, was to overcome difficulties faced by many students in Tarim in finding accommodation (Imron & Hary, n.d., pp. 99–100). The Rubat was founded with the support of wealthy Hadhrami *sayyids* in the diaspora and in Hadhramaut. In this institution, students receive instruction in one purpose-built school which also includes boarding facilities (Boxberger, 2002, p. 167). Students are organised into classes based on ability and principle of progression and follow a strict four-year curriculum (Freitag, p. 284). Like the Dar al-Mustafa, the school adheres to the Shafi'i school of Islamic jurisprudence and maintains Sufi traditions (Bubalo, et al., 2011, p. 36). The school still adheres to the *halaqa* method, a traditional way of teaching where students sit in a circle on the floor to receive instruction from a teacher (Imron & Hary, n.d., p. 105). Each *halaqa* has a different level of advancement. The study session starts after prayer either in the morning, noon, afternoon, or at night. Students learn various disciplines of Islamic studies, such as Islamic legal law (*fiqh*), Arabic grammar (*nahw*), hadith, exegesis (*tafsir*), and Islamic monotheism (*tauhid*). The school became a favourite destination, along with a new rubat in Say'un, for Hadhrami communities in the East Indies (now Indonesia), East Africa, and India (Boxberger, 2002, p. 168). Under the regime of the People's Democratic Republic of Yemen (South Yemen), the school was closed but later reopened after unification (Bubalo, et al., 2011, pp. 35–36). The current director of the Rubat Tarim is Habib Abdul Qadir al-Jailani b. Mahdi b. Abdullah b. Umar Al-Shatiri. He replaced his uncle, Habib Salim b. Abdullah b. Umar Al-Shatiri, who passed away in 2018.

Yemen's return to peace has also revived the practice of sending Indonesian students to Rubat Tarim. Students come from several cities in Indonesia but largely from Java and South Kalimantan. There were about 250–300 Indonesian students who studied at the Rubat in 2010 (Bubalo, et al., 2011, p. 36; Interview with Syarif, March 3, 2013). Some senior *habaib* in Indonesia have facilitated the registration, student selection, short training, and travel to Rubat Tarim. I met some graduates who have become preachers in Jakarta and South Kalimantan. They told me that they registered through the Rubat's representative in Jakarta and also the former graduate, Habib Abdurrahman b. Syech Alatas. Habib Abdurrahman is a senior *habib*, the leader of Al-Attas clan (*munsib*) in Indonesia, and has served as advisor in the Rabithah Alawiyah. He owns a travel and tourism business that serves to facilitate the sending of students and pilgrims to Yemen. He also established the *pesantren* Masyhad al-Nur in Sukabumi, West Java, and claims that it is a branch of the Rubat Tarim. Once students who have passed the selection test, they must attend his *pesantren* for about three months in order to equip themselves with basic skills in Arabic and Islamic knowledge before flying to Yemen. The prospective students are also required to pay a fee of around $5,000 USD which covers return flight fare, tuition fee, accommodation, and living costs for four years of study (Interview with Syarif, March 3, 2013).

Unlike the Dar al-Mustafa which concentrates on *dakwah* activities, the Rubat places a greater emphasis on the mastery of Islamic knowledge through reading and analysing authoritative texts (Interview with Muhiddin, October 20, 2013). A student is not encouraged to undertake *dakwah* unless he has read the key texts in Islamic studies. A graduate from South Kalimantan told me that most of his fellow graduates in this region spread their knowledge by teaching in traditionalist *pesantren* rather than establishing popular sermon groups like the Dar al-Mustafa's graduates (Interview with Syarif, March 3, 2013).

Al-Ahgaff University

The third major destination for Indonesian students is Al-Ahgaff University. The university was established in 1995 and is accredited by the Ministry of Higher Education and Scientific Research, Yemen (Al-Ahgaff University Profile, 2014). The central office, language centre, and main faculties are located at Mukalla, a main seaport and the capital city of Hadhramaut. However, the shari'a faculty is located in Tarim, a place regarded as conducive to enhancing the intellectual and spiritual capacity of the students who study Islamic law (Imron & Hary, n.d., pp. 116–117). The shari'a faculty combines the traditional method with the modern educational system. The traditional method lies in the textual analysis of the classical literature with regard to the subjects of *usul fiqh* (the philosophy of Islamic law) and Shafi'i

90 *Reviving Yemeni Traditionalist Networks*

Islamic legal school. According to this method, students have to master the major classical texts in detail under the supervision of senior *sayyids* in Tarim, including those from Rubat Tarim. The modern method involves a critical analysis of contemporary literature under the instruction of lecturers who hold master and doctoral degrees. However, the lecturers usually only summarise the content of books without much detailed discussion. The subjects under study are secondary and complimentary resources related to exegesis (*tafsir*), prophetic tradition (*hadith*), and Islamic economy (Imron & Hary, n.d., pp. 118–119). Unlike previous traditional institutions, Al-Ahgaff University provides a formal degree for its graduates.

More Indonesian students are enrolling in Al-Ahgaff University. According to an Indonesian student, Muhammad Sunni Ismail, there are special scholarships provided for about 100 Indonesians every year. The scholarship covers tuition fee, accommodation near campus, three meals a day, electricity, and water. There is a representative of Al-Ahgaff foundation in Indonesia who manages the student selection test. If the students pass the selection, they need to pay $2,000 USD for a student visa and five years' fees in advance. Due to the low cost of living and availability of scholarship funding, the number of Indonesian students attending the university is growing. Muhammad estimates that in 2015 there were about 500–600 Indonesian students (male and female) studying at the Al-Ahgaff campuses in Tarim and Mukalla. Each year, there are around 120–150 new students coming from Indonesia to study at this university (Pers. communication with Muhammad Sunni Ismail, March 1, 2015). Although Al-Ahgaff has several faculties, international students from Southeast Asia, including Indonesia, are only allowed to enter the Faculty of Shari'a and Islamic Studies (Imron & Hary, n.d., p. 119).

The academic atmosphere at the university is more relaxed for students as they have more free time to do other activities. Moreover, they are not closely monitored and strictly supervised like those in the previous institutions. Therefore, the Al-Ahgaff's students could utilise their free time for doing sports, joining student organisations, or attending *halaqa* in the Rubat Tarim and Dar al-Mustafa (Berkuliah, 2014). Despite this relaxed atmosphere, the university is rigorous in its evaluation and examination system. When a student fails to achieve a minimum score in their exams, they will be provided alternatives with remedial test and a chance to repeat their studies in the following year. If they fail again, the student will be expelled from the university (Pers. communication with Muhammad Ismail Sunni, March 4, 2015).

Building Global and Local *Dakwah* Network

Expanding Prophetic Dakwah *Style*

Besides revitalising traditionalist education in Hadhramaut, as explained above, *sayyids* have also created and maintained *dakwah* networks among religious scholars (ulama) across the world, especially in Southeast Asia. The key actors in creating and expanding this network are the Indonesian Yemeni graduates who have returned to their home countries. Graduates of Dar al-Mustafa, Hadhramaut, have

Reviving Yemeni Traditionalist Networks   91

been actively spreading the religious mission of their respected teacher, Habib 'Umar al-Hafiz. They admit that Habib 'Umar always monitors and asks about their progress in *dakwah* when he visits Indonesia. Based on my observation in Indonesia, there are three institutions of *dakwah* established by the graduates: sermon groups (*majelis ta'lim*), traditional *pesantren*, and Islamic media. The three types appear to follow the steps undertaken by Habib 'Umar in Yemen. Habib 'Umar is tireless in spreading *dakwah* by travelling to various places in Yemen. He travels all over the world and visits Indonesia every year. He has also visited various countries in Southeast Asia, the US, Australia, or Europe to deliver sermons and lectures. Furthermore, he has used visual and audio media as well as DVD and the internet to spread his message.

The sermon group Majelis Rasulullah is a good case study of the influence and direction of Habib 'Umar upon his former student in Indonesia. The major influence of Habib 'Umar on Habib Munzir is *dakwah* activism. It has become the main platform for spreading the *sayyid* style of traditional Islam under the banner of devotion to the Prophet. This kind of *dakwah* has been called the Prophetic *dakwah* (*dakwah nabawi*). Two aspects have often been mentioned in Habib Munzir's messages: first, this *dakwah* is a way of continuing the Prophet's mission; second, the *dakwah* emphasises the practice of traditional rituals as a way of loving and pleasing the Prophet. To express his devotion to the Prophet, Habib Munzir often appeared in public dressed in traditional garments believed to be the type of clothing worn by the Prophet; he also employed symbols and messages related to the Prophet in his performances as well as sermons. When Habib Munzir returned to Indonesia in 1998, the first thing he did was conducting *dakwah*, a mission which is emphasised in the Dar al-Mustafa. He was dressed in a Hadhrami-*sayyid* long robe and turban (*imama*) when delivering his sermons. This was in contrast to the appearance of other popular preachers who wore more fashionable Muslim dress in an attempt to accommodate Muslim consumerism. When his congregation grew sufficiently large, he formalised his *dakwah* groups under the name of the Majelis Rasulullah (the Assembly of the Prophet). The name, which is linked to the Prophet, was first used by Habib Munzir and later becomes an identity and a commodity among *habaib* religious entrepreneurs.

The second element which is borrowed from Habib 'Umar is the high-mobility *dakwah* style and the adept appropriation of new media technology. Unlike sermon groups in Indonesia that regularly take place in one permanent location or building such as the Majelis Taklim Habib Ali Kwitang in Jakarta, Habib Munzir frequently moved his venue from one public place to another. This seems to be inspired by the *dakwah* style of his teacher in Yemen who travelled to many places in his vehicle and gave "fiery public sermons and lecturers at every stop" (Knysh, 2001, p. 406). Habib Munzir brought new innovation in public *dakwah* by creatively casting his sermon group's name as a banner for his religious marketing. Apart from public preaching, he and his team also produced religious merchandise that promotes him and his sermon group. Like Habib 'Umar, he utilised various media, especially DVDs, streaming videos, websites, and social media in spreading his messages to

92 *Reviving Yemeni Traditionalist Networks*

a wider audience. Through high mobility and the use new media technology, Habib Munzir quickly gained respect for himself as a teacher and preacher as well as achieving popularity for his sermon group.

The third element that Habib Munzir adopted from Hadhramaut is the popularisation of Hadhrami-*sayyid* rituals in Indonesia. As I have pointed out before, after the Yemen's unification, Habib 'Umar revived the *sayyid*'s traditional customs, including collective recitations of Sufi poetry, celebration of the Prophet's birthday, and pilgrimages to the shrines of saints and prophetic figures. During class, Habib 'Umar would encourage his pupils to conduct *ziarah* or visit the graves of saints in Hadhramaut. This ritual has also become a weekly programme of Habib Munzir's *dakwah* activity in Indonesia. Habib Munzir and his team mobilised his followers to carry out traditional rituals such as reciting *zikir*, *salawatan*, and *maulid* texts as well as visiting the sacred graves of *sayyid* saints in Jakarta and other places. The time for regular gathering of the Islamic sermon group at a mosque is Monday night. It follows the public gathering time of Habib 'Umar's in Hadhramaut. Furthermore, the *maulid* text read at the gathering is a work of Habib 'Umar entitled *al-Diya'u al-Lami* (the Shimmering Light). It has become a ritual for the Majelis Rasulullah to start their activity with a reading of *maulid texts* that takes about an hour. During the public chanting, the tambourines are played by the *hadhrah* crew intensifying the emotions of the audience. Apart from this, the visit to saints' graves has also become a weekly activity of the group. Among the popular graves in Jakarta are those of al-Habib Ali b. Abdurrahman al-Habsyi (Habib Ali Kwitang), al-Habib Ahmad b. Alwi Al-Haddad (Habib Kuncung), al-Habib Hasan b. Muhammad al-Haddad (Mbah Priok), and al-Habib Husein b. Abu Bakar Alaydrus (Habib Keramat Luar Batang). Those graves have been popular sites among traditionalist Muslims in Jakarta for many decades. In big cities, such rituals fail to attract young people who aspire to be 'modern'. However, Habib Munzir popularised this ritual among urban Muslim youths, and it has succeeded in attracting hundreds to thousands of participants in the ritual. During my observation of *sayyid* saint veneration in North Jakarta, I saw a large number of teenagers attending such rituals wearing jackets with the sign 'I am the lover of saints' on the back (*Ane pecinta wali*).

Habib 'Umar has served as spiritual father and consultant for the Majelis Rasulullah. He is popularly called 'noble teacher' (*guru mulia*) by Habib Munzir and his followers, an indication of their great reverence for him. Some staff told me that Habib 'Umar has played a great role in directing the development of the sermon group since its establishment. In dealing with serious problems and operations, Habib Munzir always consulted with Habib 'Umar. When faced with challenges from various directions, he asked for advice and support from his teacher. The close relationship of Habib 'Umar to the sermon group has been demonstrated by his regular presence in the public gathering at the end of the year, usually in November, in which he performs as a key preacher. When Habib 'Umar arrives, the stage displays the big poster welcoming his visit to Indonesia. The Majelis also regularly organises a *haul* (yearly commemoration) for Habib 'Umar's charismatic grandfather Shaikh Abubakar b. Salim who is regarded as a great ulama and revered saint in Hadhramaut. The *haul* regularly takes place in Cidodol, South Jakarta, and

Reviving Yemeni Traditionalist Networks 93

Figure 5.1 A special public sermon for welcoming Habib 'Umar at Monas, Jakarta
Source: Photo credit, author, 25 November 2013.

attracts a large number of participants. At the *haul*, Habib 'Umar gives a sermon and recites prayers. After spending several days with the Majelis Rasulullah, Habib 'Umar usually goes to visit his former students' institutions and several ulama in Jakarta and then moves on to Java.

The influence of Habib 'Umar on the Majelis could also be seen after the death of Habib Munzir in 2013. *Majelis* leaders gathered to discuss who would be the most suitable successor to Habib Munzir but any nomination would have to be approved by Habib 'Umar, who came to Jakarta at the end of 2013. The result was the restructuring of the Majelis which had previously had a single leader. With the approval of Habib 'Umar, the *majelis* leaders decided to divide the leadership between the *majelis syura* and the executive board (*pengurus*). The *majelis syura* consists of several senior *habaib* who give advice and make decisions concerning religious matters, while the executive board carries out the *majelis*' programmes and organise the religious gatherings. In 2015, *majelis syura* member who is also the elder brother of Habib Munzir, Habib Nabil Al-Musawa, told me that the supreme leadership of Majelis Rasulullah is the *majelis syura*; they have the authority to appoint preachers, develop the Majelis Rasulullah foundation, and monitor the executive board (Pers. communication with Habib Nabiel Al-Musawa, September 17, 2015). After Habib Munzir's death, his successors are graduates of Dar al-Mustafa and they are not his relatives. The first chairman of MR executive board

94 *Reviving Yemeni Traditionalist Networks*

was Habib Ahmad b. Novel (2014–2015). Since then, the executive board has been led by Habib Muhammad Bagir b. Yahya. According to Habib Nabil (2015), this restructuring was made because there is no one who could replace the charismatic Habib Munzir. Besides, the changing leadership is aimed at empowering the figures (*penokohan*) of the Dar al-Mustafa graduates.

Building Ulama Network of Southeast Asia

Starting from Indonesia, Habib 'Umar has moved to build a traditional Sunni network among traditionalist ulama in Southeast Asia. In 2007 he established an ulama network called the *Majelis al-Muwasholah baina Ulama al-Muslimin* (A Communication Forum for Muslim Scholars), the objective of which was "to contribute to creating and developing Godly scholars (*ulama Rabbani*) within Muslim societies" (Majelis Al-Muwasholah, 2016). The Muwasholah website states that the reason for establishing the forum is the worsening condition that besets Muslim societies in the form of moral decline, internal conflict, and increasing crime rates. They believe that in dealing with such a situation, Muslim scholars (ulama) have a responsibility to provide guidance and shepherd the umma to the corridor of God's true path. One way to realise this, according to the Muwasholah, is to push for unity, consolidation, and mutual support among the ulama across regions (Majelis al-Muwasholah Profile, 2016). The forum has conducted several meetings and training sessions (*daurah*) for teachers and ulama in Indonesia, Malaysia, and Singapore. The participants invited are mostly local popular preachers and teachers of Islamic studies (*ustadz*) who have a traditionalist orientation. The programme is not only undertaken at the national level but also in the provinces such as West Nusa Tenggara, South Kalimantan, and East Java. The forum invites a number of local traditionalist ulama to a meeting (*multaqo ulama*) and encourages unity and communication among them. On particular occasions, several *sayyid* scholars of Hadhramaut such as Habib Salim b. Abdullah al-Shatiri were invited to deliver a religious lecture or sermon to the ulama audiences. Several branches of the Muwasholah have been established in several provinces in which most of the local coordinators come from the *sayyid* figures.

In its efforts to expand the organisation and realise its programmes, Muwasholah has actively engaged with both Muslim organisations and local governments. Notably, Muwasholah has established collaborations with prominent formal Muslim organisations, with a significant focus on its partnership with the Central Board of Nahdlatul Ulama (PBNU). Commencing in 2017, Muwasholah and PBNU's *dakwah* institution have jointly organised live-streamed Islamic learning sessions emanating from Hadhramaut. These sessions feature Habib 'Umar delivering teachings on the classical texts of the NU Founder, Muhammad Hasyim Asy'ari.[2] Moreover, a pivotal event took place on September 23, 2019, when Habib 'Umar paid a visit to the former PBNU's General Chairman, Said Aqil Siradj, at his office. This encounter further solidified their shared dedication to reinforcing traditional Sunni Islam and propagating the middle path of Islam globally, including

Indonesia.[3] With respect to Muwasholah's interactions with governmental bodies, there are discernible indications that the organisation has established collaboration with local authorities to bolster its mission. This inclination became evident during the ulama meeting for the Bali and West Nusa Tenggara regions, held in Mataram in 2014, during which the governor of West Nusa Tenggara conveyed his support for the programme through his opening address (Lombok Today, 2014).

The meetings and training programmes of the Muwasholah aim to strengthen traditional Sunnism by empowering traditionalist preachers and teachers. The issues raised deal with consolidating traditionalist local ulama and organising educational events (*daurah*) regularly. The venues are usually traditionalist bases such as in *pesantren*, *habaib*'s *majelis*, or rented buildings. In South Kalimantan, for instance, the Muwasholah organised a meeting for ulama in the Pesantren al-Falah Banjar Baru in 2014. It was reported that there were about 100 ulama from various places in South Kalimantan who attended the programme (Muwasholah News, 2015). At this forum, Habib Muhammad b. Agil Assegaf was elected as the coordinator of Muwasholah for the region. A number of reports on the website have indicated that most of the Muwasholah coordinators for several provinces come from *habaib*. The domination of *habaib* in the communication forums implies that *habaib* have created venues and networks that allow them to expand their influence and religious standing among traditionalist Muslim societies.

In expanding the global ulama network, Habib 'Umar has received support from existing local networks created by his students, especially in Southeast Asia. In Indonesia, the graduates of Hadhramaut have been active in building communication among their peers. For instance, they created a communication forum for the graduates of Dar al-Mustafa called *al-Wafa' bi Ahdillah* (Realizing the Promise of God) (Pers. communication with Alwi Al-Kaff, March 12, 2015). It has branches in several provinces where the graduates are based. In East Java, the head of the local communication forum since 2011 is the young popular preacher in Malang, Habib Jamal b. Thoha Ba'agil. He estimated that there were around 200 alumni in 2013 in East Java, and most of them have established *pesantrens* and sermon groups. The alumni regularly meet once every three months in order to discuss the development of their outreach and share information and solutions in dealing with problems in the societies (Interview with Jamal Ba'agil, March 25, 2013). The alumni networks have hosted activities for Habib 'Umar and other *sayyid* scholars from the Middle East.

Another institution that helps to expand Habib 'Umar's influence across the world is the Tabah Foundation in United Arab Emirates, which was founded by his former student, Habib Ali al-Jifri in 2005. It is a non-profit organisation that

> offers suggestions and recommendations to opinion makers in order that they assume a wise approach that is beneficial to society. It also sets up practical projects that serve the exalted values of Islam and brings out its splendours as a civilization
>
> (The Tabah Fondation, 2015)

96 Reviving Yemeni Traditionalist Networks

Habib 'Umar is positioned in an advisory board along with other five Muslim scholars in the foundation. Habib Ali al-Jifri also serves as the deputy director in Dar al-Mustafa. Due to this relationship, the Tabah Foundation has helped Habib 'Umar's religious academy Dar al-Mustafa to improve the standard of its administrative organisation and increase services provided for students. The foundation also has facilitated the travel of Habib 'Umar to give lectures and sermons in Islamic institutions and universities in Africa and Europe (Mustafa, 2014). These venues, therefore, have helped to increase the profile and influence of Habib 'Umar in different parts of the world.

Promoting Hadhramautism for Authority

Promoting Hadhramaut as the Centre of 'Truly' Sunni Scholarship

Indonesian graduates from Hadhramaut have helped to promote Yemeni traditionalist education in Indonesian societies. Most of the graduates of Rubath Tarim and Dar al-Mustafa maintain an intense communication and connection with their teacher after they returned to Indonesia. Many have established traditionalist education institutions and sermon groups or joined existing ones. I met several popular preachers in Java who founded a traditional model of *pesantren* which adopts the teaching methods and subjects from Hadhramaut. New generation of students are also encouraged to continue their studies in Hadhramaut. As the graduates have an intense communication and connection with their teacher, especially Habib 'Umar, they are assigned to carry out selection tests and travel to Hadhramaut. It is different from Al-Ahgaff University which has a representative office in Indonesia that manages the selection and offers scholarship every year. Habib Jamal, a graduate of Dar al-Mustafa, is a case in point. Upon returning to Malang, he established a small *pesantren* called *Anwar Tawfiq* (the Lights of Guidance) with the financial support from a donator in his region. He states that the school's establishment was approved by his teacher in Yemen. He also admits that he borrowed the Dar al-Mustafa's model, especially in developing his students' ability to read classical religious books (*kitab kuning*) and Arabic language skills. Some of his students have graduated and continue their studies in the Dar al-Mustafa, Hadhramaut (Interview with Jamal Ba'agil, March 25, 2013).

Besides the work of graduates, several publishing houses and magazines owned by *sayyids* also play a significant role in promoting education in Hadhramaut. There are several reasons for promoting schools in Hadhramauwt. Firstly, Hadhramaut, especially Tarim, has been regarded as the eminent centres of traditional Sunnism with Shafi'i legal school in the Middle East. Several Indonesian graduates from Hadhramaut said that they prefer to go to Hadhramaut because Mecca and Medina have been infused with Salafi-Wahhabi teachings. The exception is the Ribat of Sayyid Muhammad Alwi al-Maliki, an informal institution in Mecca that bases its philosophy on traditional Sunni tenets. For the Indonesian graduates and the *sayyid* media, the Sunni tradition in Hadhramaut has long been maintained and practised by the *sayyid* communities. Several *sayyid* publications point out that the

Reviving Yemeni Traditionalist Networks 97

majority of Muslims in Hadhramaut follow Sunni theology and Shafi'i law school (Mauladdawilah & Mauladdawilah, 2012, p. 98; Baharun, 2013, pp. 69–70). They argue that the spread of Shafi'i jurisprudence in the region was due to the role of their ancestor Ahmad b. Isa who moved from Kufah, Iraq, to Hadhramaut. He was considered to have an important role in propagating the Sunni theology among the Hadhrami population which was at that time dominated by Shi'i Zaidiya and Ibadhiya (Baharun, 2013, pp. 69–70). Therefore, they feel at home in Hadhramaut as it has much in common with Indonesia in terms of theology, law school, and tradition. In fact, they argue that the similarities in theology and religious law school came about because of the roles of Hadhrami *sayyids* who disseminated Islam in Indonesia many centuries ago (Mauladdawilah & Mauladdawilah, 2012, p. 101).

Secondly, *habaib* promote Hadhramaut as a spiritual centre. During their studies in Hadhramaut, the students learned not only Islamic law and Islamic monotheism (*tawhid*) but also Sufism through literature and religious practice. These subjects are not offered in Saudi universities where puritan Salafy ideology predominates. Moreover, students learn Sufi practices that follow the teaching of *tariqa alawiya*, such as reciting *ratib al-haddad* after obligatory prayers, visiting the graves of holy saints, obtaining blessings (*tabarruk*), and maintaining ethical behaviour (*adab*) in everyday life. A graduate of Ribat Tarim Muhiddin explained:

> The place of my study (Tarim) is traditional and it has a rich heritage. The Hadhrami community really maintain the tradition (*adat*) inherited from their ancestors. So, this is a genuine teaching of the Prophet. They have adopted both Islamic knowledge (*ilmu*) and practice (*amal*) in their lives. In terms of knowledge, it might be the same as what students learn in Saudi, Egypt and Indonesia, yet in terms of blessing you will find more in Hadhramaut. Their ethics (*adab*) and behaviour (*akhlak*) are amazing. They really respect their teachers and their ancestors. Several study spaces contain blessings as many people have studied in such places before. When you study at such spaces, you will feel peaceful (*adem*).
>
> (Muhiddin, October 20, 2013)

The spiritual attractiom of Hadhramaut has been associated with the high number of graves of Muslim saints, especially *sayyids*, and sacred places. Besides the grave of the Prophet Hud, there are three cemeteries that have become pilgrimage destination: Zambal, Furaith, and Akdar (Mauladdawilah & Mauladdawilah, 2012, p. 130). Zambal is the most popular as it is the site of the graves of the Companions of the Prophet, the spiritual father of *sayyids* in Yemen, al-Imam al-Faqih al-Muqaddam, and thousands of Muslim saints and great ulama (Mauladdawilah & Mauladdawilah, 2012, p. 132). Furthermore, there are a number of old mosques believed to have the power to bestow blessings since famous Muslim saints and scholars from previous generations have studied and prayed in such places. They include the Ba'alawi Mosque, the Assegaf Mosque, the Mosque of Habib Abdullah b. Abu Bakar al-Aydrus, the Muhdor Mosque, the Mosque of Awwabin, the Mosque of Al-Fath, and the Mosque of Al-Hajir. It is believed that praying and

98 *Reviving Yemeni Traditionalist Networks*

sitting in certain spaces could lead to one's requests being granted or prayers answered and renders them peaceful and tranquil (Imron & Hary, n.d., pp. 59–71).

Lastly, *habaib* promote Tarim as a healthy environment for learning and practising Islamic piety. The *sayyid* publications state that the population of Tarim is generally pious and committed to the values of Islam. They "put forward their ethical behaviour, live with ascetic ways, ignore earthly pleasures, and avoid popularity" (Mauladdawilah & Mauladdawilah, 2012, p. 122). A graduate from Ribath Tarim recalled that he felt very peaceful when he was studying there and believed that the environment allowed him to focus on religious learning and to rid himself of material concerns (Interview with Syarif, March 3, 2013). This pious environment, according to *sayyid* publications, was due to the prayer of the Companion of the Prophet Abu Bakr after gaining the support of Tarim's population for his leadership. He prayed for three things for Tarim: the prosperity of the city, the abundance of water and blessings, and the presence of pious people in Tarim (Mauladdawilah & Mauladdawilah, 2012, p. 116). This, for some Indonesian *habaib*, theologically explains the birth of numerous scholars and saints in Tarim for many generations.

Promoting Charismatic *Sayyid* Scholars as the International Authoritative Ulama

The Venues of Promotion

The return of the Hadhramaut-educated graduates to Indonesia helps to promote the rise of *sayyid* scholars and teachers from Yemen. The intense communication between graduates and their teachers allow the former to invite the later to give sermons or lectures in Indonesia. Through such programmes, they introduce their charismatic teachers to Indonesian audiences. Habib 'Umar is the most popular; he is invited to visit Indonesia each year for the big *maulid's* festivity in Jakarta and other activities organised by his former students and ulama networks. Other popular *sayyid* scholars who have been invited include Habib Ali al-Jifri of Dubai, Habib Salim Al-Shatiri of Tarim, and Habib Zain b. Sumayt of Medina. Another popular *sayyid* scholar is the late Sayyid Muhammad Alwi al-Maliki of Mecca (1944–2004) whose works have been published by his former students' network called *Hai'ah Shofwah*. After his death, his position as teacher in a traditionalist school in Mecca has been taken up by his son Sayyid Ahmad b. Muhammad b. Alwi al-Maliki.

The print and electronic media play a significant role in promoting the *sayyid* scholars from the Middle East. Publications on the scholars are promoted not only by graduates of Hadhramaut but also by Indonesian *sayyids* and traditionalist Muslims who are interested in popularising their thoughts or marketising their works. These publications are sold in certain Islamic bookstores and by small vendors rather than in big bookstores such as Gramedia due to their reluctance to fulfil those retailers' requirements. Among the *sayyid* scholars in the Middle East, the works of Habib 'Umar and Sayyid Muhammad Alwi seem to get more attention from several publishers because of their popularity. Most publications are works

Reviving Yemeni Traditionalist Networks   99

written in Arabic and translated into Indonesian. The works of Habib 'Umar mostly contain religious advice on purifying the soul, Islamic ethics (*akhlak*), and Islamic moderation (*wasatiyya*). The translated works of Sayyid Muhammad Alwi, on the other hand, deal with doctrinal justifications for defending the traditionalist practices such as *maulid, tawassul, tabarruk*, and *ziarah*.

Book publishers and magazines which promote *habaib* profiles and writings have been growing in number. Most of these publishers are based in East and Central Java. The Pustaka Basma in Malang, East Java, promotes local *habaib* as well as *sayyid* scholars from the Middle East. Previously, it was called Karisma when it was established in 2008 (Interview with Abdul Qadir Mauladdawilah, March 22, 2013). The publishing house was founded by Habib Abdul Qadir b. Umar Mauladdawilah and his colleagues who had a concern for traditionalist *dakwah*. Since his days as a student in the Pesantren Darut Tauhid, Malang, Habib Abdul Qadir has had a hobby of collecting *habaib*'s photos and hagiographies (*manaqib*) and recording *habaib*'s sermons. This hobby eventually led him to write a best-selling book entitled *17 Influential Habaib in Indonesia* (*alKisah*, 2015). Habib Abdul Qadir told me that the idea of founding a publishing company came to him when he was attending sermon groups in Malang with his friends. They saw that the Islamic bookstores in Malang were full of Wahhabi books. As an attempt to counterbalance the Wahhabi, they started publishing books on stories and bibliographies of Muslim scholars and saints since such books can inspire people to emulate the saints and have a successful life. Habib Abdul Qadir and Arnaz told me that most of their consumers are traditionalist Muslims who buy their books from vendors around the sites of sermon groups. Several books such as *17 Influential Habaib in Indonesia* have been popular among sermon groups' participants. The Basma publisher has sold over 30,000 copies of the book not only in Indonesia but also in Malaysia and Singapore (Pers. communication with Ernaz Siswanto, March 23, 2015). Despite the book's continuing publication, Habib Abdul Qadir admits that his publisher lacks professionalism and has limited funds (Interview with Abdul Qadir Mauladdawilah, March 22, 2013).

Like book publishers, the number of Islamic magazines that promote *habaib* is also growing. The most notable magazine of this kind is *alKisah* based in Jakarta. According to Kazuhiro Arai, the magazine has an important role in introducing *habaib* and their activities to a broader Indonesian audience (Arai, 2009, p. 247). *AlKisah* was first published in July 2003 and has been led by Harun Musawa, a *sayyid* businessman who has worked in the publishing industry, and his family. He used to work as an editor at *Tempo* magazine. Later, together with his wife Nuniek, he started his own publishing business by running magazines for adolescents such as *Aneka Yes!* The distinctive element of *alKisah* is that it is dedicated to *habaib*. *Habaib*'s images adorn the cover page, and the articles inside contain religious messages, stories, and reports on past and present religious figures. The magazine used to publish pictures of celebrity Muslim figures on the cover page but has replaced these with pictures of *habaib*. According to the vice editor-in-chief, Ali Yahya, this change was not planned at the outset; it was a result of positive response from readers who wanted them to keep publishing pictures of *habaib* as

100 *Reviving Yemeni Traditionalist Networks*

their unique covers (Interview with Ali Yahya, January 2, 2013). In other words, the *habaib*'s images have a market value for the magazine. Not only does the magazine promote the newly emerging *habaib* preachers in Indonesia, it also helps to introduce the *sayyid* scholars from the Middle East to the Indonesian public. Several editions have raised the profiles and religious messages of Sunni *sayyids* from the Middle East, more notably Yemen, such as Habib 'Umar b. Hafiz, Habib Abdullah b. Salim Al-Shatiri, and Habib Ali al-Jifri. It also often reports the activities of Habib 'Umar when he comes to Indonesia on his annual visit. The magazine even devotes a whole section called *madrasah Hadhramaut* (Islamic School of Hadhramaut) to topical religious advice from the vice head of Dar al-Mustafa Habib Ali al-Jifri.

Promoting Sayyid *Scholars as the Guardians of Sunni Islam*

Various media of Indonesian *habaib*, either print or electronic, have promoted *sayyid* scholars from the Middle East as the guardians of 'true' Islam. Two *sayyid* scholars who feature predominantly in Indonesian publications are Habib 'Umar b. Hafiz and the late Sayyid Muhammad Alwi al-Maliki. *Habaib* media describe them as among the authoritative Sunni ulama from the Middle East who seek to spread the 'true' path of Islam through education and *dakwah.* The 'true' Islam in their view is traditional Sunnism formulated by *salafuna al-shalihin* (the pious predecessors). This version of Islam follows the authentic path of the Prophet, His family (*ahl bayt*), and His companions (Mauladdawilah & Mauladdawilah, 2009, p. vii).

Habib 'Umar and Sayyid Muhammad Alwi are special for *sayyid* communities and traditionalist Muslims in Indonesia for several reasons. Firstly, both are the descendants of the Prophet. Habib 'Umar's genealogy is through the line of the Prophet's grandson Husayn, while Sayyid Muhammad's is through the line of another Prophet's grandson Hasan. Secondly, they are considered to have mastered various disciplines of Islamic knowledge with genealogical chain and legitimacy to the Prophet (*sanad*). This sort of traditional knowledge certification has been in decline after the modernisation of Islamic schools. While such practices are seldom found in formal education such as Islamic senior high schools and universities, several informal learning centres such as *halaqa* and *rubat* in the Middle East, especially Hadhramaut, and *pesantren* in Southeast Asia still maintain them. The more *ijazah* (certification through oral and written form) from authoritative scholars a student obtains, the more respect he gains from his followers. It is therefore understandable to see a list of teachers or Muslim scholars displayed on a *sayyid* preacher's profile either in his book or on his website. Thirdly, they share a similar concern to maintain and protect Sunni Islam through education, written works, and *dakwah.* Sayyid Muhammad Alwi was a productive scholar whose works in various disciplines have been translated into Indonesian. He wrote books that defended the Sunni orthodox beliefs and rituals which are criticised as *bid'ah* (unlawful innovation) by Salafi scholars. The most cited work is *Mafahim Yajibu an Tusahhah* (The Views That Have to Be Corrected). The book provides doctrinal arguments in defending traditionalist rituals such as *maulid* (celebrating the Prophet's birthday),

Reviving Yemeni Traditionalist Networks 101

visiting saint's graves, *tawassul* (intercession), and *tabarruk* (gaining blessing). With regard to intercession, for instance, he refuted those who judge such practice as a part of polytheism (*mushrik*). He argues that intercession is justified by religious texts and precedents from the past believers. He stresses that intercessors only serve as mediators in order to get quick access to God's help. To support his argument, he refers to a number of Qur'anic verses and Hadith, several ulama's opinions, and the intercession practice of the previous Prophets to indicate that intercession is allowed in Islam (Al-Maliki, 2011, pp. 85–90). I observed that many *habaib* and *kiais* in Indonesia often refer to his work or his doctrinal justification in preaching and publications.

Like Sayyid Muhammad Alwi, Habib 'Umar is also a prolific writer, but most of his works revolve around religious messages in purifying soul and in following the Prophet's paths. In particular, Habib 'Umar puts emphasis on *dakwah* as a part of his teaching in reviving traditional Islam.

Promoting Sayyid Scholars as the Prophetic Exemplars

With regard to Habib 'Umar, the Indonesian *habaib* and traditionalists promote him as the rising star who manifests the 'perfect' character of the Prophet. Several informants told me that Habib 'Umar has 'precisely' emulated the character of the Prophet as well as following His ways in religious practice (*ibadah*) and human interaction (*muamalah*). Former students who have interacted with Habib 'Umar for years have used a hagiographical style in describing his life, his character, and his dedication in realising his religious mission. Habib Munzir, for instance, praised the personality of his teacher Habib 'Umar in a sermon in front of his audience:

> He is a man who has achieved a level of 'hafiz', i.e. one who has memorized 100.000 hadith with its chain (*sanad*) and its content (*matn*). He also has the title of *al-musnid*, meaning a one who has received thousands of hadith which links him with other transmitters to the Prophet. During my four years study with him in Hadhramaut I have not seen a greater person who resembles the Prophet than what I found in him. What I read from hadith on the description of the Prophet (such as the way he sits, walks, sleeps, and talks) is all found in the person of Habib 'Umar b. Hafiz.[4]

The stories on his affable personality have often been retold and spread by his students and later included in books and magazines, or posted on their websites and social media. The stories include his 'extraordinary' treatment of his students in Hadhramaut when facing hardship. A story documented in a book and spread in the social media, for instance, recounts:

> Once upon a time Habib Munzir and his friends stayed in the *ribat* of Dar al-Mustafa in a time of hardship situation due to the civil war in Yemen. The food stock had decreased as its delivery was blocked by invaders. The food was only enough for Habib 'Umar's family. However, Habib Munzir and his

102 *Reviving Yemeni Traditionalist Networks*

friends could have a meal. One day, after having a meal, he saw the child of Habib 'Umar collecting the rest of their food. When asked of what she was doing, she said 'I am collecting the rest of the food for my father who has not eaten'. That is the amazing moral (*akhlak*) of al-Habib 'Umar b. Hafiz. He and his family did not eat provided that his students were not hungry. Is there one of us who could follow his morality and altruism even in difficult situation?.

(Biografi Ulama dan Habaib, 2012)

His efforts at proselytisation (*dakwah*) are another element in promoting his Prophetic quality. He has been described as a zealous preacher who spread the religion of God in many places with patience, sincerity, and persistence (Mauladdawilah & Mauladdawilah, 2009, p. 9). Habib 'Umar is seen as a great orator and communicator who could attract his audience and move them to tears by his sermons. Some former students have called him a 'lion of the stage' (*singa podium*) illustrating his excellent skills in public communication (Mauladdawilah & Mauladdawilah, 2009). His *dakwah* travel has expanded not only in the Middle East but also in Southeast Asia, South Asia, Africa, America, and Europe. *Dakwah* in Islam has two dimensions. The first involves a call or persuasion to non-Muslims to convert to Islam, while the second means to call or remind Muslims to follow and practise the teaching of Islam. There are some accounts from Indonesian *muhibbin* (followers of *habaib*) about the success of Habib 'Umar in converting non-Muslims in the West, thanks to his soul-touch approach. However, the works and sermons of Habib 'Umar largely target Muslims urging them to go back to the true path of Islam as exemplified by pious predecessors who manifested the authentic teaching of the Prophet. This call is not different from that of the Salafi group, which asks Muslims to return to the authentic teaching. However, in Habib 'Umar's perspective, the authentic Islam means the revival of Islamic tradition rather than the purification of Islam. Indeed, many of his students believed the Salafi and other groups have strayed from Islam and therefore 'deviant'.

The glorification of Habib 'Umar and other Yemeni ulama enhances the authority of the new preachers. Several preachers, especially the graduates of Dar al-Mustafa, express their admiration and attachment to Habib 'Umar through either stories or pictures. I have observed some young preachers display the images of Habib 'Umar and other Yemeni *sayyid* scholars in their official websites and social media page as a way of basking in their reflected glory. By connecting themselves to Habib 'Umar, the preachers may convey three messages to audience: firstly, they are students of Habib 'Umar and have studied with him in Hadhramaut; secondly, they are not direct students of Habib 'Umar in Hadhramaut, but they have received certificate for teaching a subject or practising a particular litany; thirdly, they follow the Sunni religious orientation and *dakwah* path of Habib 'Umar. By displaying these connections, preachers have sought to bolster their profile and attract more participants to their *majelis.*

Conclusion

The chapter has indicated that the transnational factor contributes to the rising influence of *habaib* in Indonesia. It shows that the political and social change in Yemen that led to the unification of South and North Yemen in 1990 has paved the way for the reconnection between Indonesia and Hadhramaut, especially in the sphere of education and *dakwah*. Some scholars have analysed this phenomenon as a new form of Hadhrami connection (Ho, 2006; Slama, 2005, 2010). It is true that there is an increasing aspiration among Hadhrami-*sayyid* communities to send their children to their ancestral land or to visit the saints' graves as a way to reconnect with their homeland. However, this chapter indicates that *habaib* have framed and promoted the new link as allowing the traditional Sunni revival rather than an exclusive Hadhrami revival. In fact, the reconnection has created a new form of transnational Sunni network between Yemen and Indonesia, as well as other countries. Through these networks, the major aspiration among *habaib* is the expansion and the strengthening of traditionalist Islam (*ahl sunna wa al-jama'a*) across the world.

Despite the common platform of strengthening Sunni Islam within these networks, the quest to revive *sayyids'* position as authoritative scholars defending the 'true Islam' is apparent. The networks have been used by 'charismatic' *habaib* in the Middle East, especially Hadhramaut of Yemen, to promote their authority in Indonesia. The venue of promotion includes the returnee graduate networks and the newly established ulama communication forums, as well as print publications and online media. Such media have promoted *sayyid* scholars in Hadhramaut (and other parts in the Middle East) as the inheritors of the Prophet's teachings and morality and as the authoritative guards of Sunni Islam in the Muslim world. Furthermore, they also promote Hadhramaut as the 'sacred' land and the centre of Sunni education and model of piety.

The transnational connection in education and *dakwah* has provided Hadhrami-*sayyid* and traditionalist Muslims in Indonesia with a cultural capital. Indonesian *habaib* have used their status and their attachment to Hadhramaut as a way of enhancing their religious authority, and hence gained popularity and financial rewards. However, this does not only apply to *habaib*. There has been an increasing trend among traditionalist Muslims, especially the graduates of *pesantren*, to continue their studies in Hadhramaut. In fact, the number of Indonesian non-*sayyid* students wishing to study in Hadhramaut is larger than that of *sayyid*. They all view Hadhramaut as the preferred destination for learning the 'truly' Sunni Islam and experiencing piety in 'the land of a thousand saints'. At the same time, they aspire to gain reputation as a graduate of Hadhramaut, which could provide them a religious standing among Muslims societies. When they become preachers or Muslim scholars, their attachment to Hadhramaut in the form of stories, pilgrimage, and connection to particular charismatic scholars will also strengthen their authority among their followers in Indonesia.

104 *Reviving Yemeni Traditionalist Networks*

Notes

1 For further discussion of Salafism in Yemen, see Laurent Bonnefoy, (2011), *Salafism in Yemen*: *Transnationalism and Religious Identity* (UK: Hurst and Company).
2 See the online news at https://khazanah.republika.co.id/berita/pyaq2n320/ngaji-bareng-di-pbnu-habib-umar-bacakan-kitab-pendiri-nu (accessed on 27 August 2023)
3 See the online news at https://khazanah.republika.co.id/berita/pyaq2n320/ngaji-bareng-di-pbnu-habib-umar-bacakan-kitab-pendiri-nu (accessed on 27 August 2023).
4 See the introduction of the video at https://www.youtube.com/watch?v=y-bLW18tzyw (accessed on 26 March 2015).

6   Following Arab Saints

Muhibbin, Popular Piety, and Youth Expression

Introduction

In Indonesia today, it is no longer unusual to see big religious gatherings held at expansive public spaces such as the broad fields of the National Monument (Monas) and mosques, and on roads and intersections blocked for the occasion. One of the organisers of these religious gatherings is the Majelis Rasulullah (MR). Its religious events attract tens of thousands of young Muslims. Most of the participants arrive at the event on motorcycles, wearing *sarung* and black jackets with the group's logo and name emblazoned on the back. Some ride in convoys while carrying the group's flags and the picture of their leader, Habib Munzir b. Fuad Al-Musawa. At the site of the religious gathering, some of the sermon group's young staff are busy directing cars in the traffic jams created by the event; some are setting up the audio system and video cameras; some are erecting the white screens and unfolding mats, while at the gate others are distributing small pieces of paper containing the sermon's hadith material and sometimes a page of liturgy prayers to the incoming participants. A banner with the words 'Jakarta is the Prophet's city (*kota nabawi*)' proudly marks the site of the religious gathering. This scene illustrates the growing participation of urban Muslim youth in traditional sermon groups in the city, a space more commonly associated with the symbols of material progress, consumerism, modernity, and cosmopolitanism. In understanding this phenomenon, this chapter raises several questions: Why do young urban Muslims participate in the *habaib*'s sermon groups? What is the appeal of *habaib* preachers and their sermon groups to young Muslims?

Studies on Muslim youth in Indonesia have been written from various perspectives. Several scholars have analysed the engagement of Muslim youth in Islamic movements, their activism, and the influence of these movements on Muslim youth (Rosyad, 1995; Hasan, 2006; Salman, 2006; Fealy, 2007; Rijal, 2011; Kailani, 2012; Nisa, 2012; Sakai, 2012). Most studies have only focused on young Muslim followers engaging in the transnational Islamic movements such as Hizbut Tahrir Indonesia, the Tablighi Jamaat, the Tarbiyah movement and its political party, the Prosperous Justice Party (Partai Keadilan Sejahtera), and Salafi organisations such as Laskar Jihad. However, only a few works have been written on traditionalist or Sufi youth movements with regard to *habaib*'s followers (Alatas, 2009;

DOI: 10.4324/9781003358558-6

106 *Following Arab Saints*

Zamhari & Howell, 2012). Their studies only address in passing the popularity of the Hadhrami *dakwah* among young Muslims without providing a deeper analysis on the issue of Muslim youth. This study seeks to fill this gap by analysing the voice of young Muslim followers, their feelings, and their experience as they participate in the *habaib majelis*. Alatas (2009) and Howell and Zamhari (2012) have stressed the rise of urban Sufism in explaining the proliferation of the *habaib*'s sermon groups. While it is undoubted that the *habaib majelis* are venues of the *tariqa alawiya* (Sufi path of *sayyids*), it cannot explain why young non-*sayyid* Muslims join the *dakwah* groups in increasingly larger numbers over the last decade. Moreover, the majority of young followers view the *habaib majelis* simply as *majelis taklim* or a place for religious learning and reciting prayers and litanies rather than as a Sufi path (*tariqa*). Inspired by the works of Asef Bayat (2010) on Muslim youths in Iran and Egypt, I will argue that young Indonesian Muslims participate in the *habaib dakwah* not only for spiritual shelter but also because they see the *majelis* as sites to express both their piety and their youthfulness in the midst of uncertainty, discontent, and limited spaces for urban youth in Jakarta.

This chapter focuses on the followers or participants of the largest sermon group, the Majelis Rasululullah (MR), in Jakarta. It will relate and compare the MR's followers with those from other sermon groups, most notably the Majelis Nurul Musthofa (NM), the second largest sermon group in Jakarta, in order to better understand the range of behaviour of the young followers. Many followers of various *habaib majelis* identify themselves as *muhibbin* (lovers or devotees), meaning that they are traditionalist Muslims who love the Prophet Muhammad, His family, and His descendants. In practice, it refers to the followers, fans, and sympathisers of *habaib* who practice traditionalist rituals such as *tahlilan, salawatan,* and *maulidan.* In my conversations with the followers, they often differentiate themselves from the Salafi-Wahhabi whom they view as an extreme group that is generally hostile to Sufism and local traditions. Therefore, *muhibbin* regard Wahhabi as their enemy.

The first part of this chapter discusses the social composition of the MR followers in Jakarta. The second part looks at the structural conditions in Jakarta and their impact on young Muslims. The third part analyses the sermon groups as sites for youth expression of piety. The fourth part critically examines the views and perceptions of *muhibbin* regarding their preacher and leader Habib Munzir b. Fuad al-Musawa. The last part analyses the meaning of their engagement in the *majelis*.

Social Composition of *Muhibbin*

Based on my observation, the number of participants in a religious gathering varies depending on the event. In a regular religious gathering such as the Monday night *majelis* (*jalsatul itsnain*), the participants' number ranges from 5,000 to 10,000. However, in special religious events such as the annual celebration of the Prophet's birthday (*maulid*), there could be around 80,000–100,000 participants. It is entirely understandable, therefore, that special religious events are usually held in the large public spaces of Monas. Most of the attendees are young, aged 12–30 years.

They usually wear the MR jacket, white cap, and *sarung* for the men, while some of the women wear black veil (some wear face veil) over an Arab-style long, black robe (*abaya*) or with a long skirt.

My engagement with the followers indicates that most of them come from lower middle class to poor family backgrounds. Many of them are secondary school students whose parents work in low-paid jobs such as *angkot* (local transport) drivers, food vendors, and factory workers. Some young adult followers work in blue-collar jobs as they lack diplomas or bachelor degrees. The followers I met in Jakarta are predominantly Betawi, but some of them are Javanese, Sundanese, and Palembangese. These ethnicities are culturally close to traditionalist Islam. The Betawi, who are considered the natives of Jakarta, are strongly associated with traditionalist Muslims. Religious rituals such as *maulid, haul, ziarah,* and *tahlilan* are at the heart of their Islamic practice. They also revere *habaib* and *kiais*. Their strong attachment to religious rituals is connected to the historical roles of *habaib* and local ulama in spreading traditional Sunni Islam since the 19th century (Fadhli, 2011, p. 59). Many participants come from Muslim families who are familiar with traditionalist rituals and ways of worship, yet are not educated in formal Islamic educational institutions such as *madrasah* or *pesantren*. Many of them feel that their regular participation in the *majelis* activities has improved their knowledge of Islam and its practice, and is helping them to be a good Muslim.

Many followers began participating in sermon groups when they were teenagers, often driven by curiosity after seeing the *majelis* banners and flags, their various activities, and colourful merchandise. The big banners usually display the preacher's image in Arab dress, the perfect personification of a pious holy man (*wali*). There is also the added attraction of riding to events in convoy and meeting with groups of friends at the event. Some followers are invited by their friends and relatives to participate in the *majelis* to deepen their Islamic knowledge. Regardless of the specific attraction that first led them to the *majelis*, the majority of followers, especially in the MR, were fascinated by the charismatic personality of Habib Munzir. For them, Habib Munzir represents a friendly preacher who uses a gentle and good-humoured approach to his *dakwah*. Several followers said the *habib* had captured their hearts from the very first meeting, and this had led them to commit to the *majelis*. A female follower, Indry, said that "*habibana* (our habib) has a soft and literary style of speaking and always refers to the Prophet Muhammad as a role model" (Interview with Indry, October 19, 2013).

There is no strict membership in the *habaib majelis*. Followers are free to participate in any *majelis*. Therefore, it is not surprising to see MR followers also attending the Majelis Habib Ali Kwitang or other *majelis*. For them, all *habaib majelis* are the same in their goal but different in terms of approach and strategy. Some followers used the examples of Habib Munzir and Habib Rizieq Syihab, who share a similar goal of guarding traditional Sunni Islam (*ahl sunna wa al-jama'a*) but adopt contrasting strategies. The former uses a friendly preaching style, while the latter uses a more strident and confrontational one. Despite the absence of strict membership, followers tend to commit to one sermon group and express their commitment by participating regularly in the group and wearing jacket with the

108   *Following Arab Saints*

majelis' logo on it. Unlike ordinary followers, the staff and crew of sermon groups have particular roles and dedicate themselves to supporting the *majelis* activities. The staff work professionally for the *majelis* and are paid salaries, while crew are mostly made up of volunteers. The staff and crew help to organise events for the *majelis* and undertake fund raising through religious activity programmes and merchandising. A large amount of funds are required when convening major events such as the Prophet's birthday ceremony, which is celebrated every year at Monas.

Jakarta, Urban Youth, and Leisure

The Aspiration for Pietistic Leisure

The popularity of young *habaib* preachers among young people in Jakarta and other cities can be understood by analysing the relationship between urban spaces and youth problems. Jakarta is the capital and largest city of Indonesia. Serving as the centre of government and business activities, it has become a major destination for those in rural areas aspiring to gain material success. The increasing urbanisation of Jakarta has made it the most populous city in Indonesia and Southeast Asia. Its population in 2022 reached nearly 10.8 million (BPS DKI Jakarta, 2023).[1] The gap between available jobs and those seeking work leads to high competition among urban populations. This results in problems with economic inequality, unemployment, inadequate housing, and the poor quality of transportation and physical environment (Cybriwsky & Ford, 2001). The Central Beurau of Statistics of DKI Jakarta Province reports that the rate of poverty has increased from 480,860 in 2020 to 502,040 in 2022 (BPS DKI Jakarta, 2023).[2] Moreover, decades of rapid economic development, especially in "commercial, retail, and high-end residential space in the CBD", have caused extensive demolition and eviction of *kampung* where poorer citizens usually resided (Bunell & Miller, 2011, p. 39). As the result, Jakarta has become overcrowded and congested, which leads to hardship and stress for many of its population.

The city's numerous problems have had an especially adverse impact on young people from poor and lower-middle-class families. Young Indonesians are highly sociable and seek out lively situations (*ramai*) where they can have enjoyable interactions and experiences (Parker & Nilan, 2013, p. 128). Jakarta, however, provides limited spaces for youth to socialise and express themselves. According to Atmodiwirjo (2008), adolescents in Jakarta rarely use government-run youth centres as they are poorly maintained and unattractive. Many of them prefer to hang out in shopping malls and other public facilities such as bus stops, train stations, parking lots, school grounds, street corners, and bridges. Spending time with their friends in such spaces enables young people to entertain themselves away from the view of their parents and authorities (Atmodiwirjo, 2008, p. 345). Moreover, due to the economic constraints of their parents, poor youth cannot afford to hang out in up-market entertainment places, pursue expensive hobbies, or buy luxury clothes. Besides, their parents may restrict their social activities after school hours.

Many teenagers from low-income family background have recently found the religious activities of *habaib* a welcome outlet for their expression. While several conservative Islamic groups disapprove of leisure and entertainment because of the association with Western popular culture, the *habaib*'s groups not only encourage such activity but also successfully combine global popular culture and Islamic messages. When I talked to the followers of the NM, many of them cite the 'coolness' (*keren*) of their guru, Habib Hasan, and his sermon groups. Coolness in this sense refers to his appearance and mannerism, which seem very appealing to young followers, including his distinctive turban, beard style, bright-coloured robe decorated with various motifs, and stylish sunglasses, not to mention his use of hip street language (*bahasa gaul*). Young people find they can spend more time outside their own home and suburb by using religion as an excuse. While some youths are religiously driven, others are motivated by the pursuit of excitement and social engagement. I was surprised to see many teenagers attending *majelis*' event activity far into the night (10 or 11 pm). With large crowds of people trying to get home after an event and the resultant traffic jam, young followers, many of whom live far away from the sermon location, often do not make it home till 12 or 1 am. They say that their parents support their *majelis*' activities as it has good objective (*tujuannya baik*). Parents hope that attending such religious activities will contribute to the moral and spiritual improvement of their children. This attitude must be seen against the backdrop of the discourse on 'moral panic' that has been pervasive among Indonesian parents, media, and the state (Parker & Nilan, 2013). Therefore, youth engagement in religious learning and Islamic consumption is supported and encouraged as part of an effort to protect them from what parents view as bad 'Western' influence.

Participation in the sermon groups provides a space for city teenagers to exhibit their transition to adulthood and their growing piety. They view the sermon groups of *habaib* as a site for both learning Islam and having fun with their fellow participants. In this setting, youths can enjoy leisure without fear of censure from their elders because it is meant for the sake of religion. They use the sermon groups as a place for socialisation, having fun with peers, and facilitating social mobility. In such an environment, young people have the opportunity to gain companionship, emotional support, and new experience and experimentation (Brown & Larson, 2002, pp. 9–10; Stephan, 2010, p. 475).

The Aspiration for Saints' 'Blessing'

The social and economic problems in the big city have also inclined young people to seek spiritual shelter and saints' blessing. This particularly applies to young adults from Jakarta's lower-middle-class and poor families as well as newly settled urbanites who are seeking a better life and more prosperity in the country's capital. Some of these followers are university students, some are unemployed, and others are unskilled labourers working in various sectors. Cities are appealing to Indonesian youth who look for good jobs and prestige. However, living in the

110   *Following Arab Saints*

big city does not guarantee prosperity and a better future for its dwellers. Many find themselves jobless or underemployed in cities. According to Michele Ford, the vast majority of young people in cities end up working in the informal sector, in which "wages tend to be lower, job security poorer, and social security harder to access" (Ford, 2015, n.p.). Many young people only earn enough money to cover their living costs and the daily needs of their immediate family with no savings and investment. This situation has created anxiety and uncertainty for young adults who have to face many challenges living in Jakarta. It is understandable, therefore, that disaffected youth should seek spiritual shelter or God's intervention in order to obtain tranquillity and 'miracles', instant solutions to their problems.

Within the expanding religious marketplaces in Indonesia, young people search for and consume Islamic ideas and practice that suit with their aspirations. Their decision to commit to one Islamic group might be shaped by their family, educational, organisational backgrounds, and peer interactions. There are young people who found compatibility with Islamist groups that call for the shari'a implementation and the creation of the caliphate as the quick answer to their problems. They believe that by implementing shari'a law or establishing the caliphate system, the *umma*, including themselves, could gain prosperity, justice, and a better future. There are also young Muslims who join Islamic entrepreneurial groups that promise material rewards and prosperity by donating voluntary alms (*sadaqah* and *infaq*) and doing regular supererogatory Islamic worship such as morning prayer (*shalat duha*) (Kailani, 2015). Others feel more at home with traditionalist sermon groups that provide more opportunity for Sufi rituals, prayers, and festivities. The *habaib majelis taklim* are the best example of this group. Most of their followers and sympathisers are traditionalist Muslims who have limited knowledge of the intellectual and historical aspects of Islam. Many of them have no formal Islamic education but are familiar with traditionalist Muslim practices and rituals as they come from traditionalist family background. Due to their strong attachment of *habaib majelis* to traditional Islam, most participants are generally traditionalist Muslims. However, it is also noteworthy that some followers are from nontraditionalist and non-observant families.

Young people attend sermon groups not only for spiritual shelter but also for gaining blessings both from the *habaib* and from their engagement in the sermon groups. The concept of blessing (*berkah*) is crucial to the traditionalist followers. This is related to the presence of descendants of the Prophet in the sermon groups. *Berkah* or *baraka* (in Arabic) literally means 'divine blessings'. It also signifies "a beneficent force, of divine origin, which cause superabundance in the physical sphere, prosperity, and happiness in the psychic order" (Colin, 1978, p. 1032). According to Liyakat N. Takim, blessing is also associated with "prosperity, luck, completion, plenitude, and extraordinary power" (Takim, 2006, p. 45). According to traditional Muslims, *baraka* could be found at specific time or place, or in a holy person. Holy persons such as *habaib*, Sufi, and saints (*wali*) are believed to possess blessings. *Baraka* is found not only in living saints and sacred objects but also in dead saints and shrines (Meri, 1999, p. 65). The *habaib*, in particular, inherit blessings from the Prophet through their lineage connection. Even after death, their tombs are venerated due to their outstanding spirituality, learning, and historical accomplishment (Mandal, 2012, p. 357).

Youths beset by uncertainty and anxiety hope that by participating in the *majelis taklim* they could gain blessings from certain *habib* that will bring fortune and prosperity, as well as solutions to their worldly problems. Touching a *habib*'s hands and robes allows transmission of blessings from the Prophet to them. I met some followers who work as labourers in malls and factories. They said that although they were very busy in their daily work and lived far from central Jakarta, they tried to attend the MR *majelis* at least once a week in order to receive blessings. One follower, Ahsan, often attends the *majelis* after work before returning to his home in Bekasi. He expects that his participation could bring improvement to his living conditions and future career.

The followers also believe that rituals in the *majelis,* such as visiting a saint's graves (*ziarah*) and asking intercession (*tawassul*), serve as a medium in accelerating their access to God's favour and approval. This belief is common among traditionalist Muslims linked to the Nahdlatul Ulama (NU) organisation. Recently, this practice has become popular among Indonesian Muslim youth, thanks to the efforts of young *habaib*. Moreover, the growing business of religious tourism to saints' shrines, especially in Java, has contributed to popularising these rituals (Slama, 2009). According to the Indonesian media, thousands of students have visited the shrines of the nine saints and other saints, including the late Abdurrahman Wahid, during critical times in their lives such as before the national exam. Through rituals and prayers, they hope to obtain the saints' blessing and achieve success in their exams.[3] Followers of *habaib* in Jakarta also seek to obtain blessings from the dead saints in dealing with their various problems. Their *ziarah* ritual is more intensive in following their *majelis*' regular programmes.

Majelis as the Venue for Pietistic Youth Expression

Habaib in sermon groups have used various strategies to attract young Muslims. The primary approach is using advertisements such as billboards, big banners, and flags as well as new media such as websites and social media. Several informants admit that they became curious after seeing the big billboards and websites of sermon groups. The *majelis*' website and its community page in social media, most notably Facebook, publish the schedule of the *majelis* four weeks ahead. The use of the internet as a medium for spreading religious messages has been increasing, especially social media, in Indonesia. According to Digital 2023 Report, the number of internet users in Indonesia reached 212.9 million on January 2023, 60 percent of whom use the internet to access social media.[4] Association of Indonesian Internet Service Providers also reports that the largest Indonesian internet users in 2022 were aged between 13 and 34 years.[5] With the introduction of the smartphone, young people constantly use their free time to send and receive text messages as well as chatting and posting on Facebook and Twitter (Parker and Nilan, 2013, p. 166).

Most young followers of *majelis* are familiar with social media. They have used it as a medium for keeping up to date with the *majelis* activities and maintaining

112 *Following Arab Saints*

communication with their fellow followers. Numerous *majelis'* fan groups have been set up on Facebook. Several groups are official, but most are set up by followers. When I engaged with MR and NM's participants during my fieldwork, I could observe how significant the social media and official websites were for followers. Through these media, they could follow the coming *majelis'* schedules, watch past videos of events, and receive religious advice from the *majelis'* leaders. Moreover, websites were used for discussions and sharing information among them. For the *majelis*, social media is critical to promoting their programmes and merchandise and for requesting donations through their participation in various programmes. Here is an example of MR's posting on its Facebook community page:

> Assalamu Alaikum (Peace be upon you) Dear Participants (*Jemaah*) of Majelis Rasulullah.
> Please buy the original products of MR because by buying those you have assisted the Prophet's *dakwah* in Jakarta. Let's realize the goal of our teacher, the late Habib Munzir Al-Musawa.
> For participants who want to have a DVD on the burial of Habib Munzir, you can buy it at the Prophet's Kiosk (*Kios Nabawi*) tonight at the mosque of Al-Munawar, Pancoran.
> We hope you not to buy other versions of DVD, except those at the MR Prophet's Kiosk.
> Jazakallahu Khair (God rewards your kindness).
>
> (Majelis Rasulullah, September 30, 2013)

Besides the use of new media, merchandise, especially *majelis* jackets, have become a marker of pietistic identity and group affiliation for young people. Many followers are keen and proud to wear the jackets as a symbol of their attachment to *habaib majelis*. It means that they are pious Muslims who affiliate with traditionalist Islam. Their use of MR group symbols confirms what the classical sociologist of religion calls 'the social representation' of religion (Durkheim, 2002). Habib Munzir was among the first to recognise the importance of merchandise as a means for *dakwah*. The success of his *dakwah* later inspired many young *habaib majelis* to use new media and merchandise, such as jackets and sermon DVDs, to attract followers. According to Mara Einstein, the consumption of particular brands of faith has defined the personal identity of the consumers (Einstein, 2008, p. 72). In this regard, "it is the marketers who give them (products) meaning, and it is that meaning that is the product" (Einstein, 2008, p. 71). In relation to this theory, MR's brands on the Prophet signify that it offers religious teaching and practice as taught by the Prophet. The association of the group with the Prophet has been strengthened by having preachers who have a blood connection to Him.

The new type of *majelis* provides spaces for young Muslims to express their youthfulness. *Majelis taklim* in the past were normally attended by middle-aged and older people with only a few young people. It was popular among women, especially married women, in urban areas. The *majelis* met at a fixed time and always in mosques, public spaces, and private homes (Millie, 2011, p. 156). The new

Following Arab Saints 113

type of *habaib majelis*, however, is dominated by Muslim youth. Unlike Islamic movements and organisations that have special programmes for recruitment and inculcation for new members, the *majelis* is open to the public and no formal membership is required. However, the *majelis* advises participants to show commitment (*istiqamah*) so that they can deepen their Islamic knowledge as well as contributing to the expansion of the Prophet's *dakwah*. From my engagement with the *majelis* crew, it seems that the *majelis*' activities have become a site for them to, as Asef Bayat puts it, "claim and reclaim their youthfulness" (Bayat, 2010, p. 8). Bayat defines youthfulness as:

> a particular habitus, behavioural and cognitive dispositions that are associated with the fact of being 'young' – that is, a distinct social location between childhood and adulthood, where the youngster experiences 'relative autonomy' and is neither totally dependent (on adults) nor independent, and is free from responsibility for other dependents.
>
> (Bayat, 2010, p. 28)

I met with some MR crew who felt proud to be crew members. They use particular signs that distinguish them from ordinary followers. Words like 'CREW' or 'AKTIVIS' (activists) appear on the front of their jacket. They usually look busy making preparations prior to the religious events. One of them boasts that it is not easy to be a crew member as they have to follow regular religious learning (*pengajian*) at the *majelis* centre and have to earn the trust of the sermon group leader. They normally wear the MR jacket with a *sarung* and white cap, a religious appearance commonly associated with rural and traditional Muslims. They voluntarily work in making preparations for the religious event and participate in fundraising activities for the *majelis*. A crew member of the MR, Syaiful Anwar, told me that he has been appointed the coordinator of the saint's grave visitation (*ziarah*) programme for the Cidodol branch in South Jakarta. The *ziarah* programme only runs twice in a year. He receives no salary but feels proud of his position. He said, "I have no idea whether crew receive salary or bonus. For me, I swear to God (*wallah*), I am sincere and volunteered (*ikhlas*) to work as the coordinator of Cidodol's saint grave visits" (Interview with Syaiful Anwar, December 16, 2013).

Activity, mobility, and leisure are key indicators of youth expression. In the *majelis*, young Muslims meet their peers who share common aspirations and experiences. Their commitment to the *majelis* has made them active and mobile since the *majelis* operates in several places. Their task is quite similar to that of the crew of event organisers and requires them to build a network of communication with other crew. In this respect, many followers, whether crew or committed participants, create online groups through mailing lists and social media, especially Facebook, and chat groups through mobile phones such as Blackberry Messenger and WhatsApp group. During my fieldwork, I joined their online groups, and I have followed their informal chats and their discussions through such daily media. In the WhatsApp group, members are active in coordinating and sharing information on various issues related to their *majelis* or other *majelis*. Some information and conversation

114   *Following Arab Saints*

are serious, but often they also share funny stories and images for their amusement. The atmosphere in these chat groups is so relaxed that members can make jokes and poke fun at each other without fear of giving offence.

Social engagement among crew and participants is another feature of youth expression in the *majelis*. The regular events and meetings among crew and participants have become occasions for sociability and social expressions. Many followers have interacted with their fellows in online MR communities without meeting them physically. To strengthen relationship and commitment among the followers of the *majelis*, especially among online group participants, MR staff also organise an informal meeting outside the formal religious events of the *majelis* or what they call 'Kopi Darat' (meeting and hanging out), abbreviated as Kopdar. The term, which sounds secular in tone, refers to the meeting of online friends. However, such activity is in fact a small-scale *majelis*. It is usually held at the house of a volunteer follower and includes activities such as welcoming speech from the host, reciting the Prophet's stories and prayers, listening to a short sermon delivered by the MR's habib and staff preachers, playing the traditional Arab musical instruments, and having lunch together. I attended a Kopdar in May 2013 to observe their activities. Several MR staff attended the programme. One of them gave a welcoming speech and updated the group on the condition of their leader, Habib Munzir, who was ill and receiving medical treatment. He encouraged the participants to show their commitment in their *dakwah* by creatively mobilising funds through various groups such as the MR helmet groups (bikers), the mailing list group, the grave visit (*ziarah*) group, and local groups based in the area. Participants were asked to suggest ideas for fundraising for the yearly large event, namely the celebration of the Prophet's birthday (*maulid akbar*) that regularly takes place at the National Monument's public spaces. By attending various events of the *majelis*, like Kopdar, participants strengthen their bond; by sharing their experiences, they can become more motivated and committed to the *majelis*.

Participation in the *majelis* does not prevent some young followers from enjoying their leisure time and romance. Unlike other Islamist movements where the interaction among men and women is restricted, the interaction among *muhibbin* is relaxed. While the staff have worked to separate men and women during the religious events, in many cases participants simply remove the barrier to sit together with their boyfriend or girlfriend during the event. I observed many male followers in MR jackets coming to the religious events on motorcycles together with their girlfriends. Romantic lines and sayings also appear in their social media account status. Some *majelis*' teen followers like to post pictures of them with their boyfriends or girlfriends from the same *majelis*.

Habaib as the Charismatic Saints and Moral Exemplars

The popularity of the MR among Muslim youth cannot be isolated from its charismatic leader, the late Habib Munzir b. Fuad al-Musawa. As I have discussed his profile and his *majelis* in Chapter 5, I will not repeat them here. Most interviews and conversation I had with *muhibbin* confirmed that Habib Munzir was a

Following Arab Saints 115

charismatic preacher whose style and rhetoric left a deep impression on his followers. This is in stark contrast to the followers of the NM who rarely mentioned the personal appeal of their preacher, Habib Hasan b. Ja'far Assegaf. Both staff or ordinary members felt amazed by the personality of Habib Munzir, which for them closely mirrored that of the Prophet. One of the female followers, Puput, narrated that she became curious and wanted to know more about the MR when she saw their banners along the major roads in Jakarta. Her eyes were captivated by the picture of an Arab preacher who looked charismatic and erudite in Islamic knowledge. Puput was in senior high school at that time, and several of her friends had been actively participating in the MR. Given the information from her friends, she went for the first time to the *maulid akbar* (Great Festivity of the Prophet) held in the National Monument's yards. Seeing Habib Munzir and listening to his preaching, she found the appeal of Habib Munzir's personality and his preaching. She recalled

> I have never met a preacher who has such a kind and soft-hearted personality. I have never seen a figure when I see him it can enhance my loving (*mahabbah*) to God and His Prophet. I have never met a preacher when he speaks as if he only talks to me and not to the thousands of audiences. He preaches as if he knows the problems that beset me.
>
> (Interview with Puput, September 20, 2013)

An MR staff member talked about his impression of Habib Munzir's character when they were working together in the MR office:

> Habib Munzir has a good character as the Prophet had from any perspective. If one of his students has done something wrong to him, he only smiled, forgave him and prayed for him so that he would not repeat that again. And he has a great love to the Prophet Muhammad and to his teacher Habib Umar b. Hafiz. Because of his great love to the Prophet, Allah called him in the great love and longing to the Prophet. Once upon a time, I made a mistake and made him angry, but in several minutes he apologized to me for his angriness. He often apologized to his audience when he cancelled his invitation to come due to his illness.
>
> (Tim milist MR, 2013, p. 42)

The charisma of Habib Munzir has been enhanced by his media team and other *habaib*'s publications. His sacred genealogy as a descendant of the Prophet and his expertise in traditional Islamic sciences endowed him what Bourdieu calls a 'religious capital' (Bourdieu, 1986). Religious capital refers to religious qualification or 'accumulated symbolic labor' through which religious specialists are able to monopolise the legitimate exercise of religious power over the laity and the administration of the religious goods and service (Bourdieu, 1991, p. 22; Swartz, 1996, p. 75; Rey, 2004, p. 340). However, Habib Munzir would not have gained popularity and religious capital had it not been for the market strategies and new media. Through various media, Habib Munzir has been marketised as a promising new

116   *Following Arab Saints*

preacher, a descendant of the Prophet, and a Muslim saint. His personal biography and photos have been displayed in *habaib*'s magazine such as *alKisah* and *Cahaya Nabawy*. Although his father is not an ulama, his journey to Hadhramaut and his studies under the supervision of the charismatic ulama Habib 'Umar b. Hafiz add to his marketability and authority. Furthermore, the symbols of ulama and Muslim saint he wears in addition to his Arab appearance contribute to enhance his appeal to audiences. The banners and advertisements depict him as a pious and good-looking saint who raises his hands praying to God. His *majelis* also becomes more saleable as his teacher Habib 'Umar and some of his fellows, from either Hadhramaut or other countries, are frequently invited to give sermon at his public preaching.

Some followers told me that among aspects that interest them is that Habib Munzir has an authoritative Islamic knowledge with a connection to the past authoritative ulama (*sanad*). This is due to the fact that Habib Munzir studied under several Sunni teachers in Hadhramaut who emphasise the genealogical chain of Islamic knowledge to the Prophet as the basis of religious authority. Since Habib Munzir has such cultural capital, he often mentioned his teachers from Hadhramaut to strengthen his religious messages. This capital is different from that of Habib Hasan who did not receive religious education in Hadhramaut. However, Habib Hasan has blood connection to the famous saint in Bogor, West Java, Al-Habib Abdullah b. Muhsin Al-Attas. Therefore, Habib Hasan in his preaching refers much to his grandfather's religious messages and life experience. Furthermore, due to his habib status, he frequently speaks of his style of *dakwah* as emulating that of the nine saints (*Wali Songo*) whom he claims were from Hadhramaut. In the latest development, he and his brothers have travelled to Hadhramaut to visit the saints' graves in Tarim and meet some Yemeni scholars, including the charismatic scholar Habib 'Umar. He also invited Hadhrami scholars from Yemen to give a sermon in his public preaching in March 2015. Such visits to Yemen and the presence of Yemeni guests in his *majelis* are often published on his social media pages and YouTube, reinforcing the profile and authority of his *majelis* to his followers and the wider audience.

The media advertisements and religious merchandise of Habib Munzir meet the expectations of the young Muslims who are seeking a religious and moral figure for their role model. They found that Habib Munzir provides both Islamic knowledge and spiritual shelter. Although many of them said that they participate in the MR just to study Islam (*ngaji* or *belajar agama*), they also say that they achieve a sense of tranquillity and the lessening of burdens when participating in the MR's rituals. One MR male follower stated:

> The thing that made me interested in the MR is the feeling of tranquillity and peace I got when attending the *majelis*. I never experienced such feeling before in other *majelis*. For me, the Majelis Rasulullah is full of peace and tranquillity combined with a plenty of praises and religious advises...
> (Interview with Anwar, December 6, 2014)

This feeling, however, can also be found in the NM and other *habaib majelis*. For the MR followers, Habib Munzir is more authoritative than Habib Hasan in terms

Following Arab Saints 117

of Islamic knowledge. His learning experience in Yemen and his close connection to Habib Umar are the main factors. Some followers told me that Munzir's *majelis* is a serious *majelis* and that you could get deep Islamic knowledge and spirituality, while Habib Hasan's *majelis* is only a place for having fun (*main-main*) for young Muslims. Furthermore, besides delivering Islamic messages in the eloquent and literary ways that impress his followers, Habib Munzir also presents himself as a moral exemplar. Several accounts of his followers express the 'amazing' character of Habib Munzir, which has been spread by the MR crew. One story that is commonly circulated in the MR media is that Habib Munzir never wore sandals when he was studying in Hadhramaut out of respect for the dead saints buried there. Habib Munzir also confirms this in his practice. I once saw Habib Munzir delivering a sermon even though he was ill. Habib Munzir was brought by an ambulance to the *majelis'* area while he was sitting on the hospital mattress with the infusion tubes still inserted into his hand. He delivered the sermon sitting on the mattress inside the mosque. At the end of the sermon, he was taken back to the hospital for further treatment. Various stories from the media of his exemplary moral practices have become an important element in enhancing his appeal among his followers.

Unlike Habib Munzir, Habib Hasan's followers did not mention him as a moral exemplar or an authoritative source of Islamic knowledge. Their narratives are dominated by the youth's fascination with his *majelis'* coolness, creativity, and entertainments. Echoing Habib Munzir's strategy but taking his ideas one step further, Habib Hasan sells religious merchandise that are more colourful and orchestrate entertainments during a public preaching event. For instance, while the MR only has one black *majelis* jacket, the NM has produced various jackets and sweaters with colourful motifs and writing crafts which resemble to stylish Western products for youth.

The NM holds its regular *majelis* on Saturday night reasoning that it is a time that youth identify with fun and dating. Habib Hasan's brother, Habib Abdullah, said that the NM was the first *majelis* that conducted a regular religious event on Saturday night targeting urban Muslim youth. By selecting this time, Habib Hasan sought to change youth behaviour, as they usually spend Saturday nights for leisure, dating, and hedonism (Interview with Abdullah b. Ja'far, June 13, 2013). During the *majelis'* processions, the NM uses various forms of entertainment such as singing religious song with Arab traditional musical instruments and launching fireworks either at the beginning or half way through preaching. With regard to this entertainment, one female follower gives her reason for choosing NM rather than MR:

> In MR, the participants have to focus on what is being said by Habib Munzir because he uses high language. If you miss his preaching for a while you will not understand the next explanation. Furthermore, the MR's *salawat* singing (praises to the Prophet) is just a small portion, so it could make you sleepy. Yet in the NM, Habib Hasan uses local Betawi daily language which makes it simple and easy to understand for teens. Moreover, the intense *salawatan* during preaching makes us stay awake even though it is late at night.
> (Interview with Siska, September 15, 2013)

118 *Following Arab Saints*

For his followers, Habib Hasan is a celebrity saint and spiritual guru. Habib Hasan with his crew actively advertises his image, his profile, and his *majelis* through new media and religious merchandise. He actively delivers messages, through either publications or preaching, urging participants to follow the path of Muslim saints (*wali*), especially the Hadhrami saints, in order to obtain blessing and easy access to God. Through such messages, he indirectly promotes himself as a saint due to his *habib* status and his kinship ties to the late saint Habib Muhsin in Bogor. However, during my engagement with the NM followers and their media, I never heard stories about his supernatural power (*karamah*) and his exemplary moral character as found in Habib Munzir's movement. In many ways, Habib Hasan and his brothers have a strategic way in approaching the youth, especially teenagers. He and his brothers often wear stylish, bright-coloured long robes and turban in religious performances. They sometimes wear black sunglasses even at night to appear stylish and modern to their audiences. Given the various attractions of the NM, it is not surprising that a large number of his followers are young people aged around 12–20 years. For his followers, Habib Hasan is a modern saint and idol who also serves as a guru and source of religious guidance and blessing in their lives. I found several followers in the social media who attach their last name with Habib Hasan's 'Assegaf' to express their emotional attachment to and idol worship of Habib Hasan.

Their attachment and commitment to Habib Hasan led them to defend him when he was reported to have committed sexual abuse against underage male followers in 2011 and 2012. Making this case the front cover story, the *Gatra* magazine (2012) ran a report that Habib Hasan had been abusing 11 of his teen followers since 2002 in the name of saint devotion and spiritual healing. The case went public after several young victims gave their statements to the Indonesian Commission for Child Protection (*Komisi Perlindungan Anak Indonesia*) in February 2012. The regional police in Jakarta (Polda) had received the report in December 2011 but mishandled the investigation by questioning Habib Hasan as a witness in March 2012. Habib Hasan rejected the allegation and considered it slander towards him and his sermon group. However, the case was not pursued any further by the police as they were reluctant to investigate a case of sexual abuse that happened several years ago. A rumour spread that some *habaib*, including Habib Munzir and Habib Rizieq Syihab, went to the police and asked them to drop the case because it could create a huge backlash from Habib Hasan's mass following as well as ruining the image of *habaib* in general. The sexual abuse allegations, however, did not affect the number of Habib Hasan's followers. The NM staff, crew, and followers strongly believe that it is a false accusation trumped up by their enemy, namely the Wahhabi group, who has been trying to undermine the traditional Sunni *dakwah*. Habib Hasan and his brothers often speak in front of their followers regarding the challenges they receive from their enemy that they depict as *fitnah* (false accusation) to their *majelis*. This counter-allegation has even enhanced the commitment of their followers to the group.

Engaging in a *Dakwah* Mission: Making Jakarta as the Prophet's City

The engagement of young Muslims in the MR leads them to strive to achieve Habib Munzir's religious mission (*dakwah*). On various occasions, Habib Munzir has called on his followers to transform Jakarta into the 'Prophet's city' (*kota nabawi*). The term implies that Habib Munzir seeks to implement Islamic values in Jakarta through *dakwah*. An MR publication states:

> In essence, the *dakwah* of Habib Munzir aims at reintroducing the personality of the Prophet among the populations in Jakarta and other cities which are too busy with mundane business. It hopes that there emerges the revived spirit of Muslims in loving and defending the traditions (*sunnah-sunnah*) of the Prophet. Slowly but surely, they will become the soldiers of the Prophet, not the soldiers who spread the teaching of the Prophet through violence but through the ethical model exemplified by the Prophet.
>
> (Guntur & Tim MR, 2013, p. 31)

The *dakwah* mission of Habib Munzir is connected to the teaching of his Yemeni teacher Habib Umar. The important feature of Habib Umar and his followers' religious view is that they place a great value on devotion to the Prophet and His descendants by reviving the old *sayyid* customs which were abolished by the socialist regime (Knysh, 2001, p. 408). He established the Dar al-Mustafa with an emphasis on propagation (*dakwah*). Habib Munzir was among the first cohort of his students from Indonesia. After his students graduated and returned to their countries, Umar keeps in contact with them and builds a *dakwah* network among them; he also actively monitors their *dakwah* development. Habib Umar visits Indonesia every year and gives a sermon in Habib Munzir's *majelis* and other places. With regard to *dakwah* mission, Habib Jamal b. Ba'agil, a former student of Habib Umar and chairman of the Dar al-Mustafa's alumnae for East Java stated:

> In the Dar al-Mustafa, we were encouraged to apply our Islamic knowledge or propagate it to those who have knowledge: *dakwah ila-llah* (call to God). Therefore, every month we were asked to give a sermon in several villages in Hadhramaut calling people to virtue. Some students stayed in one night, others did not, even I used to spend forty days for *dakwah*. This is like an internship for university students. So, we spread our knowledge during our study, not after graduation.
>
> (Interview with Jamal b. Ba'agil, March 25, 2013)

The emphasis on *dakwah* led the DM's graduates to establish various venues for *dakwah* when they returned home. Some graduates established sermon group and media, while others established *pesantren* with classical curriculum. When I met several *habaib* preachers, most of them had a sermon group or small *pesantren*. They maintain that *dakwah* is manifested not only in preaching but also through media and educational institutions.

120 *Following Arab Saints*

The success of Habib Munzir in preaching can be explained by his ability to mobilise young Muslims to support his religious mission. Under the slogan 'to transform Jakarta into the Prophetic city', he invited young participants to form the MR team of staff and crew. The staff receive religious education in his headquarters and are paid for their work depending on the amount of funding assistance available at the time. The religious education they received from Habib Munzir and his moral example inspired them to commit to the *majelis*. Their close relationship with Habib Munzir led them to refer to him in such terms as *habibana* (our *habib*) or *guru kita* (our teacher).

The MR team works as event organisers and marketers. They help promote the *majelis* through marketing strategies and a range of religious merchandise. In their view, marketing MR's merchandise means supporting the mission of the Prophet. Moreover, they actively establish small groups of volunteers among followers for the purpose of fundraising for the MR events. They, for instance, establish the helmet group for bikers, the milist group for those active in the MR mailing list, the *ziarah* (pilgrimage) group, the *kopdar* group (hanging out group), and so forth. There are also followers who form groups based in their local area such as MR Bekasi, MR Depok, MR Cijantung, MR Cibubur, and MR Cilincing. Each group voluntarily mobilises donations from their members and compete with other groups in fundraising. The staff sometimes encourage groups to compete with one another to see who can collect the most donations. More financial assistance is usually required for the yearly *maulid* (the Prophet's Birthday Celebration). One example of fundraising is through religious pilgrimage programme from Jakarta to Cipanas on 12 January 2014. The announcement was spread in MR mailing list, encouraging members to participate. One staff reported in the mailing list that they had collected Rp. 19,400,000 (about $1300 USD) from the pilgrimage and *kopdar* group. He encouraged members to participate in the next round in order to make the coming *maulid* event a big success. The registration fee was Rp. 110.000 (about $8 USD) which covered return transport and lunch. The pilgrimage destinations at that time included the grave of Habib Munzir, the grave of an Arab saint in Keramat Empang Bogor, the grave of Habib Munzir's father Habib Fuad b. Abdurrahman Al-Musawa in Cipanas, and obtaining blessings through objects (*tabarruk*) in Habib Munzir's house.

In the view of *muhibbin*, dedication to the MR means dedication to the Prophet. Habib Munzir and his staff frame their religious activities as ways of pleasing the Prophet. On the MR website, Habib Munzir stated that the naming of the *majelis* after the Prophet was because most of its messages are related to the teachings of the Prophet, and Muslims are directed to love God and His Prophet (Majelis Rasulullah, 2015). The emphasis on the Prophet's *dakwah* seems appealing to Muslim youth. By engaging in the MR, the followers feel that they are fighting for the Prophet's *dakwah* mission. This kind of activism provides a meaning for the Muslim youth in pursuing their worldly lives. Moreover, they feel that they can get blessings through Habib Munzir who is seen as the representative of the Prophet. In traditionalist Muslim views, the blessings of the Prophet are transferred through His descendants. It is therefore a common view in *habaib majelis* to see a flock of

Following Arab Saints   121

participants stand up and greet *habaib* preachers by kissing their hands either before or after the *majelis* in order to obtain their blessings. Many participants in the *majelis* bring a bottle of water with them during praying time to capture the powerful effect of prayers that could later be used for healing physical and mental sickness. During the chanting of the Prophet's praises (*maulid* texts), the participants believe that the Prophet's spirit is present among them and bestowing blessings on the congregations. Furthermore, for the followers, sending prayers to the Prophet and Muslim saints will lead them to obtain *Syafa'at* (help) from the Prophet in the hereafter. In their belief, the Prophet's help will enable them to obtain special access to the heaven regardless of their sins on earth.

For the marginalised youth in the big city, being active in the *majelis* provides spiritual tranquillity and blessing in dealing with various problems in life. In Sufi literature, Muslim saints (*wali*) have served as intercessors for ordinary Muslims in order to seek divine assistance in dealing with mundane affairs (Gilsenan, 1973, p. 43). This belief is held by Habib Munzir's followers, many of whom often ask prayers from him to deal with their problems such as illness, study, family matters, and employment. Students, who wish the best for their studies especially in exams, ask for prayers from their *habib*. Those working in low-paid jobs express their commitment to attend the *majelis* due to the spiritual tranquillity and blessing they hope will help improve their economic condition.

The MR followers believe that Habib Munzir's Islamic teachings represent the true version of Islam. They regard his teachings as the authentic version based on the teachings of the pious predecessors (*salafuna shalihin*). In this regard, the followers call it the teachings of *ahl sunna wa al-jama'a* (*aswaja*), a traditional Sunnism which is associated with NU's religious orientation. Rather than mentioning NU as the group affiliation for their religious view and practice, they simply understand that *aswaja* is the Islamic teachings taught by *habaib* and *kiai* who suggest that they conduct traditionalist rituals. Like other *habaib*'s followers, they claim *aswaja* to be the true teaching and regard other groups, especially the Salafi-Wahhabi, as deviant. When asked about the challenges they face in *dakwah*, some crew mention the challenges from Wahhabi in the form of virus attacks on their *dakwah* website. Another challenge comes in the shape of criticisms from a Salafi preacher, Firanda Adirja, who wrote a particular book that condemns and criticises Habib Munzir's message as teaching *bid'ah* (unlawful innovation) to Muslim populations. Given their shared mission with other *habaib*'s followers, the MR followers contribute to spreading *aswaja dakwah* in the media and warn of the danger of Wahhabi teachings in Indonesia.

Conclusion

This chapter has examined the young followers' views and experiences in the largest *habib*'s sermon group, MR, in Jakarta. This examination is a way of understanding the rising trend of *habaib* influence and popularity among urban Muslim youths in Indonesia. I have shown that the participation of young Muslims in the sermon group is not merely due to the attraction of Sufism or spiritual revivalism.

122 *Following Arab Saints*

I argue that Indonesian Muslim youth see the group as an avenue for expressing both piety and 'youthfulness' at the same time. The appeal of MR to young people cannot be separated from the strategy of Habib Munzir in stylising his *dakwah* through various means that meet the need and aspiration of urban youth. Such means include the utilising of new media (the internet and social media), logos, symbols and merchandising, staging performance, and creation of social groups of followers. The *muhibbin* use their engagement not only for learning about Islam but also to have ethical fun and interact socially with their peer followers. This case, therefore, confirms the significant roles of new media and popular culture as mediums for drawing youth to religion and sites for expressing religiosity.

This study also shows that the *habib* factor is central to attracting youth followers. This resonates with the popularity of celebrity preachers in Indonesia due to their attractive speakers and their public communication skills. Habib Munzir, however, combined aspects of *sayyid* status, his graduation from Yemen (under the charismatic Habib 'Umar), and the Prophet-centred preaching for his promotion. The youth view Habib Munzir as a charismatic saint, authoritative scholar, and exemplary model of the Prophet by whom they can learn and follow as well as asking his blessings in dealing with their mundane problems. Habib Munzir came to the city where poor urban youth and lower-middle-class families have been marginalised by the country's rapid development, inequality, and mismanagement of the megacity. They are uncertain and insecure youths who have experienced the hardships of living and uprooted from their tradition. By joining or participating in the *majelis* with its various activities, the youth found tranquillity, pietistic identity, and hopes through *habib*'s blessings and prayers in making them stronger and optimistic in dealing with their lives and their future.

Notes

1 See BPS DKI Jakarta https://jakarta.bps.go.id/indicator/12/111/1/jumlah-penduduk-provinsi-dki-jakarta-menurut-kelompok-umur-dan-jenis-kelamin.html (accessed on 29 April 2023)
2 See BPS DKI Jakarta https://jakarta.bps.go.id/indicator/23/645/1/garis-kemiskinan-jumlah-dan-persentase-penduduk-miskin-di-daerah-menurut-kabupaten-kota-di-provinsi-dki-jakarta.html (accessed on 29 April 2023)
3 The online news include http://nasional.inilah.com/read/detail/2194883/jelang-un-pelajar-ziarah-ke-makam-gusdur, http://video.liputan6.com/news/jelang-un-ratusan-pelajar-berziarah-makam-667249 (accessed on 27 April 2015).
4 See Digital 2023 Special Report Digital 2022 at https://wearesocial.com/uk/blog/2023/01/digital-2023/ (accessed on 27 May 2023).
5 See Indonesian Internet Profile 2022 by APJII at https://apjii.or.id/download/cf790057f-dac70557a6655945479b5ab (accessed on 30 May 2023).

7 Conclusion

The rise of *habaib* with their preaching activities has become a vivid manifestation of the revival of traditional Islam in contemporary Indonesia. In many Muslim countries, the long decline in authority of traditionalist Muslim leaders has accelerated over recent decades, especially as a result of modernisation, mass education, and new media technology – all of which have challenged or eroded the previously high standing of such religious leaders (Eickelman & Anderson, 2003; Mandaville, 2007; Turner, 2007). While historically religious authority was centred on traditionalist ulama, lay interpreters of Islam, who come from secular education background, began to emerge (Mandaville, 2007). Many were popular preachers with a talent for using new communication technologies and Western management knowledge to deliver religious messages that tapped into Muslim aspirations for greater prosperity and piety (Muzakki, 2008; Kailani, 2015; Hoesterey, 2016). As the most populous Muslim country in the world, Indonesia has experienced such a transformation of religious authority.

The Rising Popularity of *Habaib* within Indonesian Islam

The emergence and popularity of young *habaib* preachers in contemporary Indonesia are the focus of this book. These are religiously learned men from the *sayyid* community who, due to their descent from the Prophet, are highly revered among traditionalist Muslims. Before Indonesian independence, *habaib* played important roles in Islamisation by establishing Islamic schools (*pesantren*) and sermon groups (*majelis taklim*). Their students and followers were predominantly traditionalist Muslims who lived in rural areas and small towns in Indonesia (Liddle, 1996, p. 622). Scholars in the mid-1900s often doubted the contribution that traditionalist leaders, such as *habaib* and *kiai*, with their old-fashioned Islamic education could make to Indonesia's development as a new nation (Geertz, 1960). Many assumed that traditional Islam was not compatible with modernity, particularly as found in urban populations. In recent decades, this expectation of traditionalist waning, however, has been debunked by the rapid growth of traditionalist institutions and practices, such as Sufi centres and study groups, in large cities in Indonesia. Julia Howell (2001) argued that the revitalisation of Sufism helped to break down the polarisation between traditionalists and modernists since the producers and consumers

DOI: 10.4324/9781003358558-7

124   *Conclusion*

of Sufism came from various segments including modernists. My study contends that the rise of *habaib* preachers after 1998 points to a different phenomenon. The *habaib* have propagated traditional Islam not only using long-standing themes such as Sufism and other spiritual rituals but also pushing for a more conservative Sunni theology. Central to their form of traditional Islam was a narrower understanding of the concept of *aswaja* than commonly found in mainstream Nahdlatul Ulama (NU) groups. While they claim to spread moderate and peaceful Islam, the preachers are also socially and legally conservative. These two inclinations are evident in their emphatic rejection of puritanical Salafism and 'deviant' sects such as the Shi'a and Ahmadiyah, as well as their criticism of liberal Islamic thought and socially progressive campaigns regarding gay and minority rights. Their social conservatism appears to have found favour in the Muslim community as the *habaib* attract large audiences from traditionalist communities across Indonesia, especially in urban areas.

Several scholars have analysed the ongoing role of traditional Muslim scholars (ulama) in the contemporary era. Most of their analysis points to the capacity of ulama to adapt their discourse to suit changing social and political developments (Zaman, 2002; Burhanudin, 2007). In the case of Indonesian *habaib*, Ismail F. Alatas, who studied the Majelis Habib Ali Kwitang of Jakarta in post-colonial Indonesia, argued that *habaib* adapted their Sufi teaching to the assimilationist discourse of the new nation by shifting emphasis to Prophetic piety and reshaping their rituals in order to include non-Arab local scholars (*kiai*) (Alatas, 2009, 2011). Arif Zamhari and Julia D. Howell (2012) categorised *habaib* sermon groups as a new form of Sufi pietism and argued that they are successful because they appeal to the desire of urban Muslims for entertainment and also because of their ability to summon religious emotion among their followers. While this line of analysis explains important aspects of the preachers' attraction, it does not capture the deeper phenomenon behind the emergence and popularity of the *habaib*.

Turning Threat into Opportunity

My study contends that the rise of *habaib* is inseparable from broader forces at work within the Indonesian society. A central focus of this book has been the contestation between traditional Islam (*aswaja*) and its more puritanical rivals, such as Salafis and other transnational Islamist groups. This doctrinal battle has produced both push and pull factors for the preachers. *Habaib* viewed the Salafi challenge as a threat to the authority of their own traditional Islam, and thus felt compelled to defend their creed. But it is also true that countering the threat to *aswaja* opened up opportunities to elevate their own position among traditionalist Muslim community and advance their socio-economic status. Thus, they have both been drawn into a religious contest and self-consciously used the opportunity for their own benefit. The commitment to defending traditional Islam appears deeply and genuinely held, but so is the motivation to make the most of their rising profile. The Salafi challenge to traditional Islam has allowed these preachers to build their power and prestige through their Yemeni heritage and religious commodification.

Conclusion 125

Habaib and New Conservatism

I have further demonstrated in this book that, in addition to opposing Salafism, the *habaib* also campaign against the Shi'a and liberal Muslim intellectuals on the grounds that such movements also deviate from and pose a threat to 'true' Islamic teachings. In this regard, the *habaib* are socially conservative rather than progressive.

By opposing both Salafism and liberalism, the *habaib* have adapted their *dakwah* to tap into deeper sentiment within the traditional community, which is resistant to change, be it hardline puritanical or challengingly progressive. *Habaib* have allied with traditionalist Muslim leaders and activists who have a similar concern to protect 'core' traditional Islamic values. In their *dakwah*, they propagate that *aswaja* is the most 'authentic' teachings of Islam and rebut Salafi claims that traditionalists follow unsound practices. *Habaib* advance their arguments by using textual reasoning and opinions of authoritative traditionalist ulama from the Middle East, particularly from Yemen. They argue for consideration of social and cultural aspects when deciding on proper Islamic practices and declare that traditional Islam is deeply and legitimately rooted in Indonesian history and culture, while Salafism is an imported belief system which not only is incompatible with Indonesian life but also produces tension and violence. Moreover, they promote the authority of traditionalist scholars such as *habaib* and *kiai* as the 'true' conveyors of Sunni Islam. They emphasise that their criteria for religious authority have greater validity than those of the Salafi since they received Islamic knowledge through direct person-to-person transmission (*sanad*) of classical teachings, and not just through books.

Habaib's Performance and Aesthetic Dimension of Religious Authority

While social and political context is a highly significant factor, my study underlines that traditionalist preachers also require what Bourdieu calls 'cultural capital' to enhance their authority. In other words, bearing the title *habib* or *kiai* is not sufficient to attract followers. I concur with scholars who emphasise the critical role of new media technology and live performance in building religious authority. Several recent studies on the popular Malian Muslim preacher, Cherif Haidara, and Pentecostal pastors in contemporary Africa have underlined the importance of 'the aesthetic dimensions' in producing religious leadership (Meyer, 2009; Kalmbach, 2015; Schulz, 2015; Witte et al., 2015). The aesthetic dimension in this regard refers to multi-sensory appeal of figures in the media and live performance and how this helps in "persuading people of religious truth and linking religious forms/knowledge and followers" (Witte et al., 2015). *Habaib* follow this growing pattern without eschewing their traditionalist characteristics. This is in contrast to most Indonesian celebrity preachers who minimalise traditionalist elements to attract a wider Muslim audience. One traditionalist characteristic that *habaib* uphold is high reverence for both living and dead charismatic Muslim leaders and saints (*awliya*). For their followers, *habaib* perform as Muslim saints who embody the Prophet's exemplary morality and spirituality.

126 *Conclusion*

The extensive use of symbols and texts evoking the Prophet in their media sites and performances highlights the status of *habaib* as heirs of the Prophet.

Middle East and Contested Islamic Legitimacy and Authenticity

This study also confirms the power of the Middle East as a source of religious legitimacy and cultural capital for Muslim preachers. It sees Arabness as a vital contributing factor in bolstering the profile of *habaib* preachers. Many scholars (Hasan, 2006; Casey, 2008; Hamid, 2009; Ghoshal, 2010; Poljarevic, 2012; Chaplin, 2014; Mandaville, 2022) identified Arabisation as identical with Salafi-Wahhabi project of authentication and purification of Islam from unwarranted local innovations. They argue that Salafi leaders and preachers in countries such as Indonesia, Nigeria, India, and Britain propagated Saudi Arabia as the paramount source of religious authority, authenticity, and social ideals. I have shown, however, that perceptions of the Middle East is multifaceted and contested. *Habaib* refer to Hadhramaut in Yemen as a central source of authority, piety, and cultural capital. This is also a form of resistance to Saudi hegemony which they regard as hostile to traditionalism. In sermons and media, *habaib* promote Hadhramaut as the 'true' place of Sunni education, which is free from insidious Salafi influences. The growing number of Indonesian traditionalists, especially *pesantren* graduates, who study in Hadhramaut indicates its growing reputation in Indonesia. The *habaib*'s heavy promotion of Yemen is an indirect way of buttressing their own authority, since their ancestors are Hadhrami and they themselves also studied in Hadhramaut. The promotion is expressed, *inter alia*, through narration of their spiritual and learning experiences in Hadhramaut and glorification of their former Yemeni teachers, especially the popular Habib 'Umar b. Hafiz.

The Appeal of *Habaib* to Young Muslims and the Role of New Media and Popular Culture

Adaptation to Muslim youth aspirations and tastes is another important aspect that heightens the appeal of *habaib* preachers. This finding contrasts with those of many other scholars who are inclined to see Indonesian Muslim youths as more oriented to modernist expressions of piety. My study on *habaib*'s followers (*muhibbin*) suggests that traditional Islam remains very popular among young Muslims. The case of two sermon groups in Jakarta, Majelis Rasulullah and Nurul Musthofa, indicates that the accommodation of youth entertainment, such as musical performance and the creation of tight-knit group identities, such as *majelis* jackets and flags, is important in attracting young participants. The sermon groups have served not only as religious space but also as the site for urban youth to enjoy their leisure time in a morally safe environment.

This book indicates that the engagement of young Muslims in *habaib* sermon groups suggests an interrelationship between socio-economic factors, youth culture, and religion. Most of the young followers come from the lower-middle-class and poor family background. They live in big cities and have to face problems such as poverty, unemployment, congestion, and the lack of youth facilities. This causes

Conclusion 127

insecurity and uncertainty. The emergence of *habaib*'s *majelis* provides them with free venues and opportunities for learning more about Islam, gaining blessings, and expressing their youthfulness. They feel that their participation and activism in the *majelis* help to support the *habaib*'s mission, namely to turn Jakarta into the Prophet's city. They believe that their regular involvement will bring good fortune and prosperity.

This book contributes to the growing scholarship of religious authority which is largely focused on 'new preachers' from secular education backgrounds by emphasising the roles of new media. The study of new preachers in the Muslim world, such as Cherif Haidara in Mali, Africa (Schulz, 2015), Amr Khaled in Egypt (Svetlova, 2014; Olsson, 2015), and Abdullah Gymnastiar in Indonesia (Muzakki, 2007; Hoesterey, 2016), has pointed to the pivotal role of new media and communication skills in augmenting their popularity. My study indicates that new preachers who come from traditionalist educational backgrounds and perform as traditionalists can also become popular through the use of new media and popular culture. While the new preachers in Indonesia tend to tailor their religious messages to appeal to a broad Muslim constituency, *habaib* promote traditional Islam and its rituals that are central to traditionalist Muslims. Therefore, the market segment of the *habaib* is limited to traditionalists. However, since traditionalists form the majority of Indonesia's Islamic community, this kind of *dakwah* has become a lucrative niche for *habaib* as it exploits a bourgeoning Islamic market.

Despite the roles of *habaib* in defending traditional Islam and resisting transnational Islamic groups, their social conservatism is at odds with the mainstream Indonesian desire for plurality and tolerance. Their conservative thought, especially in Islamic theology, aligns with that of the conservative wing of NU, which is predominantly based in East Java. *The habaib* alliance with NU conservatives in *dakwah* activities is growing, and it challenges the authority of NU's progressive religious scholars, such as Mustofa Bisri and Said Aqil Siroj, whom they see as deviating from Sunni orthodoxy. Given that they are now active in *dakwah*, through preaching, publications, internet, and training, it is likely that their impact in shaping the discourse of traditional Sunnism will grow in coming decades.

Appendix

List of Interviewees

Abdul Qadir Mauladdawilah, March 22, 2013
Abdullah b. Ja'far Assegaf, Juni 13, 2013
Achmad Zein Al-Kaff, March 13, 2013
Ahmad Fauzi (MR IT Team), October 5, 2013
Ahmad Muhammad Alatas, July 3, 2013
Ali Hasan Al-Bahr, March 8, 2013
Ali Yahya, January 2, 2013
Alwi Shahab, May 23, 2013
Dian Kusumaningrum, November 2, 2013.
Ernaz Siswanto, March 23, 2015
Fahmi, April 5, 2015
Febry, December 16, 2014
Geys Amar, February 11, 2013
Hasan Daliel Alaydrus, January 28, 2013
Husin Ali Alattas, March 8, 2013
Husin Maskati, July 4, 2013
Indry Rahmawati, October 19, 2013
Ismail Sunni, March 4, 2015
Jamal, September 29, 2013
Jamal b. Thoha Ba'agil, March 25, 2013
Jindan b. Novel, April 8, 2013
Mahdali, June 3, 2013
Mahmud b. Umar Al-Hamid, July 14, 2013
Mas'ud, October 20, 2013
Muhammad Al-Bagir b. Alwi b. Yahya, February 8, 2013
Muhammad Alwi Al-Kaff, March 12, 2013
Muhammad Bawazir, September 11, 2013
Muhammad Ghazi Alaydrus Gazi, February 14, 2013
Muhammad, February 14, 2013
Muhammad Rizieq b. Syihab, April 4, 2013
Muhiddin, October 20, 2013
Muhsin Al-Hamid, September 25, 2013
Nabiel Al-Musawa, September 17, 2015
Noval b. Muhammad Alaydrus, September 2, 2013

130   *Appendix*

Puput, September 20, 2013
Quraish Shihab, August 22, 2013
Said Sungkar, April 16, 2013
Siska, February 13 & September 15 2013
Syafiq, August 12, 2015
Syaiful Anwar, 16 December 2013
Syarif, March 3, 2013
Syauqi Al-Gadri, February 2, 2013
Syukron Makmun, October 9, 2013
Thobary Syadzily, October 20, 2013
Ulfa, September 20, 2013
Yusuf Usman Baisa, July 4, 2013
Zeyd Al-Hiyed, April 16, 2013

List of Institutions

Ahbabul Musthofa in Solo
Ahlul Bait Indonesia (ABI) in Jakarta
Albayyinat (Anti-Shia Group led by *habaib*) in Surabaya
Al-Irsyad Al-Islamiyyah in Jakarta
AlKisah Magazine in Jakarta
Basma Publisher in Malang
Darul Aitam (Orphanage managed by *habaib*) in Jakarta
Front Pembela Islam (FPI) in Jakarta
Gemira (Gerakan Muslim Indonesia Raya) in Jakarta
Hai'ah Shofwah (A Network of the students of Sayyid Muhammad Alwi Al-Maliki) in
     Surabaya
Jamiatul Khair (*sayyid* Islamic school) in Jakarta
Majelis Ar-Raudah in Solo
Majelis Nurul Musthofa in Jakarta
Majelis Rasulullah in Jakarta
Majelis Ta'lim Ar-Ridwan in Batu, Malang
Majelis Ta'lim Habib Ali Al-Habsyi in Jakarta
Majelis Taklim & Dzikir Al-Mubarak in Makassar
Majelis Ta'lim & Tadzkir Al-Anwar in Jakarta
Majelis Warotsatul Musthofa in Jakarta
Markaz Syariah of FPI in Jakarta
Nabawy Magazine in Pasuruan
Pengurus Besar Nahdlatul Ulama (PBNU) in Jakarta
Perhimpunan Al-Irsyad in Jakarta
Pondok Pesantren Dar Lugah wa *Dakwah* in Pasuruan (*habaib*-led Islamic Boarding School)
Pondok Pesantren Darul Hadits Al-Faqihiyyah in Malang (*habaib*-led Islamic Boarding
     School)
Rabithah Alawiyah in Jakarta and Malang
Sarjana Kuburan, Sarkub (an online network of *Aswaja* activists who oppose Salafi movement
     in Indonesia) in Tangerang, Banten

Bibliography

Books, Thesis, and Articles

Abaza, M. (2004). Markets of Faith: Jakartan Da'wa and Islamic Gentrification. *Archipel*, *67*(1), 173–202.

——— (2007). More on the Shifting Worlds of Islam. The Middle East and Southeast Asia: A Troubled Relationship? *The Muslim World*, *97*(3), 419–436.

Abidin, F.A. (2012). Ketika Sang Habib Dikritik: Membuka Mata dan Hati, Meniti Jalan Kebenaran. N.p.: Naashirusunnah.

Abushouk, A.I. & Ibrahim, H.A. (2009). *The Hadhrami Diaspora in Southeast Asia: Identity Maintenance or Assimilation?* Leiden; Boston, MA: Brill.

Affandi, B. (1976). *Shaykh Ahmad Al-Surkati: His Role in Al-Irshad Movement in Java in the Early Twentieth Century*. MA thesis. Canada: McGill University.

——— (1999). *Syaikh Ahmad Syurkati (1874–1943): Pembaharu & Pemurni Islam di Indonesia*. Jakarta: Pustaka al-Kautsar.

Ahmad, H. (1976). *Latar Belakang Sosial Budaya Masyarakat Keturunan Arab dan Sejarah Pertumbuhan dan Perjuangan Partai Arab Indonesia*. Bandung: Lembaga Kebudayaan Universitas Padjadjaran.

Alatas, I.F. (2005). Land of the Sacred, Land of the Damned: Conceptualizing Homeland among the Upholders of the Tariqah 'Alawiyah in Indonesia. *Anthropologi Indonesia*, *29*(2), 142–158.

——— (2009). *Securing Their Place: The Habaib, Prophetic Piety and Islamic Resurgence*. MA thesis. Singapore: National University of Singapore.

——— (2011). Becoming Indonesians: The Ba 'Alawi in the Interstices of the Nation. *Die Welt des Islams*, *51*(1), 45–108.

——— (2021). *What Is Religious Authority?: Cultivating Islamic Communities in Indonesia*. Princeton, NY: Princeton University Press.

Alatas, S.F. (1997). Hadhramaut and the Hadhrami Diaspora: Problems in Theoretical History. In U. Freitag & W. Clarence-Smith (Eds.). *Hadhrami Traders, Scholars and Statesmen in the Indian Ocean, 1750s–1960s* (pp. 19–34). Leiden; New York, NY; Köln: E.J. Brill.

——— (1999). The Tariqat Al-Alawiyyah and the Emergence of the Shi'i School in Indonesia and Malaysia. *Oriente Moderno*, *18*(79), 323–339.

Alaydrus, H.N.M. (2011). *Ahlul Bid'ah Hasanah: Jawaban untuk Mereka yang Mempersoalkan Amalan Para Wali*. Surakarta: Taman Ilmu.

Algadri, H. (1988). *Politik Belanda terhadap Islam dan Keturunan Arab di Indonesia*. Jakarta: Haji Masagung.

132 Bibliography

Al-Maliki, S.M.A. (2011). *Meluruskan Kesalahfahaman: Ijtihad Menurut Dalil dan Pandangan Para Ulama.* Bandung: Rosdakarya. Translated from Mafahim Yajib an Tusahha.

Al-Mashoor, A.A. (2011). *Sejarah, Silsilah & Gelar 'Alawiyin: Keturunan Imam Ahmad bin Isa Al-Muhajir.* Jakarta: Maktab Daimi-Rabithah Alawiyah.

Al-Masyhur, I.A. (2010). *Sejarah, Silsilah & Gelar Keturunan Nabi Muhammad SAW di Indonesia, Singapura, Malaysia, Timur Tengah, India dan Afrika.* Jakarta: Saraz Publishing.

Al-Musawa, I.F. (2014). *Meniti Jalan Pemuda Nabawi: Biografi Pendiri Majelis Rasulullah Saw Habib Munzir bin Fu'ad Almusawa.* Jakarta: Majelis Rasulullah.

Al-Musawa, M.F. (2008). *Kenalilah Akidahmu 1.* Jakarta: Majelis Rasulullah SAW.

——— (2009). *Kenalilah Akidahmu 2.* Jakarta: Majelis Rasulullah SAW.

Anthony, B. et al. (2011). *Talib or Taliban?: Indonesian Students in Pakistan and Yemen.* Sydney: Lowy Institute for International Policy.

Arai, K. (2012). The Sayyids as Commodities: The Islamic Periodical alKisah and the Sayyid Community in Indonesia. In M. Kazuo (Ed.). *Sayyids and Sharifs in Muslim Societies: The Living Links to the Prophet* (pp. 247–266). New York, NY: Routledge.

Assegaf, H.B.J. (2011). *Mengenal Para Wali: Bersama Al-Habib Hasan bin Ja'far Assegaf.* Malang: Pustaka Basma.

——— (2013). *Inilah Jalan Para Leluhurku.* Jakarta: Pilar.

Atmodiwirjo, P. (2008). The Use of Urban Public Places in Jakarta for Adolescents' Hanging Out. *Journal of Asian Architecture and Building Engineering, 7*(2), 339–346.

Azra, A. (2002). *Islam Nusantara: Jaringan Global dan Lokal.* Bandung: Mizan.

——— (2004). Political Islam in Post-Soeharto Indonesia. In V. Hooker & A. Saikal (Eds.). *Islamic Perspectives on the New Millennium* (pp. 133–149). Singapore: Institute of Southeast Asian Studies.

——— (2006). A Hadhrami Scholar in the Malay-Indonesian Diaspora: Sayyid Uthman. In *Islam in the Indonesian World: An Account of Institutional Formation* (pp. 245–249). Bandung: Mizan.

Azra, A. & Kaptein, N.J.G. (Eds.). (2010). *Varieties of Religious Authorities: Changes and Challenges in 20th Century Indonesian Islam.* Singapore: ISEAS.

Ba'Alawi, M.B.A.H. (2012). *Mutiara Ahlu Bait Dari Tanah Haram.* Malang: Ar-Roudho. Translated from Lawami'un Nur As-Sani fi Tarjamah Syaikhina Al-Imam As-Sayyid Muhammad bin Alawi Al-Maliki Al-Hasani.

Badjerei, H.H. (1996). *Al-Irsyad Mengisi Sejarah Bangsa.* Jakarta: Presto Prima Utama.

Baharun, A.H. (2013). *Mazhab Para Habaib and Akar Tradisinya.* Malang: Pustaka Basma.

Bajunid, O.F. (1996). The Arab in Southeast Asia: A Preliminary Overview. *Hiroshima Journal of International Studies, 2,* 21–56

Bamualim, C.S. (2011). Islamic Militancy and Resentment against Hadhramis in Post-Suharto Indonesia: A Case Study of Habib Rizieq Syihab and His Islamic Defenders Front. *Comparative Studies of South Asia, Africa, and the Middle East, 31*(2), 267–281.

Bang, A.K. (2003). *Sufi and Scholars of the Sea: Family Networks in East Africa, 1860–1925.* London: Routledge.

Bayat, A. (2010). *Being Young and Muslim: New Cultural Politics in the Global South and North.* New York, NY: Oxford University Press.

Berg, L.W.C.V.D. (1989). *Hadramaut dan Koloni Arab di Nusantara.* Jakarta: INIS. Translated from *Le Hadhramout Et. Les Colonies Arabes Dans L'Archipel Indien.*

Bonnefoy, L. (2011). *Salafism in Yemen: Transnationalism and Religious Identity.* UK: Hurst and Company.

Bibliography   133

Bourdieu, P. (1986). The Forms of Capital. Translated by Richard Nice. In John G. Richardson, *Handbook of Theory of Research for the Sociology of Education* (pp. 241–258). Westport, CT.: Greenword Press.

———— (1990). *The Logic of Practice*. Translated by Richard Nice. Redwood City, CA: Stanford University Press.

———— (1991). Genesis and Structure of the Religious Field. *Comparative Social Research, 13*, 1–44.

Boxberger, L. (2002). *On the Edge of Empire: Hadhramaut, Emigration, and the Indian Ocean, 1880s–1930s*. Albany: State University of New York Press.

Brown, B.B. & Larson, R.W. (2002). The Kaleidoscope of Adolescence: Experiences of the Worlds Youth at the Beginning of the 21st Century. In B.B. Brown, R.W. Larson & T.S. Saraswathi (Eds.). *The World's Youth: Adolescence in Eight Regions of the Globe* (pp. 1–20). Cambridge: Cambridge University Press.

Bruinessen, M.V. (1994). *NU: Tradisi, Relasi-Relasi Kuasa, Pencarian Wacana Baru*. Yogyakarta: LKIS.

———— & Howell, J.D. (Eds). (2007). *Sufism and the 'Modern' in Islam*. London: I.B. Tauris.

———— (Ed.). (2013). *Contemporary Developments in Indonesian Islam: Explaining the Conservative Turn*. Singapore: Institute of Southeast Asian Studies.

Bubalo, A. et al. (2011). *Talib or Taliban? Indonesian Students in Pakistan and Yemen*. Sydney: Lowy Institute for International Policy.

Bujra, A.S. (1971). *The Politics of Stratification: A Study of Political Change in a South Arabian Town*. London: Oxford University Press.

Bunell, T. & Miller, M.A. (2011). Jakarta in Post-Suharto Indonesia: Decentralisation, Neo-Liberalism and Global City Aspiration. *Space and Polity, 15*(1), 35–48.

Burhani, A.N. (2012). Al-Tawassut wa-l I'tidal: The NU and Moderatism in Indonesian Islam. *Asian Journal of Social Science, 40*(5–6), 564–561.

Burhanudin, J. (2007). *Islamic Knowledge, Authority, and Political Power*. PhD thesis. Netherlands: Leiden University.

Bush, R. (2009). *Nahdlatul Ulama and the Struggle for Power within Islam and Politics in Indonesia*. Singapore: ISEAS.

Campo, J.E. (2009). *Encyclopedia of Islam*. New York, NY: Facts On File.

Casey, C. (2008). Marginal Muslims: Politics and the Perceptual Bounds of Islamic Authenticity in Northern Nigeria. *Africa Today, 54*(3), 67–92.

Chaplin, C. (2014). Imagining the Land of the Two Holy Mosques: The Social and Doctrinal Importance of Saudi Arabia in Indonesian Salafi Discourse. *Austrian Journal of South-East Asian Studies, 7*(2), 217–236.

Chumaidy, A.F. (1976). *The Jam'iyah Nahdlatul Ulama: Its Rise and Early Development (1926–1945)*. MA thesis. McGill University.

Colin, G.S. (1978). *Encyclopedia of Islam*. Leiden: E.J. Brill.

Cybriwsky, R. & Ford, L.R. (2001). City Profile: Jakarta. *Cities, 18*(3), 199–210.

Dhofier, Z. (1982). *Tradisi Pesantren: Studi tentang Pandangan Hidup Kyai*. Jakarta: LP3ES.

DPP Rabithah Alawiyah. *Anggaran Dasar & Anggaran Rumah Tangga Rabithah Alawiyah*. Jakarta: Rabithah Alawiyah.

Durkheim, E. (2002). The Elementary Forms of Religious Life. In M. Lambek (Ed.). *A Reader in the Anthropology of Religion* (pp. 34–47). London: Blackwell.

Eickelman, D.F. (1992). Mass Higher Education and the Religious Imagination in Contemporary Arab Societies. *American Anthropological Association, 19*(4), 643–655.

134   Bibliography

——— & Anderson, J.W. (2003). *New Media in the Muslim World: The Emerging Public Sphere*. Bloomington: Indiana University Press.

Einstein, M. (2008). *Brands of Faith: Marketing Religion in Commercial Age*. London; New York, NY: Routledge.

Fadhli, A. (2011). *Ulama Betawi (Studi tentang Jaringan Ulama Betawi dan Kontribusinya Terhadap Perkembangan Islam Abad ke-19 dan 20)*. Jakarta: Manhalun Nasyi-in Press.

Fealy, G. (1998). *Ulama and Politics in Indonesia: A History of Nahdlatul Ulama, 1952–1967*. PhD thesis. Monash University.

——— (2007). Hizbut Tahrir in Indonesia: Seeking a 'Total' Islamic Identity. In S. Akbarzadeh & F. Mansouri. *Islam and Political Violence: Muslim Diaspora and Radicalism in the West*. London; New York, NY: I.B. Tauris.

——— (2007). The Political Contingency of Reform-Mindedness in Indonesia's Nahdlatul Ulama: Interest Politics and the Khittah. In A. Reid & M. Gilsenan (Eds.). *Islamic Legitimacy in a Plural Asia* (pp. 154–166). New York, NY; Canada: Routledge.

Fealy, G. & Barton, G. (1996). *Nahdlatul Ulama, Traditional Islam and Modernity in Indonesia*. Melbourne: Monash Asia Institute.

Fealy, G. & White, S. (Eds.). (2008). *Expressing Islam: Religious Life and Politics in Indonesia*. Singapore: Institute of Southeast Asian Studies.

Feener, R.M. (2007). *Muslim Legal Thought in Modern Indonesia*. New York, NY; Cambridge: Cambridge University Press.

——— (2014). Muslim Religious Authority in Modern Asia. *Asian Journal of Social Science*, *42*(5), 501–516.

Feillard, A. (2010). From Handling Water in a Glass to Coping with an Ocean: Shifts in Religious Authority. In A. Azra & N.J.G. Kaptein (Eds.). *Varieties of Religious Authorities: Changes and Challenges in 20th Century Indonesian Islam* (pp. 157–176). Singapore: ISEAS.

Formichi, C. (2014a). Violence, Sectarianism, and the Politics of Religion: Articulations of Anti-Shi'a Discourse in Indonesia. *Indonesia*, *89*, 1–27.

——— (2014b). From Fluid Identities to Sectarian Labels: A Historical Investigation of Indonesia's Shi'i Communities. *Al-Jami'ah*, *52*(1), 101–126.

——— (2014c). Shaping Shi'a Identities in Contemporary Indonesia between Local Tradition and Foreign Orthodoxy. *Die Welt Des Islam*, *54*(2), 212–236.

Freitag, U. (2003). *Indian Ocean Migrants and State Formation in Hadhramaut*. Leiden; Boston, MA: Brill.

Freitag, U. & Clarence-Smith, W. (Eds.). (1997). *Hadhrami Traders, Scholars and Statesmen in the Indian Ocean, 1750s–1960s*. Leiden: E.J. Brill.

Gause, F.G. (2011). *Saudi Arabia in the New Middle East. Council Special Report 63, December*. USA: Council on Foreign Relations-Center for Preventive Action.

Geertz, C. (1960). The Javanese Kijaji: The Changing Role of a Cultural Broker. *Comparative Studies in Society and History*, *2*(2), 228–249.

Gellner, E. (1981). *Muslim Society*. London: Cambridge University Press.

Ghoshal, B. (2010). Arabization: The Changing Face of Islam in Asia. *India Quarterly*, *66*(1), 69–89.

Gilsenan, M. (1973). *Saint and Sufi in Modern Egypt: An Essay in the Sociology of Religion*. UK: Oxford University Press.

Graham, W.A. (1993). Traditionalism in Islam: An Essay in Interpretation. *The Journal of Interdisciplinary History*, *23*(3), 495–522.

Guntur & Tim Majelis Rasulullah. (2013). *Habib Munzir Menanam Cinta untuk Para Kekasih Rasulullah*. Jakarta: Qultum Media.

Bibliography   135

Haidar, M.A. (1994). *Nahdlatul Ulama dan Islam di Indonesia*. Jakarta: Gramedia.

Haikal, H. (1986). *Indonesia-Arab dalam Pergerakan Kemerdekaan Indonesian (1900–1942)*. PhD thesis. Jakarta: The University of Indonesia (UI).

Halverson, J.R. (2010). *Theology and Creed in Sunni Islam: The Muslim Brotherhood, Ash'arism, and Political Sunnism*. New York, NY: Palgrave Macmillan.

Hamby-Wells, J.K. (2009). 'Strangers' and 'Stranger-kings': The Sayyid in Eighteenth-century Maritime Southeast Asia. *Journal of Southeast Asian Studies, 40*(3), 567–591.

Hamid, S. (2009). The Attraction of 'Authentic Islam': Salafism and British Muslim Youth. In R. Meijer (Ed.). *Global Salafism: Islam's New Religious Movement* (pp. 384–403). London: Hurst and Company.

Hariyadi. (2013). *Islamic Popular Culture and the New Identities of Urban Muslim Young People in Indonesia: The Case of Islamic Films and Islamic Self-Help Books*. PhD thesis. Perth: The University of Western Australia.

Hasan, N. (2005). *Laskar Jihad: Islam, Militancy, and the Quest for Identity in Post-New Order Indonesia*. PhD thesis. Netherlands: Utrecht University.

——— (2006). *Laskar Jihad: Islam, Militancy, and the Quest for Identity in Post-New Order Indonesia*. Ithaca, NY: Cornell Southeast Asian Program.

——— (2007). The Salafi Movement in Indonesia: Transnational Dynamics and Local Development. *Comparative Studies of South Asia, Africa and the Middle East, 27*(1), 83–94.

——— (2009). The Making of Public Islam: Piety, Agency, and Commodification on the Landscape of the Indonesian Public Sphere. *Contemporary Islam, 3*, 229–250.

——— (2010). The Failure of the Wahhabi Campaign: Transnational Islam and the Salafi Madrasa in Post-9/11 Indonesia. *Southeast East Asia Research, 18*(4), 657–705.

Heiss, J. & Slama, M. (2010). Genealogical Avenues, Long-Distance Flows and Social Hierarchy: Hadhrami Migrants in the Indonesian Diaspora. *Anthropology of Middle East, 5*(1), 34–52.

Ho, E. (2006). *The Graves of Tarim: Genealogy and Mobility across the Indian Ocean*. Berkeley; Los Angeles; London: University of California Press.

Hoesterey, J.B. (2008). Marketing Morality: The Rise, Fall, and Rebranding of Aa Gym. In Fealy, G. & White, S. (Eds.). (2008). *Expressing Islam: Religious Life and Politics in Indonesia* (pp. 95-112). Singapore: Institute of Southeast Asian Studies.

——— (2012). Prophetic Cosmopolitanism: Islam, Pop Psychology, and Civic Virtue in Indonesia. *City and Society, 24*(1), 38–61.

——— (2016). *Rebranding Islam: Piety, Prosperity, and a Self-Help Guru*. Redwood City, CA: Stanford University Press.

Howell, J.D. (2001). Sufism and the Indonesian Islamic Revival. *The Journal of Asian Studies, 60*(3), 701–729.

——— (2008). Modulations of Active Piety: Professors and Televangelists as Promoters of Indonesian Sufism. In G. Fealy & S. White (Eds.). *Expressing Islam: Religious Life and Politics in Indonesia* (pp. 63–85). Singapore: Institute of Southeast Asian Studies.

——— (2014). Christendom, the Ummah and Community in the Age of Televangelism. *Social Compass, 6*(2), 234–249.

——— (2015a). Revitalised Sufism and the New Piety Movements in Islamic Southeast Asia. In B.S. Turner & Salemink (Eds.). *Routledge Handbook of Religions in Asia* (pp. 276–292). New York, NY: Routledge.

——— (2015b). Revival Ritual and the Mobilization of Late-Modern Islamic Selves. *Journal of Religious and Political Practice, 1*(1), 47–57.

Ida, L. (2004). *NU Muda: Kaum Progresif dan Sekularisme Baru*. Jakarta: Erlangga.

136 Bibliography

Imron, A. & Hary, S. (n.d.). *Hadramaut Bumi Sejuta Wali*. Surabaya: Cahaya Ilmu and Duta Mustafa.

Institute for Policy Analysis of Conflict (IPAC). (2013). *Weak, Therefore Violent: The Mujahidin of Western Indonesia*. IPAC Report, 5, 2 December.

International Crisis Group (ICG). (2004). *Indonesia Backgrounder: Why Salafism and Terrorism Mostly Don't Mix*. ICG Asia Report, 83, 13 September.

Jacobsen, F.F. (2009). *Hadrami Arabs in Present-Day Indonesia: An Indonesia-Oriented Group with an Arab Signature*. London; New York, NY: Routledge.

Jaiz, H.A. (2011). *Kuburan-Kuburan Keramat di Nusantara*. Jakarta: Pustaka Al-Kautsar.

Jamhari & Jahroni, J. (2004). *Gerakan Salafi Radikal di Indonesia*. Jakarta: Raja Grafindo Persada.

Jones, S. (1984). The Contraction and Expansion of the "Umat" and the Role of Nahdlatul Ulama in Indonesia. *Indonesia, 38*, 1–20.

———— (2013). *IPAC Report 2 December.*

Jonge, H.d. (1993). Discord and Solidarity among the Arabs in the Netherlands East Indies, 1900–1942. *Indonesia, 55*.

———— (2004). Abdul Rahman Baswedan and the Emancipation of the Hadhramis in Indonesia. *Asian Journal of Social Science, 32*(3), 373–400.

———— & Kaptein, N. (Eds.). (2002). *Transcending Borders: Arabs, Politics, Trade, and Islam in Southeast Asia*. Leiden: KITLV.

Kailani, N. (2012). Forum Lingkar Pena and Muslim Youth in Contemporary Indonesia. *Review of Indonesian and Malaysian Affairs, 46*(1), 33–53.

———— (2015). *Aspiring to Prosperity: The Economic Theology of Urban Muslims in Contemporary Indonesia*. PhD thesis. Canberra: University of New South Wales.

Kalmbach, H. (2015). Blurring Boundaries: Aesthetics, Performance, and the Transformation of Islamic Leadership. *Culture and Religion, 16*(2), 160–174.

Kaptein, Niko J.G. (2014). *Islam, Colonialism and the Modern Age in the Netherlands East Indies: A Biography of Sayyid 'Uthman (1822–1914)*. Leiden; Boston, MA: Brill.

Kathirithamby-Wells, J. (2009). 'Strangers' and 'Stranger-Kings': The Sayyid in Eighteenth-Century Maritime Southeast Asia. *Journal of Southeast Asian Studies, 40*(3), 567–591.

———— (2012). Hadrami Projections of Southeast Asian Identity. In G. Wade & L. Tana (Eds.). *Anthony Reid and the Study of the Southeast Asian Past* (pp. 271–302). Sigapore: Institute of Southeast Asian Studies.

Keddie, N.R. (1972). *Scholars, Saints, and Sufis: Muslim Religious Institutions in the Middle East since 1500*. Berkeley; Los Angeles; London: University of California Press.

Kersten, C. (2015). Islamic Post-Traditionalism: Postcolonial and Postmodern Religious Discourse in Indonesia. *Sophia, 54*, 473–489.

Kertzer, D.I. (1988). *Ritual, Politics, and Power*. New Haven, CT; London: Yale University Press.

Kitiarsa, P. (Ed.). (2008). *Religious Commodification in Asia: Marketing Gods*. London; New York, NY: Routledge.

———— (2010). Toward a Sociology of Religious Commodification. In Bryan S. Turner (Ed.). *The New Blackwell Companion to the Sociology of religion* (pp. 563–583). West Sussex: Wiley-Blackwell.

Knysh, A. (1999). The Sada in History: A Critical Essay on Hadhrami Historiography. *Journal of the Royal Asiatic Society, 9*(2), 215–222.

———— (2001). The Tariqa on a Landcruiser: The Resurgence of Sufism in Yemen. *The Middle East Journal, 55*(3), 399–414.

Bibliography   137

Kramer, G. & Schmidtke, S. (Eds.). (2006). *Speaking for Islam: Religious Authorities in Muslim Societies*. Leiden; Boston, MA: Brill.

Leaman, O. (Ed.). (2015). *The Biographical Encyclopedia of Islamic Philosophy*. London: Bloomsbury.

Lekon, C. (1997). The Impact of Remittances on the Economy of Hadhramaut, 1914–1967. In U. Freitag & W. Clarence-Smith (Eds.). *Hadhrami Traders, Scholars and Statesmen in the Indian Ocean, 1750s–1960s* (pp. 264–280). Leiden; New York, NY; Koln: 1997.

Liddle, R.W. (1996). The Islamic Turn in Indonesia: A Political Explanation. *The Journal of Asian Studies*, *55*(3), 613–634.

Mandal, S.K. (1994). *Finding Their Place: A History of Arabs in Java under Dutch Rule, 1800–1924*. PhD thesis. New York: Columbia University.

———— (2011). The Significance of the Rediscovery of Arabs in the Malay World. *Comparative Studies of South Asia, Africa and the Middle East*, *31*(2), 299–300.

———— (2012). Popular Sites of Prayer, Transoceanic Migration, and Cultural Diversity: Exploring the Significance of Keramat in Southeast Asia. *Modern Asian Studies*, *46*(2), 355–372.

Mandaville, P. (2007). Globalization and the Politics of Religious Knowledge: Pluralizing Authority in the Muslim World. *Theory, Culture & Society*, *24*(2), 101–115.

———— (2007). *Global Political Islam*. London; New York, NY: Routledge.

Manger, L. (2010). *The Hadhrami Diaspora: Community-Building on the Indian Ocean Rim*. New York, NY: Berghahn Books.

Mauladdawilah, A.Q.U. & Mauladdawilah, A.Q.A. (2009). *17 Habaib Berpengaruh di Indonesia*. Malang: Pustaka Bayan.

———— (2009). *Habib Umar bin Hafiz Singa Podium*. Malang: Karisma.

———— (2010). *Dakwah Pemuda Ibu Kota*. Malang: Pustaka Basma.

———— (2012). *Tarim Kota Pusat Peradaban Islam*. Malang: Pustaka Basma.

Meijer, R. (2009). *Global Salafism: Islam's New Religious Movement*. New York, NY: Columbia University Press.

Meri, J.W. (1999). Aspects of Baraka (Blessings) and Ritual Devotion among Medieval Muslims and Jews. *Medieval Encounters*, *5*(1), 46–69.

Meuleman, J. (2011). Dakwah, Competition for Authority, and Development. *Bijdragen tot de Taal-, Land- en Volkenkunde*, *167*(2/3), 236–269.

Meyer, B. (2009). Introduction: From Imagined Communities to Aesthetics Formation: Religious Mediations, Sensational Forms, and Styles of Binding. In B. Meyer (Ed.). *Aesthetic Formations: Media, Religion and the Senses* (pp. 1–30). New York, NY: Palgrave-Macmillan.

Millie, J. (2009). *Splashed by the Saint: Ritual Reading and Islamic Sanctity in West Java*. Leiden: KITLV Press.

———— (2011). Islamic Preaching and Women's Spectatorship in West Java". *The Australian Journal of Anthropology*, *22*(2), 151–169.

———— (2012). Oratorical Innovation and Audience Heterogeneity in Islamic West Java. Indonesia, 93, 123–145.

Mobini-Kesheh, N. (1997). Islamic Modernism in Colonial Java: The Al-Irshad Movement. In U. Freitag & W. Clarence-Smith (Eds.). *Hadhrami Traders, Scholars and Statesmen in the Indian Ocean, 1750s–1960s* (pp. 231–248). Leiden: E.J. Brill.

———— (1999). *The Hadrami Awakening: Community and Identity in the Netherlands East Indies, 1900–1942*. New York, NY: Cornell Southeast Asia Program.

138 Bibliography

Muzakki, A. (2008). Islam as a Syimbolic Commodity: Transmitting and Consuming Islam through Public Sermons in Indonesia. In P. Kitiarsa (Ed.). *Religious Commodifications in Asia: Marketing God* (pp. 205–219). London; New York, NY: Routledge.

Newby, G. (2002). *A Concise Encyclopedia of Islam*. England: One World.

Nisa, E.F. (2012). Embodied Faith: Agency and Obedience among Face-Veiled University Students in Indonesia. *The Asia Pacific Journal of Anthropology*, *13*(4), 366–381.

Noer, D. (1980). *Gerakan Modern Islam di Indonesia 1900–1942*. Jakarta: LP3ES.

——— (1987). *Partai Islam Di Pentas Nasional*. Jakarta: Pustaka Utama Grafiti.

Nuhrison, M.N. (2010). Gerakan Paham dan Pemikiran Islam Radikal Pasca Orde Baru (Gerakan Dakwah Salafi di Kec. Lembar, Kab. Lombok Barat, Nusa Tenggara Barat). In W. Sugiyarto (Ed.). *Direktori Kasus-Kasus Aliran, Pemikiran, Paham, dan Gerakan Keagamaan di Indonesia* (pp. 23–28). Jakarta: Kementerian Agama RI Badan Litbang dan Diklat Puslitbang Kehidupan Keagamaan.

Olsson, S. (2015). *Preaching Islamic Revival: Amr Khaled, Mass Media and Social Change in Egypt*. New York, NY: I.B. Tauris.

Parker, L. & Nilan, P. (2013). *Adolescents in Contemporary Indonesia*. New York, NY: Routledge.

Pimpinan Pusat Al-Irsyad Al-Islamiyyah. (2012). *Mabadi' Al-Irsyad dan Penjelasannya*. Jakarta: Al-Irsyad Al-Islamiyyah.

Poljarevic, E. (2012). In Pursuit of Authenticity: Becoming a Salafi". *Comparative Islamic Studies*, *8*(1–2), 139–164.

Qomar, M. (2002). *NU "Liberal": Dari Tradisionalisme Ahlussunnah ke Universalisme Islam*. Bandung: Mizan.

Ramli, M.I. (2010). *Buku Pintar Berdebat dengan Wahhabi*. Jawa Timur: Bina Aswaja and LMB NU Jember.

——— (2013). *Bekal Pembela Ahlus Sunnah Wal Jamaah Menghadapi Radikalisme Salafi-Wahabi*. Surabaya: Aswaja NU Center.

Reid, A. (1972). Habib Abdur-Rahman Az-Zahir (1833–1896). *Indonesia*, *13*, 36–59.

Rey, T. (2004). Marketing the Goods of Salvation: Bourdieu on Religion. *Religion*, *34*, 331–343.

——— (2007). *Bourdieu on Religion: Imposing Faith and Legitimacy*. New York, NY: Routledge.

Riddel, P.G. (2010). Arab Migrants and Islamization in the Malay World during the Colonial Period. *Indonesia and the Malay World*, *29*(84), 113–128.

Rijal, S. (2011). Indoctrinating Muslim Youths: Seeking Certainty through An-Nabhanism. *Al-Jami'ah*, *49*(2), 253–280.

Robinson, F. (1993). Technology and Religious Change: Islam and the Impact of Print. *Modern Asian Studies*, *27*(1), 229–251.

——— (2008). Islamic Reform and Modernities in South Asian. *Modern Asian Studies*, *42*(2/3), 259–281.

——— (2009). Crisis of Authority: Crisis of Islam? *Journal of the Royal Asiatic Society*, *19*(3), 339–354.

Roof, W.D. (1999). *Spiritual Marketplace: Baby Boomers and the Remaking of American Religion*. New York, NY: Princeton University Press.

Rosyad, R. (1995). *A Quest for True Islam: A Study of the Islamic Resurgence Movement among the Youth in Bandung, Indonesia*. Canberra: ANU E-Press.

Rudnyckyj, D. (2010). *Spiritual Economies: Islam, Globalization, and the Afterlife of Development*. Ithaca, NY: Cornell University Press.

Bibliography 139

Rumadi. (2008). *Post-tradisionalisme Islam: Wacana Intelektualisme dalam Komunitas NU*. Cirebon: Fahmina Institute.

Saat, N. (2014). "Deviant" Muslims: The Plight of Shias in Contemporary Malaysia. In B. Platzdasch & J. Saravanamuttu (Eds.). *Religious Diversity in Muslim-Majority States in Southeast Asia: Areas of Toleration and Conflict* (pp. 359–378). Singapore: ISEAS.

Sakai, M. (2012). Preaching to Muslim Youth in Indonesia: The 'Dakwah' Activities of Habiburrahman El Shirazy. *Review of Indonesian and Malaysian Affairs*, *46*(1), 9–31.

Saleh, F. (2001). *Modern Trends in Islamic Theological Discourse in Twentieth Century Indonesia: A Critical Survey*. Leiden; Boston, MA; Koln: Brill.

Salman. (2006). The Tarbiyah Movement: Why People Join This Indonesian Contemporary Islamic Movement. *Studia Islamika*, *13*(2), 171–241.

Schulz, D.E. (2015). Mediating Authority: Media Technologies and the Generation of Charismatic Appeal in Southern Mali. *Culture and Religion*, *16*(2), 125–145.

Sekretariat DPR-GR (n.d.). *Seperempat Abad Dewan Perwakilan Rakyat Republik Indonesia*. Jakarta.

Sheffer, G. (Ed.) (1986). *Modern Diasporas in International Politics*. London: Croom Helm.

Shihab, A. (2001). *Islam Sufistik: Islam Pertama dan Pengaruhnya Hingga Kini di Indonesia*. Bandung: Mizan.

Shihab, M.Q. (2007). *Sunnah-Syiah Bergandengan Tangan Mungkinkah?: Kajian atas Konsep Ajaran dan Pemikiran*. Tangerang: Lentera Hati.

Sila, M.A. (1998). *In Search of Union with Allah (Ma'rifatullah) among the Sayyid People in Cikoang, South Sulawesi*. MA thesis. Canberra: Australian National University.

———— (2001). The Festivity of Maulid Nabi in Cikoang, South Sulawesi: Between Remembering and Exaggerating the Spirit of the Prophet. *Studia Islamika*, *8*(3), pp. 1–56.

———— (2015). *Maudu': A Way of Union with God*. Canberra: ANU Press.

Slama, M. (2005). Indonesian Hadhramis and the Hadhramaut: An Old Diaspora and Its New Connections. *Antropologi Indonesia*, *29*(1), 107–113.

———— (2010). Genealogical Avenues, Long-Distance Flows and Social Hierarchy: Hadrami Migrants in the Indonesian Diaspora. *Anthropology of the Middle East*, *5*(1), 34–52.

———— (2011). Paths of Institutionalization, Varying Divisions, and Contested Radicalism: Comparing Hadhrami Communities on Java and Sulawesi. *Comparative Studies of South Asia, Africa and the Middle East*, *31*(2), 331–342.

———— (2011). Translocal Networks and Globalisation within Indonesia: Exploring the Hadhrami Diaspora from the Archipelago's North-East. *Asian Journal of Social Science*, *39*(2), 238–257.

———— (2014a). Hadhrami Moderns: Recurrent Dynamics as Historical Rhymes of Indonesia's Reformist Islamic Organization Al-Irsyad. In V. Gottowik (Ed.). *Dynamics of Religion in Southeast Asia: Magic and Modernity* (pp. 113–133). Amsterdam: Amsterdam University Press.

———— (2014b). From Wali Songo to Wali Pitu: The Travelling of Islamic Saint Veneration to Bali. In B. Hauser-Schaublin & D.D. Harnish (Eds.). *Between Harmony and Discrimination: Negotiating Religious Identities within Majority-Minority Relationships in Bali and Lombok* (pp. 112–143). Leiden; Boston, MA: Brill.

Soares, B.F. (2004). Muslim Saints in the Age of Neoliberalism. In B. Weiss (Ed.). *Producing African Futures: Ritual and Reproduction in a Neoliberal Age* (pp. 79–105). Leiden: Brill.

————. (2005). *Islam and the Prayer Economy: History and Authority in a Malian Town*. Ann Arbor: The University of Michigan Press.

140 Bibliography

Stassen, G.H. (2012). God's Vision for the Church-Kingdom Discipleship. In D.P. Gushee (Ed.). *A New Evangelical Manifesto: A Kingdom Vision for the Common Good* (pp. 50–56). Des Peres, MO: Chalice Press.

Stephan, M. (2010). Education, Youth, and Islam: The Growing Popularity of Private Religious Lessons in Dushanbe, Tajikistan. *Central Asian Survey*, *29*(4), 469–483.

Svetlova, K. (2014). The New Media and Islamic Activism: The Case of 'Amr Khalid. In E. Daphna, H. Meir & D.F. Eickelman (Eds.). *Religious Knowledge, Authority and Charisma: Islamic and Jewish Perspective*. Salt Lake City: University of Utah Press.

Swartz, D. (1996). Bridging the Study of Culture and Religion: Pierre Bourdieu's Political Economy of Symbolic Power. *Sociology of Religion*, *57*(1), 71–85.

——— (1997). *Culture and Power: The Sociology of Pierre Bourdieu*. Chicago, IL; London: The University of Chicago Press.

Takim, L.N. (2006). *The Heirs of the Prophet: Charisma and Religious Authority in Shi'ite Islam*. Albany: State University of New York Press.

Tim Milist MR. (2013). *Mengenal Lebih Dekat Habib Munzir Almusawa*. Jakarta: Majelis Rasulullah SAW.

Tim Pustaka Basma. (2012). *Memahami Pribadi Suci Baginda Nabi Saw Melalui Maulid Dhiya'ullami*. Malang: Pustaka Basma.

Turner, B.S. (2007). Religious Authority and the New Media. *Theory, Culture & Society*, *24*(2), 117–134.

——— (Ed.). (2011). *The New Blackwell Companion to Sociology of Religion*. UK: Wiley-Blackwell.

Urban, H.B. (2003). Sacred Capital: Pierre Bourdieu and the Study of Religion. *Method and Theory in the Study of Religion*, *15*(5), 354–389.

Wacquant, L.J.D. (1987). Toward a Reflexive Sociology: A Workshop with Pierre Bourdieu. *Sociological Theory*, *7*, 26–63.

Wahid, A. & Ma'arif, M.S. (Eds.). (2009). *Ilusi Negara Islam: Ekspansi Gerakan Islam Transnasional di Indonesia*. Jakarta: Wahid Institute.

Wahid, D. (2014). *Nurturing the Salafi Manhaj: A Study of Salafi Pesantrens in Contemporary Indonesia*. PhD thesis. Utrecht: Utrecht University.

Wai-Weng, H. (2012). Expressing Chineseness, Marketing Islam: The Hybrid Performance of Chinese Muslim Preachers. In S. Sai & C. Hoon (Eds.). *Chinese Indonesians Reassessed: History, Religion, and Belonging* (pp. 178–199). London; New York, NY: Routledge.

Weber, M. (1978). *Economy and Society: An Outline of Interpretive Sociology*. Berkeley; Los Angeles; London: University of California Press.

Witte, M.d. et al. (2015). Aesthetics of Religious Authority: Introduction. *Culture and Religion*, *6*(2), 117–124.

Woodward, M. et al. (2012). Ordering What Is Right, Forbidding What Is Wrong: Two Faces of Hadhrami Dakwah in Contemporary Indonesia. *Review of Indonesian and Malaysian Affairs*, *46*(2), 105–146.

Zada, K. (2002). *Islam Radikal: Pergulatan Ormas-ormas Islam Garis Keras di Indonesia*. Bandung: Mizan.

Zaman, M.Q. (2002). *The Ulama in Contemporary Islam: Custodians of Change*. Princeton, NJ; Oxford: Princeton University Press.

Zamhari, A. & Howell, J.D. (2012). Taking Sufism to the Streets: Majelis Zikir and Majelis Salawat as New Venues for Popular Islamic Piety in Indonesia. *Review of Indonesian and Malaysian Affairs*, *46*(2), 47–75.

Zulkifli. (2013). *The Struggle of the Shi'is in Indonesia*. Canberra: ANU E-Press.

Bibliography   141

Magazines and Websites

alKisah No. 04, February 11–24, 2008.

alKisah No. 20, September 30–October 13, 2013.

alKisah No. 22, October 31–November 13, 2011.

alKisah No. 24, November 25–December 8, 2013.

Gatra No. 26, May 7, 2009.

Gatra No. 15, 16–22 February 2012.

Tabloid Media Ummat No. 161, 2013

Albayyinat. (n.d.). *Apa dan Siapa Albayyinat*. Retrieved October 20, 2014, from http://www.albayyinat.net/ind1.html

Alhabib Omar Official Website. (2011). *A Brief Biography of Habib Umar*. Retrieved March 5, 2015, from http://www.alhabibomar.com/About.aspx?Lang=EN&SectionID=12

Al-Irsyad. (2009). *Al-Irsyad Tidak Haramkan Pemilu dan Kafirkan Anggota DPR*. Retrieved July 8, 2015, from http://alirsyad.net/?s=sekolah+cabang+2009

Al-Irsyad. (2006). *Pemerintah Hanya Akui Al-Irsyad yang Disahkan Mahkamah Agung*. Retrieved July 7, 2015, from http://alirsyad.net/pemerintah-hanya-akui-al-irsyad-yang-disahkan-mahkamah-agung/

AlKisah. (n.d.). *Habib Habib Abdul Qadir bin Umar Mauladawilah: Memelihara Jejak-jejak Salaf Ash-Shali*. Retrieved March 22, 2015, from http://majalah-alkisah.com/index.php/figur/26-profile-tokoh/357--habib-abdul-qadir-bin-Umar-mauladawilah-memelihara-jejak-jejak-salaf-ash-shalih

APJII [Asosiasi Penyelenggara Jasa Internet]. 2022. Profil Internet Indonesia 2022 [Indonesian Internet Profile 2022]. https://online.fliphtml5.com/rmpye/ztxb/#p=1 (accessed on 30 May 2023).

Arrahmah. (2014). *Habib Zein Al-kaff: Habib yang Jadi Syiah Adalah Pengkhianat Rasulullah*. Retrieved July 7, 2017, from https://www.arrahmah.id/habib-zein-alkaff-habib-yang-jadi-syiah-adalah-pengkhianat-nabi-muhammad/

Ar-Raudhah Majelis Ilmu & Dzikir. (n.d.). *Tentang Majelis*. Retrieved November 2, 2014, from http://ar-raudhah.info/tentang/

Badan Kontak Majelis Taklim (BKMT). (2016). *Sejarah BKMT*. Retrieved May 1, 2016, from https://bkmt.or.id/wp/sejarah-berdirinya-bkmt/

Biografi Ulama dan Habaib. (2012). *Kisah Kemuliaan Akhlak al-Habib Umar bin Hafidz*. Retrieved March 26, 2015, from http://biografiulamahabaib.blogspot.com.au/2012/12/kisah-kemuliaan-akhlak-al-habib-umar.html

Berkuliah. (2014). *Yaman: Pengalaman Studi di Timur Tengah? Inilah Kisah dari Muhammad Ismail Sunni (an Interview)*. Retrieved March 4, 2015, from http://www.berkuliah.com/2014/09/yaaman-pengalaman-studi-di-timur-tengah.html

BPS [Badan Pusat Statistik] DKI Jakarta. 2023. Jumlah penduduk provinsi DKI Jakarta menurut kelompok umur dan jenis kelamin 2020–2022 [The number of population of Jakarta based on age and gender between 2020 to 2022]. https://jakarta.bps.go.id/indicator/12/111/1/jumlah-penduduk-provinsi-dki-jakarta-menurut-kelompok-umur-dan-jenis-kelamin.html (accessed on 29 April 2023).

BPS[Badan Pusat Statistik] DKI Jakarta. (2023). Garis kemiskinan, jumlah, dan persentase penduduk miskin di daerah menurut kabupaten/kota di Provinsi DKI Jakarta 2020–2022 [Poverty line, number and percentage of poor people in regions by district/city in DKI Jakarta Province 2020–2022] https://jakarta.bps.go.id/indicator/23/645/1/garis-kemiskinan-jumlah-dan-persentase-penduduk-miskin-di-daerah-menurut-kabupaten-kota-di-provinsi-dki-jakarta.html (accessed on 29 April 2023).

142 *Bibliography*

Debat Ustadz Wahabi vs Ustadz Aswaja di Batam. (2014). *Video File*. Retrieved November 5, 2014, from https://www.youtube.com/watch?v=HkCIfDrQqUU

Firanda. (2011). *Habib Munzir Mencela Imam Masjidil Haram Syaikh Dr. Abdurrahman as-Sudais!!!*. Retrieved March 19, 2020, from https://abunamira.wordpress.com/2011/11/24/habib-munzir-mencela-imam-masjidil-haram-syaikh-dr-abdurrahman-as-sudais/

Ford, M. (2015). *Making Their Way*. Retrieved April 20, 2015, from https://www.insideindonesia.org/editions/edition-120-apr-jun-2015/making-their-way

Galeri Kitab Kuning. *Ditakuti Wahabi, Ini Biografi dan Biodata KH. Muhammad Idrus Ramli*. Retrieved April 15, 2022, from https://www.galerikitabkuning.com/2021/02/biografi-kh-idrus-ramli-musuh-wahabi.html

Inilah. (2011). *Jelang UN Pelajar Ziarah ke Makam Gus Dur*. Retrieved April 27, 2015, from http://nasional.inilah.com/read/detail/2194883/jelang-un-pelajar-ziarah-ke-makam-gusdur

Jakarta. n.d. *Tentang Jakarta*. Retrieved January 5, 2022, from https://www.jakarta.go.id/tentang-jakarta Kontras. (2013). *Desakan Penyidikan Komprehensif Kasus Penyerangan Pondok Pesantren Darul Sholihin, Puger, Jember, Jawa Timur*. Retrieved June 7, 2015, from http://www.kontras.org/home/index.php?module=pers&id=1774

Lombok Today (2014). *Multaqo Ulama Indonesia Perkuat Persatuan Umat*. Retrieved February 10, 2015, from https://lomboktoday.co.id/20141123/multaqo-ulama-indonesia-perkuat-persatuan-umat.html

Majelis Rasulullah. (2007). *Forum Majelis Rasulullah*. Retrieved April 15, 2013, from http://majelisrasulullah.org/index.php?option=com_simpleboard&Itemid=&func=view&catid=7&id=9654#9654

Majelis Rasulullah SAW. (2013, September 30). *Assalamualaikum wahai jama'ah Majelis Rasulullah SAW, beli lah produk Majelis Rasulullah SAW yg asli. Karena dg anda membantu produk Majelis Rasulullah SAW, yg ASLI. Anda sudah membantu Dakwah Rasulullah saw, di Kota Jakarta ini. Wujudkanlah [Facebook status update]*. Retrieved January 10, 2015, from https://www.facebook.com/Majelis-Rasulullah-SAW-89898810391/?fref=ts

———— (n.d.). *Biografi Majelis Rasulullah*. Retrieved January 21, 2015, from http://www.majelisrasulullah.org/biografi-majelis-rasulullah/

———— (n.d.). *Profil Majelis Rasulullah*. Retrieved April 15, 2013, from http://majelisrasulullah.org/index.php?option=com_content&task=view&id=2&Itemid=26

Majelis Al-Muwasholah. (n.d.). *Tentang kami*. Retrieved March 5, 2016, from https://majelisalmuwasholah.com/sekilas-tentang-majelis/

Majelis Rasulullah Habib Umar bin Hafidz 2013 (video file). (n.d). Retrieved March 26, 2015, from https://www.youtube.com/watch?v=y-bLW18tzyw

Mustafa, Tariq. (2014). *The Future of Political Sufism. Islam Affairs*. Retrieved May 9, 2015, from: http://islamaffairs.com/blog/future-political-sufism/

Muwasala. (n.d). *About Muwasala*. Retrieved March 5, 2015, from http://muwasala.org/about/

Pustaka Muhibbin. (2013). *Satu Gedung Warga Inggeris Semuanya Masuk Islam Berkat Habib Umar bin Hafidz*. Retrieved March 26, 2015, from http://pustakamuhibbin.blogspot.com.au/2013/11/satu-gedung-warga-inggris-semuanya.html

Republika. (2013). *Kontras Desak Penyelidikan Kasus Penyerangan Ponpes*. Retrieved July 8, 2015, from http://nasional.republika.co.id/berita/nasional/hukum/13/09/21/mtg6nx-kontras-desak-penyelidikan-kasus-penyerangan-ponpes

Republika. (2014). *Salah Kaprah Sebutan Habib di Masyarakat*. Retrieved December 15, 2014, from http://www.republika.co.id/berita/nasional/umum/14/10/11/nd9vk0-salah-kaprah-sebutan-habib-di-masyarakat

Bibliography 143

Republika. (2019). *Ngaji Bareng di PBNU, Habib Umar Bacakan Kitab Pendiri NU.* Retrieved September 24, 2019, from https://khazanah.republika.co.id/berita/pyaq2n320/ngaji-bareng-di-pbnu-habib-umar-bacakan-kitab-pendiri-nu

Rodja. (n.d). *Profil Radio Rodja dan Rodja TV.* Retrieved March 25, 2015, from http://www.radiorodja.com/about/

Sarkub. (2013). *KH. Thobay Syadzily: Mengawal Aswaja Sampai Dunia Maya.* Retrieved October 20, 2014, from http://www.sarkub.com/2013/kh-thobary-syadzily-mengawal-aswaja-sampai-dunia-maya/#ixzz2Zl13GGHD

Sarkub. (n.d.). *Tim Sarkub bertemu Ust Hartono Jaiz.* Retrieved October 15, 2014, from http://www.sarkub.com/densus-99-sarkub/densus-hartono/

———— (n.d.). *Visi Misi Sarkub.* Retrieved October 15, 2014, from http://www.sarkub.com/about/

Sanad Media. (2020). *Selayang Pandang Lembaga Pendidikan di Hadhramaut.* Retrieved March 3, 2021, from https://sanadmedia.com/post/selayang-pandang-lembaga-pendidikan-di-

Tabah Foundation. (n.d). *About Tabah Foundation.* Retrieved March 27, 2015, from http://www.tabahfoundation.org/en/about/

Tagar. (2019). *PBNU Sambut Kunjungan Habib Umar ke Indonesia.* Retrieved August 27, 2023, from https://www.tagar.id/pbnu-sambut-kunjungan-habib-umar-ke-indonesia

Tv Shia. (n.d.). *Kronologi Kejadian Penyerangan PP. Darul Sholihin Dalam Rangka Peringatan Maulid Nabi SAW Ke-28.* Retrieved July 7, 2015, from http://www.tvshia.com/indonesia/index.php/news/299-kronologi-kejadian-penyerangan-pp-darus-sholihin-dalam-rangka-peringatan-maulid-nabi-saw-ke-28

Univerzites. (n.d.). *Al-Ahgaff University Profile.* Retrieved March 3, 2015, from http://www.univerzities.com/yemen/al-Ahgaff-university/

Video Liputan6. (2011). *Jelang UN Ratusan Pelajar Berziarah ke Makam.* Retrieved April 27, 2015, from http://video.liputan6.com/news/jelang-un-ratusan-pelajar-berziarah-makam-667249

Winn, Phillip. (2012). *Women's Majelis Taklim and Gendered Religious Practice in Nothern Ambon. Intersections: Gender and Sexuality in Asia and the Pacific, 30, November.* Retrieved March 10, 2015, from http://intersections.anu.edu.au/issue30/winn.htm

Wearesocial. 2023. *Digital 2023.* https://wearesocial.com/uk/blog/2023/01/digital-2023/ (accessed on 27 May 2023).

Index

Abaya 107
Abdullah Jaidi 36
Abdurrahman Baswedan or A.R. Baswedan 24, 25, 26
Abdurrahman Wahid or Gus Dur 52, 111
Achmad Zein Al-Kaff 28
Ahbabul Musthofa 76
ahl bayt 27, 42
ahl hadith 55
ahl sunna wa al-jama'a or *Aswaja* 41, 42, 50, 55, 57, 58, 103, 107, 121
Ahlul Bait Indonesia 14, 30
Ahmad Bahmid 26
Ahmad Surkati 21, 22, 24, 33, 34, 36, 37, 38, 39
Ahmad Syafii Maarif 33
Ahmadiyah 10, 32, 53, 124
Akidah 52
al-Ahgaff University 86, 89–90, 96
al-Ash'ari 42
al-Dhiya al-Lamiy 75
Al-Irsyad 9, 14, 16, 18, 22–24, 27, 33–39, 42–43
Al-Irsyad Al-Islamiyah 18, 33–39
al-Khairaat 8
Al-Maturidi 42
Al-Qadri family 5
al-Wafa' bi Ahdillah 95
Albayyinat 30–33, 54
Ali Alatas 26
alKisah 14–15, 51, 63–64, 66, 74, 99, 116
Alwi Shihab 26
anti-Salafism 41, 44
Anwar Tawfiq 96
'aqida 46, 88
Ar-Riyadh Mosque 47
Ash'arite 53, 55
Aswaja dakwah 41, 44, 46–47, 50, 54
aswaja habaib 54

Awad Sungkar Al-Urmei 21
Ayatollah Khomeini 29, 30, 39

Baraka 58–59, 72, 110
bid'ah 44, 48, 52, 54, 55, 56, 57, 100, 121
bid'ah hasanah 48, 52
bid'ah madzmumah 56
bid'ah mahmudah 56

celebrity preachers 6, 61, 79–80, 122, 125
Clifford Geertz 2–3, 121

Dar al-Zahra 86
Dar al-Mustafa 58, 66, 68, 85, 86, 87, 88, 89, 90, 91, 93, 94, 95, 96, 100, 101, 102, 119
Daurah 94–95
DDII 45

egalitarianism or *musawa* 36, 38–39

Farid Ahmad Okbah 35, 40
Farouk Zein Bajabir 34
Firanda 51
Fitrah Foundation 29
Forum *Al-Husainy* 29
Front Pembela Islam (FPI) 32

Geys Amar 33–39
Golongan Karya 80
guru mulia 92

Habib Abdul Qadir Al-Haddad 30, 54
Habib Abdurrahman Az-Zahir 9
Habib Achmad b. Zein Al-Kaff 30–33
Habib Ahmad Assegaf 30, 54
Habib Ahmad b. Zein Al-Kaff 30, 54
Habib Ali b. Umar al-Habsyi 32
Habib Anis b. Alwi Al-Habsyi 47, 64, 66

146   *Index*

Habib Hasan Daliel al-Aydarus 29, 30
Habib Jamal b. Ba'agil 29, 119
Habib Muhammad b. Ali al-Habsyi 10
Habib Muhammad b. Luthfi b. Yahya *or*
  Habib Luthfi 11–12
Habib Muhammad Rizieq b. Syihab (Habib
  Rizieq) 10, 30, 32, 53, 53–54, 65,
  107, 18
Habib Muhdhor al-Hamid 33
Habib Munzir 93–94, 101, 105–107, 112,
  114–122
Habib Nabiel Al-Musawa 68–69, 93
Habib Syech 10, 61
Habib Thohir b. Abdullah Al-Kaff
  30, 54
Habib Zen Umar b. Smith 5
Habibana 107, 120
Haddad Alwi 31
Hadhrami Diaspora 3, 8, 82–83
Hamid Algadri 26
Hartono Ahmad Jaiz 51
haul 15, 43, 92–93, 107
hisab 35
Hizbut Tahrir 41, 45, 50, 53, 105
Houthi rebel movement 87
Husein Shahab 28, 29
Husin Maskati 37

ICC 29
ijazah 58, 64
ijtihad 43
imamah 61, 70
Irsyadi basic principles 37
isbal 35, 38
isnad paradigm 58

Ja'far Umar Thalib 35
Jalaluddin Rakhmat 28
Jamal al-Din al-Afghani 21, 43
Jamiat Khair 14, 18, 21, 27–28, 30, 39

kafa'ah 8, 23, 73
karama 74
Kemusyrikan 57
kenduri 43
kewalian 72
Kharijism 42
Kharijite 42, 56
Khazanah 57
Khittah 1926 44
Kios Nabawi 67, 78, 112
kitab kuning 49–51, 96
Komite Hijaz 43
Kopi darat 50, 75, 114

L.W.C. van den Berg 7, 84
Laskar Jihad 35, 105
Lembaga Bahtsul Masail (LBM)
LIPIA 35, 45

Mabadi' 36–37, 39
Madrasah Al-Khairiyyah 28
Madzhab 52, 56
Majelis Ali Kwitang 11
majelis syura 68, 93
Majelis Tabligh 24
Majelis Ulama Indonesia (MUI) 51
Masyumi 26, 28, 44
Matn 101
Maturidite 53, 55
maulid 43, 46, 57, 68, 76–79, 92, 98–100,
  106–107, 114, 120–121
Maulid akbar 114–115
MIAI 44
Muhammad 'Abduh 21, 43
Muhammad Alwi Al-Maliki 58, 96, 98, 100
Muhammad Bawazir 33–34, 37
Muhammad Hasyim Asy'ari 94
Muhammad Idrus Ramli 48–51
Muhammad Nasiruddin al-Albani 59
Muhammad Quraish Shihab 26, 31, 33, 54
Muhammadiyah 6, 24, 33–34, 36
Muhibbin 78, 102, 105–106, 114, 120,
  122, 126
multaqo ulama 94
munsib 89
Mustofa Bisri 127
muwallad 7, 19, 23–25

nahda hadhramiyya 20
Nahdlatul Ulama (NU) 6, 26, 33, 42–43,
  47, 94, 111, 124
Nawawi Al-Bantani 51
Netherlands East Indies 7, 18, 19
New Conservatism 52, 125
non-*sayyid* 8–9, 16, 18, 21–22, 24, 39, 82,
  103, 106
Nurul Musthofa 11, 15, 16, 62, 64, 65,
  74–81, 106, 126

Partai Amanat Nasional 80
Partai Keadilan Sejahtera (PKS) 105
Partai Nasional Indonesia (PNI) 26
Partai Sosialis Indonesia (PSI) 26
PBNU 47, 49, 94
pengajian 51, 66, 90, 113
peranakan 24–25
Perhimpunan Al-Irsyad 14, 18, 33–35, 37
Persatuan Islam (Persis) 42–43

Index 147

pesantren 3, 28–29, 32–33, 35, 45–49, 51, 63, 66, 70, 87–89, 91, 95–96, 99–100, 103, 107, 119, 123, 126
pesantren ar-Riyadh 28
PKB 44
Pondok Pesantren Darul Lughah wad Dakwah (Dalwa) 47, 64
Ponpes Darul Sholihin 32
Post-traditionalism 52
Prophet's city (*Kota Nabawi*)

qabail 19–20
quburiyyun 50

Rabithah Alawiyah 5, 14, 18, 22, 33, 72, 89
ratib 47
ratib al-haddad 88, 97
Rodja Radio 38, 46
Rubat Tarim 86–90, 97
ru'ya (sighting moon) 35

Said Agil Husin Al-Munawar 26
Said Aqil Siradj 33, 47, 59, 94
Said Bahreisj 26
Said Sungkar 35–36
Salafi-Wahhabi 34–35, 47–48, 50–51, 56, 96, 106, 121, 126
Salafism 18, 26, 35, 37–39
Salawat 76, 107
Salawatan 56, 75, 77, 92, 106, 117
Sanad 58–59, 100, 101, 116, 125
Sarkub *or* Sarjana Kuburan 50–52, 57
Saudi Arabia 45, 52, 56–57, 85–86, 126
Saudi Salafism 37, 45
sayyid 97–103, 106, 119; communit(ies) 11–12, 14, 18, 27, 29, 31, 33, 39, 73, 96, 100, 103; preachers 5, 12; sayyidness 73–74; Shi'i 18; social status or group identity 5
Sayyid Ali b. Ahmad Shahab 27
Sayyid Aqil b. Zainal Abidin 27
Sayyid Husein al-Habsyi 28
Sayyid Muhammad b. Ahmad al-Muhdar 27
Sayyid 'Uthman 9
Sayyid Zein Umar b. Smith 5
sayyida 4, 19, 21
SBY 79
Shalat duha 110
Sharaf 20
Sharifa 4, 19, 21, 73
Shi'ism 18, 26–33, 39–42, 49–50, 53–54

singa podium 102
siwak 73
Soeharto 10, 39, 44; post-Soeharto era 8, 41, 44, 55, 61, 70; Soeharto regime 84
Sunni orthodoxy 41, 49, 53, 127
Sunni tradition 41, 96
Sunni traditionalists 42
Sunnism 95–96, 100, 121, 127
Susilo Bambang Yudhoyono 79
syafa'at 77, 121

Tabarruk 56, 97, 99, 101
Tablighi Jamaat 45, 105
tahlilan 56–57, 106–107
takfiri 53
talqin 43
taqiyya 27
taqlid 36, 43
Tarbiyah movement 105
Tarim 85–90, 96–98, 116
tariqa 106
Tariqa 'Alawiya 30
tawassul 57, 99, 101, 111
Thariqat Sarkubiyah 50
traditional Sunnism 11, 39, 59, 95–96, 100, 121, 127
TRANS7 57
tuan guru 12
Tutty Alawiyah 70

ulama Rabbani 94
Umar Yusuf Umar Manggus 22
umma 78–81, 90, 94, 110
usalli 43

Wahhabi 35–39, 43, 45, 50–51, 56, 58, 99, 106, 118, 121
Wahhabism 35, 46, 50
wali 72
Wali songo 56, 74, 116
Waratsatul Musthofa 76
Wasatiyya 99
wulaiti 19, 23–25, 39

YAPI 28–29
Yusuf Usman Baisa 35, 37

Zainal Abidin 51
Zeyd Al-Hiyed 35–36
Ziarah 15, 43, 50, 56–57, 77, 92, 99, 107, 111, 113–114, 120

Printed in the United States
by Baker & Taylor Publisher Services